PLANNING AND EXPENDITURE ON EDUCATION

PLANNING AND EXPENDITURE ON EDUCATION

Dr. Gooru Sreeramulu

KALPAZ PUBLICATIONS
DELHI-110052

Planning and Expenditure on Education

Rs. 690

ISBN: 81-7835-215-X

Published in 2004 in India by
Kalpaz Publications
C-30, Satyawati Nagar
Delhi - 110052
e-mail : kalpaz@hotmail.com

Laser Typesetting at : Shree Vaishnavi Creations, Delhi
Printed at : Mehra Offset Press, Delhi

Contents

List of Tables

List of Graphs

Foreword

I am very glad that Dr. Gooru Sreeramulu, Lecturer in the Department of Political Science has made a maiden attempt to bring out a book entitled "Planning and Expenditure on Education."

He has presented every chapter in the book very systematically and has produced a work that is very useful to those researching in Education, Economics, Public Administration in general and Political Science in particular. The author has made a very sincere attempt to analyse the budgetary documents from 1948-2000.

The author has also used appropriate statistical techniques to analyse the data collected such as NSDP at deflator, educational expenditure at Current ad Constant Prices, Consumer Price Index, Annual Average Rate of Growth, Primary Educational Per Capita Expenditure, Percentage of Variation in Per Capita Educational Expenditure, Index of total Educational Allocations and Expenditure and Compound Growth Rate.

The work is all the more useful because, the author has analysed the allocations and expenditure for all sectors of education not only in the state of Karnataka, but also in the States of Maharashtra, Kerala, Tamil Nadu, Pondichery and Andhra Pradesh.

The conclusions drawn from the study are of great relevance not only to the academicians but also to those in administration so that they can turn their attention towards initiating effective legislative measures to improve and enrich the quality of education, at primary, secondary, higher and technical levels. I wish Dr. Gooru Sreeramulu the very best and still greater research contribution in the future.

DR. V.B. COUTINHO
Vice-Chancellor
Gulbarga University

Acknowledgements

The present book is an outcome of the research work done at the Department of Education, Bangalore University, Bangalore, under the able supervision and guidance of Dr. M.S. Talawar, Professor in the Department to whom I am indebted for his invaluable suggestions, academic inspiration and constant encouragement in completing this work.

I am sincerely thankful to Prof. M. Khajapeer, former Professor, Dean and Chairman, Department of Education, Bangalore University, Bangalore, presently Vice-Chancellor, Karnataka University, Dharwad for his valuable suggestions, help and co-operation without which this work would have not been completed.

My sincere thanks are to Dr. Smt. C.K. Degaonkare, Professor, Department of Economics, Gulbarga University, Gulbarga for her valuable suggestions, timely help and co-operation in the completion of the present research.

The staff of Planning, Budget Section, Finance, Directorate of Economics and Statistics, State Income Department, Record Room, Archives and Library, (Vidhana Soudha) Government of Karnataka, Bangalore all of them deserve my appreciation for their whole-hearted support and kindness in providing me necessary data for the present research.

I am specially grateful to my Father, Mother, Brother, Sister-in-laws and my wife Smt. Sangeeta and my daughter Sahana for their encouragement and moral support.

I also thankful to Amit Garg Director, Gyan Publishing House for their cooperation and help.

Gooru Sreeramulu

1

Introduction

In recent years human resource planning is being identified as a critical component in the process of development. This chapter provides a brief account of its meaning, scope and progress of education in India and in the state of Karnataka. The first section deals with human resource development and planning. The second section deals with Educational Planning in India and finally in the third section a brief historical sketch of Karnataka, land, people, culture and progress of education in Karnataka are dealt.

SECTION-1

Human Resource Planning

"In rapidly changing times like those which have characterized the second-half of the 20th century and which promise to proceed at an equally heady pace, planning for human resources will be a challenging task. With an increasingly competitive environment, projected labour shortages, changing demographics and increased pressure on government to protect employee rights, organization will need to be flexible and remain aware of the dynamics of their environments".

- J.A.F. Stoner & R.E. Freeman
(Management)

Dag Hammarskjold, Secretary General, UNO, while addressing International Law Association (May 30, 1956) opined that: "Man is the key to our problems, not money. Competent people can work miracles even with small resources and draw wealth out of barren land". Hammarskjod's views highlight on the need for systematic planning of all men and material accessible.

Definition and Meaning of Human Resource Planning

Human resource planning is a systematic approach to ensure that the right people will be in the right place at the right time. It may be looked upon as a strategy for the acquisition, utilization, improvement and preservation of an enterprise's human resources. The purpose is to evolve a process by which an organisation can move from its current human resources position to its desired human resources position, which results in both the organization and the individual receiving maximum long run benefits. This has to be an integrated approach in which the planning aspects of the personnel function are performed in order to have a sufficient supply of adequately developed and motivated personnel. Human resources planning, then, can be seen as a set of activities designed to make available the necessary number of people with the necessary qualifications in order to realize the organization's goals along with the interests of individual employee.

Importance of Human Resource Planning

Human resource planning may be viewed as serving two broad objectives. Firstly, it is an attempt to prepare for the future. Secondly, human resource planning gives to the organisation a valuable knowledge about present resources which needs to adapt quickly and adequately to sudden changes in such factors as technological advances, new market demands, political and economic pressures, etc. Moreover, human resource planning is the first and most important step to be taken with the objective of effective and meaningful utilization of human resources. As automation and computerization takes their stride the jobs that are left require more decision taking and the exercise of greater discretion. Even more importantly, manpower is pre-eminently an income-generating resource and must be seen as the organization's greatest asset. But what is ironic is accounting conventions look at inanimate things, such as plant and machinery as assets and human resources as an expense. As Gareth Stainer puts it, "This treatment really epitomizes all that is mistaken in industrial perspectives on manpower." In fact, a glance at the budget of any enterprise in India, particularly in the public sector, reveals that an annual expense, manpower is more than twice as treat as capital investment.

Need for Human Resources Planning

The upsurge of interest in Human Resource Planning in recent years has been brought about by a number of influences that have underscored the utility of this powerful tool as an imperative in enterprise management. These influences are briefly outlined below:

I. Technological Change: The rapid change in the technology of work has created a situation the world over and particularly in India, where potential employees with appropriate skills frequently not available in the labour market. Employers across the board, therefore, are gradually waking up to the fact that they must plan the recruitment and training of candidates for posts well in advance of it heir becoming vacant.

II. Decreasing or Increasing Growth of Organizations: The manner, the pace and the direction in which an organization is growing also dictate the need for a human resource plan. Years of comfortable growth may give rise to slower growth prospects or even reduced growth prospects. Conversely, there might be an immediate expectation of accelerated growth. Either way, if the organization has not planned its manpower levels and requirements in accordance with growth expectations, it is likely to run into considerable difficulties and costs.

III. Size: The need for human resource planning is increasingly being perceived as directly proportional to the size of the organization. The larger the size, the greater, the need. Size brings with it, the attendant features of complexity, variability, uncertainty, and requires a careful planning to obviate chaos.

IV. Irregular Age Structure: Many organizations are saddled with situations where the actual age distribution of employees is irregular because of the manpower policies of the past. Such irregular age distributions frequently occur where organisation size has changed rapidly or recruitment has taken place in only a few age groups. In situations where the proportion of older employees to younger employees is skewed, one has to forecast future human resources requirements as well as availability, both qualitatively and quantitatively.

V. Labour Costs: Since the cost of manpower is a major factor in the price of most goods and services and there is constant pressure for enhanced productivity, managers needs to examine means of controlling labour costs. These processes has been reinforced by legislation as well as court pronouncements which gives workers great security of employment and a minimum level of wages. The effect, in most cases, has been that labour costs, from being a variable cost, have become a quasi-fixed cost in the operation of an enterprise.

VI. The Human Resources Decision-making process: Decisions, with regard to human resources policies have a great impact on the organization and on individual employees. Therefore, such impacts have to be studied in detail. Moreover, many deliberations at various levels, such as at top or middle management, work councils, etc., increase the demand for information about the consequences of alternative human resource policies, capacities of training institutions, finance and so on.

Good manpower planning can provide this information by forecasting requirements and availability of personnel, both quantitatively and qualitatively.

VII. Attrition: Even when there are no significant changes in the growth, expansion, or down-sizing of an enterprise, the phenomenon of attrition or wearing out occurs. That is, because of wastage, turnover, separations, retirement or mobility on account of transfers, promotions, etc. gaps would inevitably emerge, needing to be filled up.

VIII. Lead Time: By anticipating the need for various types of skill requirements and level of personnel, well in advance, a manpower plan will be able to provide adequate lead time for recruitment, selection and training. Human resources planning become all the more crucial because the lead time for obtaining the required personnel is often a dilatory process and the needed skill or experience may not readily bee available. Non-availability of suitable manpower or undue delays in getting required people results in postponements, time and cost overruns, rescheduling, interruptions, stoppages both in ongoing and projected programmes and these inevitably lead to inefficiencies, escalating costs and reduce profitability.

Human Resources Planning in India

With the concept of human resources planning having gained worldwide acceptance and having been shown to yield definite results, it would worthwhile to examine how the process has worked in India.

We have seen that the 80's and 90's have been replete with major economic and political changes with significant implication for India. Formation of trading blocks, increasing pressures for reduction in trade barriers, the threat of ecological disaster and India's epoch-making campaign of economic liberalization have all contributed to a new and complex environment where India could be so easily isolated and marginalised unless it responds with greater vision and timely action.

As Reddy puts it, "There is an undeniable move towards greater globalisation and increasing competitiveness. Protectionism and ideologically dictated soft economic approaches seem to be disappearing in a new international order which is singing in chorus for attaining developmental advantage through unsympathetic competition. In the context of globalisation, the country would lose opportunities and will be pushed to the margin unless it responds quickly and strategically in the race."

It is against this background that the winds of change have at last begun blowing across the Indian economy. Political and economic perceptions have coalesced into a firm belief that regulations and controls, which have stifled us so far, must go and unproductive expenditure pared to the bone. Greater competition has painted a scenario where losing enterprises have no place and maximum utilization must be derived from the available resources. Government, in its turn, is left with no option but to work in close harmony with business and shed its cloistered image as a regulatory and policing instituting. Corporate objectives have to be linked and integrated with national economic objective both in perception and action.

What are the implications of the new and complex politico-economic environment on the management of human resources in India? Our basic problem has been in the spheres of both utilization and availability of education and trained human resources. It was also necessary to provide information to the educational administrations regarding the quantities of manpower needed for economic and development purposes. This work was undertaken in the first year of independence itself when a Scientific Manpower committee was formed in 1947. In the course of time, many other committees were formed. These committees and working groups highlighted the paucity of the data to make precise quantitative estimates. Therefore, as a part of the manpower policies of the Government of India, it was felt that research bodies should be set up for performing the crucial functions of manpower planning.

Systematic research on manpower planning was started under the Planning commission itself in the mid-50's for comprehensive studies were initiated under the Scientific and Technical Manpower Division. The Institute of Applied Manpower Research was set up in 1962. There was simultaneously a significant expansion of facilities for technical education. Courses were diversified for meeting the needs of specific categories of manpower and advanced centers of education. In the course of time, agencies for conducting research in manpower areas were set up in large numbers.

There is certainly no difference of opinion relating to the view that the national wealth of India can be better produced and distributed when trained personnel with improved knowledge and skills entering the labour market, are fully absorbed into productive employment. What has been a major lacuna is the inadequate relationship between educational planning and human resources planning in India. Yet, India has over the years, produced a rich complement of skilled manpower in high-tech areas. In a host of foreign countries, Indians have proved their worth and occupied prestigious positions in key sectors. The efforts of our government in raising this rich crop cannot be altogether discounted. Our primary drawback has been the inability of most organizations to channelise our human resources output in achieving desired results. It is only through such a process that the investment in education and training of manpower would be utilized in a productive manner. This may be regarded as one of the most important guidelines to human resources planning in the future. High rates of industrial sickness and mortality, discouraging export performances, low returns on investments and high capital to output ratios have underscored our signal failure in managing our human resources.

The dimensions of manpower planning in India can only be visualized when confronted with the sheer numbers involved. An unfortunate assumption, often made in a developing country like India, is that there is a large amount of trained human resources available for any specific skill requirements. We are paying dearly today for this misconception. Specific skills, and in many cases, professional become scarce as technology becomes more complex and the demand for skilled manpower increases. The complacency regarding easy availability of skills will result in our paying a heavy penalty particularly as we approach the turn of the century and plan for technological changes, expansions and diversifications.

The overall picture of human resources planning in India continues to be dismal. Dominated by a budget approach, and paid lip-service to by personnel executives who have little role or power in human resource planning. Most enterprises, whether in the public or in the private sector, have neither established their systems for a detailed and strategically responsive personnel plan nor have they demonstrated effectively the desire to do such work overtime. Reddy points out that "it is for this reason of adhoc approaches that organizations often suffer from over endowment and mal-allocation of human resources. That is on the whole, there is over-manning, but there are areas and skills which are inadequately manned too. This is especially noticeable in the case of the service sector, government departments and programmes".

Human Resources Development

In the last 40 years nations have become increasingly development oriented. Economic development is, of late, a major issue in international politics. An adequate definition of economic developments is not easy to construct because of the vast disparities in natural endowments, economic structure, cultural heritage and social and political institutions that exist between different regions of the world today. However, economic development can be regarded as the process by which one economy transfer itself from very low or sometimes even negative growth rate per capita income into one that registers a higher rate of growth of per capita income.

There is no denying that the level of state expenditure on education in a country is regarded as a reliable indicator of its march towards economic prosperity. The extent to which a country can exploit and utilize its resources depends largely on the quality and quantity of its educated and the technological transformation of the country. The rate of the economy's output is a function not only of the employment level of capital, labour and land, but also of the technology and skills used in production and the socio-cultural environment in which the economy functions. The countries are backward not because of inadequate supply of physical and financial resources but because of acute shortage of skilled personnel and technicians. Education promotes and develops an openness of mind, tolerance, cooperation, and ability to adjust to the changes.

Dension on the basis of Cobb- Douglas production, estimated the return on education and as well as on physical capital for the period 1929-57. His estimates shown that, the growth in education and skill per worker contributed to the GNP of the USA at an annual average of 0.67 per cent while the increase in the quantity of physical capital per person employed contributed only 0.15 per cent annually. According to Slow's estimates, which are based on the assumption of Linear Homogeneous Production Function, about 87.5 per cent of increase in output during the period 1909-49 was attributable to the increase in the human capital.

Human capital contributes to economic growth in several ways. The most appropriate processes through which it contributes to the increased productivity per man hour are:

1. Human capital contributes to the GNP by increasing the productivity of labourers;
2. Education develops not only common understanding and general ability of the labour force but it leads to specialization;
3. Skilful handling of the machines and tools lengthens the durability of the capital assets; and
4. Education helps economic growth by increasing the adaptability of a society to the new technology.

   Normally, one can look forward to an increase in the expenditure on education when a traditional society ventures to move away from stereo typed learning to an intensive course in science and technology. In the early stages of this transition period, constraints arising out of low national income levels and inadequate management practices may come in the way of achieving the desired prospects. But keeping pace with the expansion of economy, the level of educational expenditure is expected to accelerate.

The international community at the World Conference of Education for All (WCEFA), held in March 1990 in Thailand, adopted a declaration calling for measures to solve the debt crisis and reduce disparities among, nations to enable developing countries to funnel over resources into education. It declares, "Time, energy and funding directed to basic education is perhaps the most profound investment on people and in the future of a country which can be made".

World Bank studies revealed that economic returns from investment in education are higher than those from most other forms of investment. Also, a number of major reports on education in the US have stated that mediocrity in education could jeopardize national prosperity. Greek philosopher Plato maintained more than 2300 years ago that "Education has an economic value... a considerable part of the wealth must be invested in education".

However, in many of the developing countries spending on education fell as a proportion of total public spending throughout the 1980's; in some there was a decrease in expenditure per student and per teacher at the primary level. At the same time major literacy campaigns have undergone severe cut in their budgets.

But, there are developing countries which have successfully ensured education and schooling for their populace. A number of developing countries have managed to double or triple their literacy rates in the last decade. Reducing the military budget to zero, Costa Rica, of late, started to spend over ten per cent of its GNP on education and health. In Zimbabwe, which achieved Independence in 1980, education now receives a remarkable allocation of budget, more than that of health and defense combined.

A country like India, which has the second largest population and adequate natural resources, could not be pulled out of poverty despite the vigorous efforts made during the planning era. Indian economy is still backward and underdeveloped. Coupled with other factors, the sizable shortage of skilled human capital has played a dominant role in pegging the economy to poverty. The deep-rooted poverty remains and possesses a serious challenge to national libber unless sufficient attention is paid to revolutionize the human resources. In India the major emphasis has been on physical capital formation than on human capital formation. Also, there is big gap between the percentage of students in science and technology and humanities.

Findings of Prakash and Chowdhury of the National Institute of Educational Planning and Administration (NIEPA) may be relevant to mention here. Between 1951 and 1987 enrolment in educational institutions in India expanded at a rate of 5.04 per cent a year. The country's population during the same period expanded at 2.16 per cent a year; while the net national product at current prices went up by almost 9.6 per cent. These rates have fallen short of the growth rate of total expenditure which increased at an annual rate of 11.65 per cent during the said years. The state's share in total education expenditure rose from 52.5 per cent in 1951 to 76.3 per cent in 1987. The findings further show that over the entire period 1951-1987, the total expenditure on education in real terms increased at an annual rate of 5.93 peer cent. Not only that, private expenditure on education too witnessed a slightly faster growth than did personal disposable incomes. So, education seems to be regarded as a superior good both at the national and the personal levels.

Due to defects in our education system, the economic growth of the country has been considerably hampered. What is most essential in the context of economic growth is well integrated and coordinated educational planning in physical and financial terms to accelerate the human capital formation. A timely and purposeful human capital formation will enhance knowledge about the wealth of inexhaustible resources and their innumerable alternative uses in the physical capital formation. It would also help the growth of technical know-how, which would save the economy from foreign dependence, and save foreign exchange at large.

Ahluwalia noted economist rightly considers that "it is necessary to open our minds rather than be content with the opening for new horizons in economy. To open our minds is indeed to open up a new vista of economic prosperity through human resource development." It is very clear from the above saying that education and national economy have close relationship with each other.

SECTION-2

EDUCATIONAL PLANNING IN INDIA

Historical Background

Origin of Educational planning in India lies with the origin of Planning Committee. After introduction of provincial autonomy in the country under the Government of India Act 1935 and the acceptance of office by the Congress in nine out of eleven provinces in 1937, the National Planning Committee was set up in 1938 under the Chairmanship of Pandit Jawaharlal Nehru. Two committees were set up in the field of education one for general education with Dr. Radhakrishnan as its Chairman and the other for technical education and development of research under Chairmanship of Dr. M. N. Saha. General Secretary of the committee brought out a volume in 1948 with broad outline for educational planning in India. Its main significance is historical, as it was the first organization to think of preparing a plan of educational development.

First comprehensive plan on education in India can be trace back to the year 1944, Sargent then Education Commissioner to the government of India, prepared a comprehensive educational plan covering the different aspects of educational planning. This document, popularly known as the Sargent Plan is the first comprehensive plan of educational development ever to be prepared in the country.

India has now record of over 50 years of planning. The first four years of independence witnessed great educational expansion on a year to year budgetary planning till the birth of the National Planning Commission in 1951, the year of launching the First Five Year Plan.

Educational Planning – Nature and Significance

"Educational Planning, in its broadcast sense, is the application of rational, systematic analysis to the process of educational development with aim of making education more effective and efficient in responding to the needs and goals of its student and society". The following generalization could be made from the above statement.

Educational planning is systems-based exercise directed towards achieving certain physical targets and objectives set by a society within certain time frame in education sector.

The procedure and practices of goal and target setting emerge from the felt-need of society and constraints before it in terms of the level of development, state of knowledge and its application.

The ultimate object of educational planing is to make education a viable effective and efficient proposition so that it could respond to the emerging needs and aspirations of the students in particular and society in general.

In education, the planning aspect has been used as an adjustment mechanism for linking human resource development with the economic growth and planning. Blaug has emphasized the need of educational planning by lining manpower requirements with economic growth.

Origin of Educational Planning

"Educational planning is the application to education itself to instill in students; a rational, scientific approach to problems. Such an approach in identifying objectives and available resources, examining the implications of alternative courses of action and choosing wisely among them, deciding on specific targets to be met within specific time limits, and finally developing the best means of systematically implementing the choices thus made. Any scheme or idea stems from its necessity. Educational planning is no exception to this testimony. History of educational planning for each country may vary in structure, design, and implementation. However, there will be certain common factors, which made a strong case of educational planning. These factors are:

- Tremendous expansion of education to meet social demand;
- Increased share of the government in funding education at all levels;
- Accountability of the government to reduce wasteful imbalances within the education system;
- To make education relevant to social and economical needs of the country.

The needed shift of emphasis in educational development strategy from linear expansion has far reaching consequences for the nature and tasks of educational planning in the future. The new concepts and methodologies of educational planning have been evolved in recent years and these have attached much attention in recent years. These concepts and methodologies have been related to educational development to social demand, manpower requirements, financial flows, economic growth and future benefits.

Salient Features of Educational Planning

The primary task of educational planning is to produce a blue print which contains the priorities, approaches, physical targets, financial allocations and strategies of implementation and achieving the set targets and goals within certain time-frame in education sector. Generally this blue print is known as Draft of Education which contains the past performance and the promises of the future in education sector. Obviously, the contents of the Draft speak about the quantitative expansion of education at different levels, and by type of education. Through quantitative expansion, a society aims at providing educational facilities to its members. It is needless to say that education is a potential force for ensuring quality of life to the members of society.

It would be misconception if the concept of educational planning is regarded as mere quantitative expansion of education. For example enrolment ratios speak about quantitative expansion, but retention rate of students is the qualitative parameters. The concept is broad-based if other parameters are also included along with quantitative indices. Education system should be viable, effective and efficient so as to respond to the emerging needs and aspirations of the society. It would imply that education system takes into account the quantitative expansion as well as qualitative dimension.

Highlights of Five Year Plans from I to VIII

Since independence, Five Year Plans have commanded systematic distribution of resources and planning of human resources. Education was considered as an important subject in all the Five Year Plans. A review of Five Year Plans with special reference to education has been presented here:

First Five Year Plan (1951-52 to 1955-56)

While it was impossible to lay down a strict order of priorities, in view of the closely inter-linked character of the various stages of education, as well as the widely varying conditions in different parts of the country, it was recommended that the highest priority should go to the improvement and remodeling of existing institutions on right lines. During the first five year plan high priority was given to experiments and research in improving educational methods, the training of teachers and the preparation of literature, basic and social education, technical and vocational education at lower level, the development of facilities for training high-grade technicians and improvement in postgraduate research.

The quantitative targets aimed at during the plan were; (i) Provision of educational facilities for 60 per cent of the population within the age group 6-11, (ii) to bring children up the age of 14 into schools, (iii) to bring 15 per cent of the relevant age group to secondary education, (iv) In the field of social education, attempt to bring 30 per cent of the people of the age group 14-40 within the purview of social education.

Second Five Year Plan (1956-57 to 1960-61)

The chapter on 'Education' begins with these remarks. "The system of education has a determining influence on the rate at which economic progress is achieved and the benefits which can be derived from it. Economic development naturally makes growing demands on human resources and in a democratic setup it calls for values and attitudes in the building of which the quality of education is an important element".

Again in the concluding part of the chapter on 'Education' the framers of the II Five Year Plan state that, "For economic development to make its full contribution to the well-being of the mass, programmes of education should be ahead of economic plans. Modern economic development calls for a wide diffusion of the scientific temper of mind, a sense of dignity in labour and disciplines in service and a readiness to adapt new techniques and new knowledge to the needs of the people. These values and attitudes will be realized in everyday life in the measure in which they are expressed through educational ideals and practice".

Main Features are

1. Emphasis on the basic education.
2. Expansion of elementary education.
3. Diversification of secondary education.
4. Improvement in the standards of college and university education.
5. Implementation of social education and cultural development programmes.

Third Five Year Plan (1961-62 to 1965-66)

Main emphasis during the third plan was on:

1. Provision of facilities for universal education for the age group 6-11.
2. Improvement of science education at the secondary and university stages.
3. Training of teachers at all grades.
4. Expansion of technical education.

Fourth Five Year Plan (1969-74)

Priority was given to the expansion of elementary education and the emphasis was made on the provision of facilities for backward communities and for girls. A survey of the deficiencies in respect of buildings and equipment of educational institutions was made with a view to removing them according to a phase programme. Other programme of importance were:

- Improvement of teacher education;
- Expansion and improvement of science education;
- raising standards of postgraduate education and research;
- Development of Indian languages
- Consolidation of technical education including reorganisation of polytechnic education and its closer linking with the needs of industry and it orientation towards self-employment;
- Increased efforts were suggested to involve people in educational programmes and to mobilize public support.

Fifth Five Year Plan (1974-78)

Broadly speaking, the Fifth Plan has laid emphasis on (i) ensuring equality of educational opportunities as apart of the overall plan of ensuring social justice; (ii) establishing closer links between the pattern of education, on the one hand, and the needs of development and the employment market, on the other; (iii) improvement of the quality of education imparted; and (iv) involvement of the academic community including students, in the tasks of social and economic development.

Sixth Five Year Plan (1980-85)

The Sixth Five Year Plan for 1980 to 1985 has laid emphasis on: (i) programmes of adult education including eradication of adult illiteracy; (ii) universalisation of elementary education; (iii) vocationalisation at the secondary stage and improvement of quality in secondary stage and higher education; (iv) better and more effective utilization on non-plan government expenditure for meeting developmental goals; (v) ensuring a rural bias in the educational programmes, to develop science education and a scientific attitude and to provide a system of non-formal education and training at all stages.

In the three decades of planed development since 1951, the number of educational institutions has been more than doubled. The number of teachers and students has gone up by about four times. Expenditure on education also went up from Rs. 153 crores in the first Plan to Rs. 901 crores in four years of the Fifth Plan. The proposed outlay for the Sixth Plan 1980-95 is Rs. 1,986 crores.

A working group of Education and Culture was set up by the Government of India in July, 1980 to suggest perspective of development for the decade. As enunciated in the Report, the important goals and tasks suggested were:

(a) To guarantee equality of opportunity in their educational planning to which the educational system and programmes need to be redirected
(b) To afford to all young people and adults, irrespective of age, the means for ample self-fulfillment within the framework of a harmonious development which reflects the needs of the community to which they belong.
(c) To provide for a continuous process of lifelong education for their physical, intellectual and cultural development and for inculcating capabilities to cope with and influence social change.
(d) To establish dynamic and beneficial links between education, employment and development with due regard for the economic and social aims of the community; and
(e) To promote values of national integration, secularism, democracy and dignity of labour.

Seventh Plan (1985-86 to 1989-90)

The Seventh Plan has given overriding priority for the realization of the objective of UEE by 1990. It was estimated that for achieving the goal, over 5 crores additional children would have to be enrolled. The new thrust in elementary education emphasised substantially on improvement in the quality of education. In 1987-88, a centrally sponsored scheme

(CSS) for restructuring and reorganization of teacher education was started as a part of NPE, New CSS for vocationalisation of higher secondary stage, improvement of science education and environmental orientation to school education were started. Improvement of quality and consolidation were main concerns in the field of higher education. Consolidation and optimum utilisation of existing infrastructural facilities, their upgradation, modernisation, identification of critical areas and creation of infrastructure in new area of emerging technology, effective management of the overall system and institutional linkage between technical education and other development sectors were important aspects during the Seventh Plan.

Eighth Plan (1992-93 to 1996-97)

Universalisation of elementary education, eradication of illiteracy in the age group 15 to 35 and strengthening of vocational education (VE) so as to realise to the emerging needs and urban and rural setting are the major thrust areas of Eight Plan. Early childhood education (ECE) was expanded by attaching pre-primary classes to selected primary school. Statutory status will be accorded to the national council for teacher education NCTE to lay down and maintain standards in institutions and courses. The expansion of secondary schools was regulated and new schools were opened on selective basis to cater to the needs of deprived sections like girls and SC/ST and rural areas in general. Other salient features are (i) Integrated approach to higher education. (ii) Excellence in higher education. (iii) Making higher education relevant in the context of exchanging socio-economic scenario. (iv) Promotion of value education.

The review of all Five Year Plans describes the trend of identification of priority areas in education. It may be remembered here that, adult education has been able to get focus in all Five Year Plans. Similarly primary education, vocational education and to some extent secondary education have drawn the attention of planners. Higher education especially research and investment on innovative practices for quality improvement seems to have relegated to backseat.

Progress of Education in India

Until the Fourth Year Plan, central assistance to the states for implementation of plan programmes within the state's jurisdiction was given in the form of schemewise allocation of funds. This resulted in rigidities and inefficiencies in the system and inequitable distribution of central assistance. The matter was raised in several meetings of National Development Council (NDC). On the basis of discussion in NDC, the concept of block assistance in the state plans was subsequently introduced. However, certain schemes continued with central assistance and they were classified as Centrally Sponsored Schemes (CSS) and monetary assistance under CSS was restricted 1/6th or 1/7th of the quantum of central assistance to State Plans.

The Sixth plan again witnessed an enlargement of CSS in terms of number as well as quantum and an expert group was setup under the chairman ship of Shri K. Ramamurthi to review the same. The review of this expert committee resulted in setting up of another committee under the chairmanship of Shri. P.V. Narasimha Rao the then Minister of Human Resource Development to review (a) the criteria for taking up new Centrally Sponsored Schemes; (b) ceiling of 1/6th or 1/7th of central plan assistance keeping (c) Consultaltion mechanism for starting new CSS; (d) Examination of CSS under implementation with a view to dropping or transferring of some of them with the modalities of transfer of the funds involved; and (e) to suggest a periodical review mechanism for transferred schemes.

The NDC committee (Narasimha Rao Committee) constituted a group of officials, headed by Shri. J.S. Bajaj, the then secretary, Planning Commission, to work out the details regarding retention or mode of transfer of CSS to state plans. The NDC approved the recommendations of the committee and nearly 68 schemes were transferred to states.

Other schemes which are retained under CSS fall in the following three categories.

(i) Bringing about greater equality through expansion of better educational facilities to the deprived sections of the society.

(ii) Improvement of the quality in education and;

(iii) Involvement of the voluntary agencies.

During eighth five year plan it was proposed that ongoing centrally sponsored schemes would ordinarily be terminated except where specific justification for continuance is forthcoming. All the CSS were classified into two lists, viz. LIST I: comprising schemes which should continue in the Eighth plan as centrally sponsored schemes which related to national goals and having a national character and LIST II: Other schemes which could be transferred to the states.

The Department of Education, at present, implements 17 centrally sponsored schemes

Centrally Sponsored Schemes

1. Operation Blackboard : The scheme of Operation Blackboard, started in 1987-88 to bring about substantial improvement in physical facilities in primary schools with the aim of improving retention has three components, namely;

(i) Atleast two reasonably large all weather rooms along with separate toilet facilities for girls,

(ii) Atleast two teachers and as far as possible one of them a woman; and

(iii) Essential teaching and learning material including blackboard, maps charts etc.

Under this teaching learning equipments were supplied to 5.23 lakh primary school and 0.27 lakh upper primary schools during the period 1987-88 to 1994-95. While additional post of teachers sanctioned were 1.47 lakh, out of these 1.18 lakh were appointed. The post of third teacher has been sanctioned to 1.9 lakh primary schools and about 1.45 lakh classrooms were constructed.

2. Non-formal Education : Despite considerable expansion of formal education, the achievement of UEE goals remain a distant dream as large group of children remain outside the formal system due to various socio-economic constraints. In order to reach these large segments of marginalised children, the Govt. of India, Dept cf Education has started a programme of non-formal education for children of 6-14 age-groups since 1979-80

3. Teacher Education : The centrally sponsored scheme of "Restructuring and Reorganization of Teacher Education" is being implemented since 1987-88. Its main objective is to impart suitable pre-service and in-service training to school teachers so that they may competently discharge their duties. Under the scheme, up to 1994-95 394 DIETs, 60 CTEs and 27 IASEs have been sanctioned.

4. Lok Jumbish : An innovative project called "Lok Jumbish", People's Movement for Education for All was started during 1992 with assistance from Swedish International Development Authority (SIDA) in Rajasthan. The basic objective of the project is to achieve education for all by the year 2000 though people's mobilization and their participation. First phase of the project was taken up for two years during 1992 with an outlay of 18 crores covering 25 blocks spread over several districts. The cost of the project was shared by SIDA, GOI and Government of Rajasthan in the Ratio of 3:2:1. The first phase of the project has been concluded on 30th June, 1994.

A joint Evaluation of the project by SIDA, GOI and GOR expressed satisfaction with the initiatives undertaken in the project and recommend its extension and continuance. Proposal for continuation of Lok Jumbish Phase-II during the period 1994-97 has recently been approved with an outlay of Rs. 80 crores.

5. Vocational Education : Scheme of 'vocationalisation of Higher Secondary Education' was introduced with effect from February 1988. The main objectives of the scheme are to enhance individual employability to reduce the mismatch between the demand and supply of skilled manpower and to provide an alternative for those pursuing higher education without particular interest or purpose. Up to 194-95 vocational courses have been introduced in 6317 higher secondary schools.

6. Science Education : The scheme of improvement of Science Education initiated during 1987-88 aims at improving the quality of science education and promoting scientific temper as envisaged in National Policy on Education 1986. Accordingly, 100% assistance is provided to the states/ UTs for upgradation of science laboratories in Government and Government-aided secondary/higher secondary schools and training of science of mathematics teachers. Up to 1994-95, science kits were supplied to 79427 upper primary schools, the science laboratories of 35421 secondary/senior secondary schools were upgraded, libraries of 35596 secondary/senior secondary schools were equipped with science books and 197 district resource centers were setup.

7. Educational Technology : The scheme of "Educational Technology' seeks to improve utilisation of the media through Radio and Television educational sector. Initiated in 1972, it has undergone many changes over the years. The scheme seeks to provide the entire cost of Radio-cum-cassette players in upper primary schools to provide access to quality education. Up to 1994-95, 3.56 lakh RCCPs and 0.62 lakh Radio-cum-cassette players have been supplied to the schools.

8. Computer Education : A pilot project on computer literacy and studies in schools (CLASS) was initiated in 1984-85 in consultation with Department of Electronics. The project aims at providing computer familiarity to secondary/senior secondary level students 2798 schools have been covered up to 1994-95.

9. Environmental Orientation to School Education : The scheme started in 1988-89 aims at providing infusion of environmental information and concepts in the general syllabus and curriculum. The scheme initially catered to the requirements of elementary sector was subsequently extended to secondary and senior secondary levels. Assistance is given to state governments for reviewing syllabus and test books for providing environment orientation. A major thrust under the scheme is to fund NGOs for developing innovative methods and reading material for school children in Th field of environment.

10. Integrated Education for the Disabled Children (IEDC) : 100% assistance is provided to the states/ Its Voluntary organisations for providing necessary facilities to disabled children in common schools. Such as books and stationery allowance, transport allowance, uniform allowance, readers allowance, equipment allowance, hostel charges etc. The scheme also provides for meeting the cost of salary of special teachers; setting up of resource rooms, carrying out of assessment of disabled children, training of special teachers, removal of architectural barriers in schools and production of instructional material.

11. Promotion of yoga : Under the scheme, financial assistance is provided for training of teachers in yoga and for building the infrastructure necessary for the purpose. In addition, institutions of all India character are given assistance for maintenance as well as developmental expenditure for promotion of basic research and/ or for teachers training programme in various aspects of yoga other than the therapeutically aspect. Financial assistance to yoga institutions for promotion of therapeutical aspect is being extended by the Ministry of Health and Family Welfare.

12. Rural Functional Literacy Programme (RFLP) : Rural Functional Literacy Project (RFLP) is one of the oldest Schemes initiated right with the launching of the National Adult Education Programme on 2nd October, 1978. It has been a center based programme. On the basis of findings and recommendations of evaluation studies and internal assessment, t he scheme of RFLP was re-organised and several structural changes were made. Following the success of Total Literacy Campaigns, the Centre based programme has been closed down in almost all the States/UTs w.e.f. April, 1f991. The Expenditure Finance Committee, however, recommended the implementation of the revamped RFLP was Scheme from 1994-95 in Jammu and Kashmir, North Eastern States, border districts of Rajasthan and other difficult terrain, hilly areas and isolated pockets. There is a provision of Rs. 6.00 crores for 1994-95 under the scheme.

13. Post Literacy and Continuing Education (PL & CE) : The scheme was launched through establishment of Jana Shikshan Nilayama (JSM's) all over the country in a phased manner. The objective of the scheme is to provide opportunity of continuity education to neo-literates to retention of their literacy skills, enable the learner to continue their learning beyond elementary literacy and to create scope for application of their learning for improvement of their living conditions.

14. Strengthening of Administrative Structure in Adult Education : Under the scheme, the States/UTs are being assisted to create necessary supportive administrative structure at State/Uts and district levels for implementation of Adult Education programme. While the central grant is meant to cover the entire expenditure on items like POL, reimbursement of medical expenses, office expenses, travelling expenses etc. are met by the state Governments.

15. Appointment and Training of Hindi Teachers in Non-Hindi Speaking States/UTs : With a view to assist the non-Hindi speaking states/ Uts for promotion and propagation of Hindi in pursuance of the provisions contained in Article 351 of the constitution of India, the central Government has started, during the Second Plan, the schemes of (I) Appointment of Hindi teachers, and (ii) opening / strengthening of Hindi Teachers Colleges. Under these schemes central assistance was provided to the non-Hindi speaking States /Uts on 100% basis. These schemes were implemented upto the seventh plan as two separate schemes. Since the objectives of these schemes are similar, these have been merged together into a single scheme entitled "Appointment and Training of Hindi Teachers in non-Hindi speaking States / Uts" in the Eight plan.

16. Financial Assistance for Promotion of Modern Indian Languages English Language : Financial Assistance is being provided to voluntary organizations as well as individual for bringing out publications as well as purchase of books with a view to promoting and propagating Modern Indian Languages and English Language. Similarly, voluntary organisations engaged in promotional activities in various Modern Indian Languages and English Language. Similarly;, voluntary organisations engaged in promotional activities in various Modern Indian languages and in English also receive central assistance. These are ongoing schemes and now being administered by the CIIL, Mysore (MIL potion) and by the CIEFL, Hyderabad (English Language portion).

17. Appointment of Urdu Teachers : A scheme for appointment of Urdu Teachers and grant of incentives for teaching and study of Urdu is under consideration in consultation with the planning commission.

The process of planning and designing various schemes especially in the education sector, has considered realities that are cropped in the field since along period of time the progress of education in India has been visualized through five year plans continuously. However, there is a feeling that allocations are inadequate when compared to the demand and need. This has to be balanced so as to achieve required targets at all levels.

Planning Education for National Development

Whatever may be the ideology of a nation, whatever may be its social setup, whatever may be the conflicting views about the functions of education, at least all civilized societies appear to reach a consensus that education system has to promote national development. The education system should promote national development by achieving the following criteria:

(1) Criteria of development
(2) Criteria of efficiency
(3) Criteria of equity
(4) Criteria of diversification

National development is treated as expedient measure not only to feed the increasing population but also to improve its quality of life. When a nation is gripping with the development problem, scarce resources should be managed efficiently. Educational planning has to be suitably designed so as to meet the challenge and to achieve efficiency. Again, when national development takes off its gains percolate downwards, obviously the level of aspirations of the masses blooms up and the expectations run high. It becomes a political expediency to adopt a policy of equity. It compels the government to open new schools, collages, and provide education at reasonable cost. Moreover, the diversification of economic activities creates demand for specialised skills and the education system should change accordingly. There lies the interface relationship between education system and educational planning.

Significance of Educational Planning with Particular Reference to Developing Societies

Educational planning should work upon as a device of intervention for fulfillment of short and long term goals and objectives of a society. The educational planning does not operate in vacuum. The base of educational planning is the educational system, which has been developed and made operative in a given social set up. The developing societies have different education system as compared to that of developed countries depending on their needs.

Though the growth of education has been very rapid at all the levels, it has been very uneven and has been coupled with the institutionalization of inequalities interms access and provisions made for different sections of the society. The growth of education precedes industrial growth and takes place when the majority of labour force is in agriculturally related occupations. There are imbalances in investment at different levels of the system. The expansion in education has been through state-supported finance and governance in majority of the developing countries. In absence of direct synchronization and relationship between the type of education and the skills required resulted mismatch between demand and supply of manpower. Coombs (1970) also identifies similar type of factors, which necessitated educational planning as a connective device in developing economies.

Planning for Future Education

While planning for the pattern of education for the next century, care should be taken to ensure that it should help the development of planetary civilisation and new world order which is just, humane and harmonious, respecting the dignity and sanctity of human personality and contributing to the advancement of liberty, equality and fraternity in the society. The great change visualised is the primacy of culture in the life of man. In the post-industrial age the rich nations must fill their leisure and regulate their consumption of material wealth by greater pursuit of the things of the mind and the spirit. For the poor, their cultural life will help people's participation in the developmental process, strengthen national integration and cultural identity, and afford a quality of life not exclusively dependent on material affluence. For both the rich and the poor of the world, culture and cultural values will be the source of cooperation upon which peace, welfare and life's quality can emerge and thrive. If the 20th century has been a century of economy and material expansion, the twenty first century may herald the primacy of culture and stress upon man's inner life and spirituality.

When one foresees the future scenario in respect to India it looks as if India has accorded one of the lowest priorities to of the most important factors of development. When examining the education prospects for the future, it is necessary to have a glance at the prevailing national figures. India, ranks 115th in the world in terms of investment in education and it is considered the lowest in the world. In the year 2000 AD nearly 50 per cent of the world's illiterate were in India. There is widespread feeling among the educationists that considerable money was being spent to chalk out a future course of action but till now the progress was at a very low ebb. The figures further point out that almost 60 per cent females and 40 per cent were males were illiterates, which brought the total illiteracy figures to 48 per cent according to 1991 census.

The present system of education which has been moulded in the light of experience of Industrial Revolution of material success, monetary profit, acquisitive competition and national ambitions, the education of the future must be devised for attainment of a higher quality of life and greater cooperation among nations and cultures. The present concept of mankind will move from its realm of abstraction to the tangible reality of the planetary civilisation.

Centre-State Financial Relation in Education

Educational finance, it has been rightly said, is like an iceberg. As with iceberg, so with financing of education, the obscure is often more important than the obvious.

The financial provisions of the Indian Constitutions are generally based on the government of India Act, 1935. Many articles relating to financial matters, as indeed several of them relating to other matters also, are reproduced verbatim from this Act. The departures that the constitution makes from its prototype, like the vesting of residuary powers in the union and the incorporation in the constitution of the statutory obligation of appointing a finance commission every five years, were those necessitated by the changed political situation.

The main financial provisions of the constitution are contained in Article 268 to 281. These deal with the division of revenues between the union and the states. The union and state lists in the seventh schedule together enumerate 31 different sources of revenue. Of these, 12 are placed in the union list and 19 in the state list.

Central assistance to the states for education falls into two broad categories. First, there are the statutory grants under the award of the finance commission. Second, there is the plan assistance given, in the form of loans and grants under the relevant articles of the constitution. The second category of assistance, which for obvious reasons is going to be the main theme of decision to follow, is plan assistance. It is estimated on schematic basis and is given partly on loan and partly on grant basis. Some schemes would involve elements of revenue as well as capital expenditure. Broadly speaking, there are two main types of schemes in the education for which central aid is available namely, the centrally sponsored schemes and the centrally assisted schemes.

Structure and Sources of Educational Finance

Education is a sub-system of the wider social system. Although, it has a separate identity, it functions autonomously to a limited extent. It has important linkages with the economic, political, religious and other sub-systems, which in turn exert powerful influence on the system of education. Education is dependent on the economic sector for funds, as it has limited resource potential and capacity to fund itself. Education is one of the sectors, which receives huge government funds. Therefore, this has to be accountable and responsible to the society.

Before attempting to analyse state's educational expenditure, it is essential to clearly understand, what constitutes the state's educational finances, its structure, sources and determinates of funding. In our country the responsibility for education of the masses devolves on the Government as constitutional obligation, as it is viewed as an essential input of human resource development. Consequently, the central and state Government made considerable allocation of funds for education in their annual budgets. These budgetary allocations cover the wide spectrum of educational activities such as primary education, secondary and higher education, inclusive of professional courses like engineering and medicine and also adult and mass education, extension education and youth activities, sports etc. Therefore, Government's role in the field of education is all pervasive and important.

In view of the perceived need to enrich human resources especially by way of promoting education and training. The networks of educational facilities are planned in such as way that equity in the provision of such facilities and efficiency in delivery of services are duly ensured for various sections of the society. India has adopted a mixed economic system where by the public sector has largely assumed the responsibility of providing infrastructural facilities, and while the private sector is to concentrate more in the main stream of economic activities such as manufacturing and production of goods and services. In this mixed system, like the other spheres of development, the private and public sectors participate in extending the educational services at almost all levels. The responsibility for making adequate provision for educational facilities, however, rests mainly on the government and even the recognised private institutions receive a considerably proportion of funds (about 55 per cent or more) from its different agencies.

The centre and the state annual allocation on education sector amounts to almost 20 per cent of the total budget allocations accounting for nearly 3 to 4 per cent of their GDP/SDP.

Over the years there has been a steady increase in the budgetary allocations on education. However, as money being a scarce resource and there are other priority and essential sector which need to be looked after, there is a limit to which state could allocate funds for education. This is an important and pertinent factor in financing of higher education, as apparently there seems to be a quantum jump in private investments in higher education. This has created at paradoxical situation, whereby state budgetary allocations for educational sector has grown disproportionately to the growth of government institutions. The analysis shows that the main beneficiary of this large growth is the private sector educational institutions.

It has to be noted that the maintenance of standards of education, however, falls under the domain of the government. Further, various federating units of the government share the responsibility of providing education. In 1976, education was included in the concurrent list of the constitution and since then education has become a joint responsibility of the centre and the states; and therefore, both levels of government are equally responsible for providing necessary finances, monitoring of educational programmes through mutual co-operation and coordination. The cost of education is thus largely borne by both the central and the state governments and partly by the individuals who benefit from education or buy education for their wards.

It could be seen that the universities and colleges are financed by the central and state governments to the extent of 80% of their total expenditure and the remaining portions if financed from fees, consultancies, endowments and philanthropic contributions. In addition, various union ministries like agriculture, industry directly extends financial assistance to universities and university level institutions. The University Grants Commission (UGC) which is mainly responsible for maintenance of standards of higher education and co-ordination of universities activities provides funds for the maintenance of standards of higher education. Central universities (CUs) and to some extent to Deemed Universities (DUs) are also funded by UGC. The institutions of National importance like IITs are directly funded by the Department of Education in the Ministry of Human Resource Development.

The states are responsible for meeting the entire financial needs of state universities and largely the colleges, while the University Grants Commission provides plan grants on a matching basis. As most of the institutions in the state of Karnataka fall under the purview of the state, the finances for the development of higher education are largely provided by it from its own resources and partly from devolution of resources received through different channels of the central government. The major portion of expenditure of Universities (about 80 per cent) comprises non-plan expenditure, as has been stated earlier, is fully borne by the states in respect of the institutions established by them.

The Development of higher education in our country is crucially dependent on the availability of financial resources and the method by which it is provided to universities determines not only the pace and direction but also the quality of higher education.

It was also observed that, private educational institutions, which seek financial support from the state governments, have been able to maintain good standard in education due to their various sources of resources. It reveals that, higher the resources and higher in quality of education.

Indian Constitution and Education

The Indian constitution provides perhaps the world's most elaborate and detailed distribution of power between the federation and its constituent units (Articles 246(2), 246(3) and 248).

Provisions relating to education are spread over several parts *of* the Indian Constitution. In part IV of the constitution relating to the directive principle of state policy, there are provisions, .which lay down the educational desiderate the country should strive to achieve. There is the provision in part XVII of the constitution; which invests the union with the responsibility to see the facilities are available to linguistic minorities for instruction in their mother language at the primary stage. Then there are the provisions in part III, which guarantee certain educational and cultural rights to individuals, and minorities based on religion or language. Finally, there the provisions that divides legislative power in education between the union and the states.

Article 45 (Part IV) directs that the state shall endeavor to provide, within a period of ten years from the commencement of the constitution for free and compulsory education for an children until they complete the age of fourteen years, it means that the local, the state and the, central governments should strive to achieving this objective.

The Article (350A) reads: "It shall be the endeavor *of* every state and every local authority within the state to provide adequate facilities for instruction in the mother tongue at the primary stage of education to children belonging to linguistic minority groups and the president may issue such directions to any state as he considers necessary or proper for securing the provision of such facilities". The main constitutional provision regarding education, however, is to be found in the seventh scheduled, at entry II of list II. The entry reads "education, including universities subject to the provisions of entries 63, 64, 65 and 66 of list I and entry 25 of list III.

Manpower Forecasting and Educational Planning

The decades of 1950s and 1960s have witnessed growing interest in manpower forecasting and educational planning in developing countries. Many countries in Asia have formulated economic and social development plans with attention given to manpower problem. A common concern has been expansion of employment opportunities to absorb ever increasing labour force so as to achieve reduction in unemployment and under employment and to develop technical skills. Manpower forecasting helps in planning education so that people with required skills are available at right time and at right place and avoids mismatch between demand and supply of manpower with any given skill. This approach has been attempted in the formulation of education plans in many countries.

The manpower approach to educational planning, however, has received some criticism in the recent decade on both methodological and functional grounds. The criticism has come particularly from those who advocate rate of return or cost-benefit approach. At the same time the search continues for solutions to the problem of optimal manpower development and utilization through programming models.

Basic Concepts in Manpower Forecasting

In making manpower forecasts for educational planning the 'education sector' and 'employment sector' may be considered as subsystems of the national economy. Manpower forecasts normally have to begin with analysis of the existing situation of education and employment, that is stocks in the sub-systems. After taking the stock projections have to be made for the intake into the 'education sub-system'. Out put of the sub-systems by levels and types of education, that is, flow within the education sub-system should consider dropout rates and demand in 'employment sub-system' by considering "replacement demand" as well as 'expansion demand'.

The term 'manpower requirements' may be used exclusively in connection with stocks, it is the total number in the labour force needed at a given time to satisfy the developmental need of the country specific to each sector, occupation, type and level of skill.

The term "annual demand for manpower" may be used in connection with flows and it represents the labour force specific to each sector and occupation each year.

Annual demand can be split into two components: replacement demand needed to adjust the stock to higher levels of activity. Expansion demand, however, depends not only on the growth of activity but also on the productivity.

The assessment of annual demand must thus logically proceed in two stages; the first is the assessment of requirements in terms of stock and the second step to convert stocks into flows that is, deriving the annual demand from the stocks. One must necessarily deal with the inter-relationships of stocks and flows. For this reason, the analysis is always a dynamic one. The assessment of 'manpower requirements' for given growth targets is usually closely linked with the apparatus used for general economic projections, but taking into consideration possible influence of technological change on the level of productivity. Science the aggregate figures are of limited value to an effective educational policy, ideally the manpower requirements must be broken down by occupation, type and level of education. Experience has shown that there is a high degree of substitutability between manpower of different occupations. Technological coefficients determining the level of labour productivity also have to be established in projecting manpower requirements.

The other side of the coin is, of course, projections on supply. The usual technique employed for projecting supply is the 'student flow analysis'. Here again the point of reference is the stock of students in different level/types of education in the system. The analysis logically starts at the point where students enter an education system or cycle. In the primary cycle, the new entrants in to the system that is grade I of primary school, after one year are promoted to the second grade or they may still remain in the first grade as repeaters or they may leave the school (drop out). Student flow between different educational cycles is usually called transition rates. These transition rates are of greater importance while assessing the supply of manpower.

The Practice of Manpower Forecasting

With the possible exception of centrally planned economics, it is very difficult to find strict matching of manpower demand and supply in terms of occupations and spatial distribution of job opportunities. In some countries attempts are made to prepare manpower planning at the sectoral level, while in some others, forecasting is made of single occupations which require very specialized skill, such as engineers, scientists, doctors, and so on. The experiences with manpower forecasting in some countries including Canada, France, Britain, Thailand, Nigeria, United States and India are documented in a volume edited by Ahmed and Blaug (1973). Some of those experiences were reviewed in the following section.

France

Manpower forecasting in France is an integral part of economic planning as a whole. The objective of manpower forecasting is to specify the number and kinds of people required to achieve the economic goal set out in the plan. These man power forecasts take the form of occupations and educational distribution of the labour force in the target year. But, manpower forecasts are also made for a date beyond the target year of the plan on a pre-education system. Manpower forecasting in the French plan also has four distinct phases: (a) the total supply of manpower, (b) sectors employment, (c) the occupational distribution of the labour force by sectors of employment and (d) the educational distribution of the labour force within a given sector and occupation.

England and Wales

In England and Wales, when there was a substantial shortage of qualified teachers they setup a National Advisory Council to draw plans to overcome the shortage. The council made projections of the future demand for teachers using pupil/teacher ratios.

The interest in forecasting the number of doctors needed to ensure the provision of adequate medical services has had a somewhat longer history than general manpower forecasting. In Britain, several attempts have been made to estimate the necessary expansion of medical schools on the basis of the manpower forecasts.

The United States

The earliest study of doctor requirements in the United States dates back to the 1930's when Lee and Jones (1933) attempted to determine doctor requirements on the basis of assumptions about the doctor population ratio. The Surgeon-General's Consultant Group (Bane Committee) also used projections of the doctor/ population ratio to make projections of doctor requirements in 1975. The US Public Health Service (1967) made projections based on (1) Professional judgements, (2) The highest doctor/population ratio, and (3) The input-output model developed by the Bureau of labour Statistics.

India

Manpower and considerations have been emphasized in India ever since independence, and a fairly elaborate machinery has been created for collecting information about manpower, preparing forecasts and formulating manpower and educational policy. Institute of Applied Manpower Research (IMAR), setup during 3rd five-year plan undertakes research on supply and demand for different categories of manpower. The main focus of the forecasting activity has been on the requirements for specific key occupations. Four major factors which determine the flow of students into the cycle are (I) the population of admission or intake age, (ii) the intake rate to the first grade, (iii) the rate of repetition at different grades; and (iv) the rate of promotion at different grades.

Canada

In its first Annual Review, the Economic Council of Canada prepared employment projection for four sectors in the economy namely agriculture, public administration, community services and commercial non-agriculture. Total employment in these four sectors was derived from demographic projections on the basis of specified assumption about fertility, mortality and net immigration. These were then transformed into labour force projections by applying projected age and sex specific participation rates and finally into employment estimates after allowing for 3 per cent of unemployment. Various methods were used to desegregate the total projections into projected employment in each of the four sectors.

Centrally Planned Economics

Manpower forecasts in centrally planned economic particularly in Eastern European countries such as Bulgaria, Hungary, Poland and German Democratic Republic are comprehensive and provide a strong basis for educational planning. In institutions of higher learning the academic programme are featured by sectoral specialization, so that the graduates are more geared towards the professional /skill requirements for operation in a particular sector such as agriculture industry, transport foreign trade, social services, and so on.

This is evident from the above that, manpower planning is prioritized in all most all nations in the world while planning for different sectors. If proper care is taken in the process of planning one could utilize resources efficiently.

SECTION – III

BRIEF HISTORICAL SKETCH OF KARNATAKA

Karnataka: An Historical Sketch

The name Karnataka is derived from 'Karunadu' literally known as lofty land. The name is entirely identified because much of Karnataka is a high plateau. Karnataka has a rich historical past. It has witnessed the rise and fall of several dynasties such as the Satavahanas, Kadambas, Banas, Gangas, Rashtrakutas, Hoysala, Vijayanagar, Wodeyars and others. It has contributed much to the main stream of Indian culture, art, architecture, literature, religion and philosophy. Its world famous temples of Belur, Halebeedu and Somanathapur, its rock cut temples of Aihole, Badami and Pattadakal, its tallest statue of Gomateshwara at Shravanabelagola, and its biggest dome of Gol Gumbaz at Bijapur, all attract lovers of art from the four corners of the world. It has been the meeting and mingling ground of different faiths such as Hinduism, Buddhism, Jainism, Christianity and Islam. It has been the cradle of a renaissance in Kannada literature enriched by Pampa, Ranna, Panna and host of other great movement in medieval times of extol love of god and love and service for people. Many social reform movements came into being, the most important of them being the movement led by Sri. Basaveswara. It has the unique distinction of resisting the colonial power by fighting four Mysore wars. The resistance of Hyderali, Tippu Sultan against the expansionist policy of the Britishers in one of the renowed historical facts. Their martyrdom for the land of Mysore State in the wars is a proof of their love to their motherland. It has produced in recent times men of great eminence in arts, literature, science and administration such as Sri. Vishveshwaraiah, C.V. Raman and Kuvempu. Indeed, Karnataka is justly pound of its rich cultural heritage and distinguished sons.

Land, People and Culture of Karnataka

The present enlarged state of Karnataka, which his co-terminus with all regions of Kannada speaking people came into existence on 1st November, 1956 under the States Reorganisation Act of 1956, but its earlier name of Mysore State was changed to Karnataka only in November 1973. It commands a unique position bounded by Arabian sea on the west, Andhra Pradesh on the east, Maharastra in the North, Tamil Nadu and Kerala in the South. In size it is the eighth largest state in India with 1,91,791 Sq. Kms in area, with 448 lakhs as its population in 1991. It is divided for administrative purpose into four revenue divisions, 20 districts and 175 taluks (Navanita Rao, 1994).

Karnataka is traversed by numerous rivers as Cauvery, Krishna, Ghataprabha, Malaprabha, Tungabhadra, Sharavathi, Nethravathi and Kalinadi, which acts as life sustaining source to the people and for generating hydroelectric power. Karnataka enjoys a congenial salubrious climate in certain parts but has dry and warm weather in certain others.

The State is endowed with varied and rich resources. The most important natural resources are its flora and fauna, climate and water resources, soils, minerals and marina resources.

The State is endowed with a number of rivers. The two important river systems of the State are Krishna and its tributaries in the north and the Cauvery and its tributaries in the south. The Cauvery with its six tributaries waters southern Mysore and in fact forms the economic life blood of the southern region. The Krishna and its tributaries waters the State's northern region. The main tributaries of Krishna viz., Ghataprabha, Malaprabha and Tungabhadra are of economic significance, as they develop rapids and falls along their courses and hence are best suited for the generation of hydro-electricity. Among the westward flowering rivers, the Sharavathi, the Kalinadi and Nethravathi are prominent.

The climate of the state may be described as essentially tropical monsoon type. Although by and large Karnataka is endowed with pleasant climate, the summers are uncomfortably hot in the northern region.

Economic Structure of the State

Karnataka embarked upon planned economic development soon after independence. The economy of Karnataka has registered a fairly balanced growth in almost all sectors.

The trends in the growth of SDP at constant prices, which reflect the growth of real output in the economy, reveal that the long term rate of growth of the State's economy has been marginally higher than that of the country. The long term growth of the State's economy is around 3.7% compound per annum as against 3.5% of the country as a whole. However, in recent years, the rate of growth in the State's economy has been lower than that of the country (Navanitha Rao, 1994).

Karnataka is the home of large number of minerals of economic importance. It contributes all the gold and silver produced in the country. Among the other minerals Iron ore, lime stone, manganese, chromate and copper are important. The department of industries and commerce has a fairly well knit structure, which actively assists small scale and cottage industries and handicrafts.

Progress of Education in Karnataka

Primary Education

There are 40,776 primary schools in the state, out which 23,383 are lower primary schools and 17,393 are Higher Primary Schools during 1993-94. Enrollment in Class I to VII is 76.72 lakhs of which 52.22lakhs are studying in classes I to IV and 24.50 lakh children are in class V to VII. Over the years enrolment rate has been increasing by 2 to 3 per cent.

Though the above achievement looks impressive, what remains to be achieved is staggering. There are still lakhs of working children who are deprived of basic education due to economic compulsions. Though the gross enrolment at primary school level is 90 per cent, we failed to retain them to finish at least primary education. The drop-out rate is as higher as 56 per cent in primary education which is of great concern.

Emphasis is being laid to make learning in Schools attractive and lessen the burden of the parents. Various incentive schemes like Vidya Vikas (supply of free books), AKSHYA, Vasthradhara (free uniform scheme) and Ahara (supply of nutritious food) are initiated to improve enrollment and encourage retention of children at the primary stage.

As a part of providing one classroom and one teacher for every class by 2000 AD, 12,000 classrooms were taken up for construction during 1993-94 with an allocation of Rs. 1610 lakhs.

Enrollment in lower primary education has gone up from 61.1 per cent in 1956-57 to 93.6 per cent in 1980-81. However girl child enrolment is lagging behind at about 85 per cent and it was estimated that one out of every four scheduled caste children is still out of school. With regard to enrollment in higher primary education, it increased from 17.9 per cent to 39.5 per cent during the same period. It is noted from a study that performance of SC's as compared to non-SC's in the growth of enrollment over the years is higher at the lower primary stage and quite low at the higher primary stage.

Government of Karnataka has offered various incentives to encourage enrolment and to increase retention rate, some of them are:

1. Attendance scholarship to girls.
2. Free supply of textbooks.
3. Mid-day meals
4. Pre-matric scholarship
5. Hostel facilities
6. Residential school facilities

To provide continuous and comprehensive in service training to the primary school teachers 16 new institutes called DIET (District Institutes of Educational Training) were established during 1993-94. Similarly 6 CTEs (Colleges of Teacher Education) have been started under a centrally sponsored scheme to provide in service training to the secondary schools teachers.

Secondary Education

Enrollment in secondary schools increased from 11.1 per cent in 1960_61 to 22.0 per cent by 1984-85. It is estimated that 13.82 lakhs of children in the age-group 14-17 will be demanding secondary education by 2000. This will be 75 per cent more of the enrolment in 1984-85. With proper balancing and through economy of scale, this demand can be met by opening additional sections in existing secondary schools, upgrading higher primary schools and limiting new locations to deprived regions.

Higher secondary education is organised in such a way that it is being handled by more than one agency. The plus two stage of education is offered by institutions called as independent Junior Colleges, which do not have either a high school section or a college attached to them. This is also offered by higher secondary schools, which are extensions of high schools, which serves as feeder institutions. The pre-university board administers junior colleges and the department of public instruction administers higher secondary schools. And pre university colleges are administered by the department of collegiate education. They have a common examination administered by the pre-University board. There are

737 higher secondary schools, 126 junior colleges and 195 degree colleges in 1984-85.

Higher Education

Higher education in Karnataka began with 12 colleges in the state in 1956-57 and steadily their number increased up to 253 (colleges in general education at degree level) by 1984-85 and further 834 by 1991-92. They are now spread over 9 universities of the state. There are also two Agricultural Universities and 4 institutions of higher learning with status of deemed universities.

The growth in the number of colleges was particularly rapid between 1980-90, wherein the number of colleges increased from 425 in 1980 to 704 in 1990 and 834 in 1991 -92. Private colleges have grown at a faster rate than the government colleges. Government colleges increased from 37 in 1960 to 159 by 1991-92. During the same period private colleges increased from 57 to 675. The growth is less than 5 times in the case of government colleges, but nearly 12 times in the case of private colleges. During 94-95 in total there are 679 general education institutes, 1458 university colleges, 52 engineering colleges, 19 allopathic medical colleges, 38 dental colleges and 37 Indian system of medical colleges. All these colleges are spread over 10 universities.

As we seen illiteracy is quite high in the state. Government of Karnataka introduced a system of non-formal education during the Fifth Plan Period for non-enrolled and dropout children in the age group of 9-14 years. Proficiencies, which required in I to IV standards in formal primary education will be imparted in two years of non formal education. Later on these students are eligible thereafter to continue formal education from V standard onwards. In addition, the government of Karnataka in 1983 introduced a programme called 'Aksara Sena' or literacy on a war footing. This includes liberal assistance to voluntary agencies for promotion of non-formal education for children (apart from an adult education component).

Adult Education

Eradication of illiteracy has been one of the major objective of the Government since independence. However, the pace of promotion of literacy is far from adequate. This Lacuna is sought to be set right with the launching of the Total Literacy Campaign, conceived and implemented by the national Literacy Mission Authority with the support of the State Government. The new strategy under the TLC is the adoption of an entire district of state for literacy drive based on voluntarism. The key to this campaign is motivation and mobilisation of every section of the people.

Karnataka is one of the first states in the country to take up the comprehensive programme of total literacy, beginning with the districts of Dakshina Kannada and Bijapur in 1990. The campaign has expanded to Shimoga, Bidar, Raichur, Tumkur, Mandya and more recently to Dharwad, Mysore, Bangalore Rural Districts, Uttara Kannada, Chickmagalore, Gulbarga, Kogadu, Kolar and Chitradurga.

One of the thrust areas in VIII five year plan is the eradication of illiteracy and providing continuing education for neo-literates. Accordingly, a detailed plan of action has been chalked out in Karnataka with the task of covering nearly 80 lakhs illiterates in the age group of 15-35 years. The scheme of Jana Shikshana Nilayas, was started during 1988-89 under adult literacy programme at the instance of National Literacy Mission. They were ment to sustain interest in reading among neo-literates and to prevent them from relapsing into illiteracy. Each Jana Shikshana Nilaya comprises a library-reading room with newspaper, magazines, audio cassette player-cum-recorder etc. In the sate there are 1175 Jana Shikshana Nilayas established during 1988-99; each Jana Shikshana Nilaya has a budgetary allocation of Rs. 14,000/- out of which Rs. 7,000/- is recurring and Rs. 7000 non-recurring in the first year and Rs. 7,000/- recurring in the subsequent years. The total budgetary allocation is Rs. 82.25 lakhs during 1993-94.

Vocational Education

Vocationalisation of Education has been a major concern in the overall transformation of the educational system in India and in providing productive employment opportunities, it assumes significance under 10 + 2 pattern of education. The scheme which was initially introduced as a centrally sponsored scheme was subsequently transferred to the state.

Initially, 52 courses were introduced in 18 institutions in three districts, with enrollment of 1275 students. Now, 1027 courses are being offered in 589 institutions having enrolment of about 30,000 students.

In an effort to make vocational education more effective by bringing about qualitative improvement, a Technical Expert Committee was appointed under the chairmanship of Dr. S. Ramegowda, Vice-Chancellor, Karnataka University. Based on the recommendations of this Expert Committee, 100 courses have been introduced. Provision for grants has been made for purchase of equipments and construction of work sheds at the rate of Rs. One lakh for each course during 1993-94, by Government of India. To provide employment to those who have been trained under vocational education Government of India have brought vocational courses under Apprenticeship Act. Accordingly, nearly 1000 candidates have been placed under apprenticeship training in different industrial organisations by the end of March 1994.

Need and Importance of the Study

This is very clear from what all has been said above that research emphasis is more either on outlays and expenditure on a sector of education or the case studies of expenditure on educational institutions. The financial allocations in five year plans received low priority for qualitative improvement. If the determination of proper priorities is the essence of educational planning, this comparative neglect of quality should be regarded as a major weakness. The fundamental difference is that the planning of expansion and the planning of qualitative improvement have not been put together and ignored by and large by our educational planners. We have not been able to raise to the occasion and the results have been rather indifferent. The expenditure orientation is the major weakness of our present educational planning. Therefore we have failed miserably in reducing wastage and stagnation phenomena at primary and secondary levels.

It is universally accepted that educational planning in India has not been linked with economic planning. Our planners have not paid adequate attention to manpower needs. Till 1968 the country did not have any national policy on education. The national policy formulated in 1968 remained, more or less, on paper. It is only in 1986, India has been able to emerge with new policy on national education with new vision and perspectives. Until this time, unfortunately, as Professor J. P. Naik has rightly pointed out, our educational planning in the post independence period has neither a clear vision nor a definite direction. As a result the expansion of education facilities has not been uniform in the whole country. There are regional imbalances expansion and across different sectors of education.

This is further evident in the statement made by Prof. V.K.R.V Rao who says, "There has been too little emphasis on actual balance between the provision of general and vocational education while there has been some diversification of education. It has not made much impact on manpower needs nor is geared to our development programme. In addition to this, wastage and stagnation is found all along the line in our educational system". A strong weakness in our planning is that inadequacy of evaluation and research.

Individuals and institutions have been done various studies to fill the gap in theory and practice in the case of educational plans. Some of the studies though dealt with all sectors of education and expenditure, no comprehensive study on the allocation and expenditure for education has been done involving the total plan periods. The strong criticism of our planning is lack of coordination between centre and the states as far as educational planning is concerned. And therefore, there is an urgent need to undertake state level studies in order to evaluate trends in allocation and expenditure for education at different levels.

Limitations of the Study

Any research is bound to be done under several limitations. These limitations arise in two respects:

1. Limitations due to topic chosen for research itself.

2. Limitations due to time constraints as well as non-availability of accurate and objective information on which generally conclusions are drawn.

The present study has both the limitations as shown below:

1. The present study analysis the allocations and expenditures made by the Government of Karnataka from 1951-52 to 1996-97. The study attempts to identify only the trends of allocations. Consequently the study has no justification beyond this.

2. The present study attempts to know financial allocations and expenditure of the state Government only. But the central allocations, financial schemes, constituency development grants through Members of Parliament (MPs), allocations of Zilla Panchayat, Taluk Panchayat, Municipal Corporation, Town Municipalities for educational development in their respective localities has not been taken in to consideration.

2

Review of Related Literature

This Chapter presents a detailed review of research studies done in the field of educational finance. Further, studies have been classified into national, international and state level studies besides the classification based on variables.

Educational financing has proved to be the most popular field of research. Several studies at the individual level and the institutional level have been conducted in this area.

Financing of education as an area of study seems to have arisen out of several quetions on aspects like patterns and processes of resource allocations, locating and mobilising resources for education, with special reference to the total national economy and inter-educational sectors. These basic questions have thus been rightly reflected in this doctoral as well as major institutional works complied and given in many documents. These studies can be analysed mainly in two ways:

(i) the studies characteristically encompassing macro systems versus micro systems, and

(ii) the studies having historical versus cross-sectional character.

In the first category, studies have been conducted on financing in less developed countries and individual Indian provinces and another feature has been analysis of financing of education as a single unit to analysing it stagewise, like higher education, elementary education, etc. In the second category, certain studies have been more of historical nature, whereas certain other studies have been somewhat problem oriented.

With increasing enrollment and the expanding scope of educational activities, coupled with decreasing resource availability for the educational sector (in view of competing claims from other sectors) the problem off finance has become increasingly formidable in all sectors of education. The problems are exprienced at three levels. First, at the level of the educational sector as a whole; secondly, at the level of sub - sectors of education; and thirdly, at the level of the individedual educational institution. These financial pressures - sectoral, sub - sectoral and institutional. would each have its own externalities on students and parents so far as the education of the household is concerned. It also has implications for the quality of education currently provided and the capability of the sector to undertake innovative programmers. Financial pressures, coupled with declining educational standards and the weakening capability of the educational sector to train and educate students according to certain requirements, have also given rise to a new class of institutions which are termed parallel, educational institution's. These trends emerged more and more clearly over the past decade or so. The general cost escalations have aggravated the problem of finance for education. In our federal framwork, irritants in inter- governmental relations have created additional dimensions to the problem. Studies in this field are therefore expected to consider new themes and issues.

During the 1990s, most studies of educational finances to examining the problem of individual educational institutions (such as those dealing with university finances sponsored by the ICSSR and UGC) and to the analysis of the prospects of individual sources of finance. From the studies that appeared during the 1980s, these seems to be a slight shift in focus, though the traditional themes have not been altgother abandoned by researchers.

Of the studies, abstracts of which are being reported in the IV the survey of educational research, three were case studies of university finances, two dealt with the problem of education. Two considered the basis question of the linkages between education finance and the problem of social justice. Five studies considered the effectiveness of scholarships as an instrument for educational equality. Two examined the possiblity of adopting an innovative approach in budgeting that, through savings within the educational sector, could provide dependable source of educational finance.

As started earlier, the studies in finances for higher education during the 1970s were largly case studies. On the same pattern, three more studies of higher education finances have been done (Singh, 1986; Jena, 1983; Tiwari, 1986). A study of higher education finances in the newly created state of Manipur since 1949 clearly shows that the problems of educational finances which have been observed since 1949 in other parts of the country are also observed in the case of Manipur, there is an unplanned growth of institutions imbalances in the course of expansion, improper budgeting systems, non-availabilty of the physical resources necessary for institutions off higher education, etc. While the expenditure of higher education in Manipur increased 727 times between 1949-50 and 1979-80, the UGC's contribution to the development of colleges was only marginal- only about 9 per cent of the total expenditure of huge colleges from 1960-61 through 1974-75. Administrative costs accounted for the bulk of university expenditure. It is intriguing that the increase in expenditure of libraries was minimal. By and large, the picture of higher education finances in Manipur presents a good idea of the crises that the higher education sector as a whole is facing in India.

Quite a good number of agencies and individuals having worked on various dimensions of the problem of financing. They are: Azad (1972, 1975), committees and commissions on education, Jha (1974), Mathur (1974), Mathur (1968), Mukerji (1974), Naik (1965a and 1975b), Nair and Pillai (1962), Nanjundappa (1975), Nigam (1974), Panchamukhi (1970,1974), Pandit (1972), Razvi (1960) and Shah (1969).

In this group of studies, a few prominent trends are discernible. The first and the foremost is the financing of Indian education as the unit. A major group of contributions to this issue are the committess and commissions on education. The Sargent Report (1944), among other things dealt with the issue of financing in terms of cost of junior and senior basis schooling, secondary education, university education, teacher training, school medical service, education of the handicapped, recreative and social activities, employment bureau and administration.The Kher Committees (1950) major task had been to find out ways and means of financing educational development in India. Education Commission (1966) has dealt with the problem more elaborately. It has devoted and exclusive chapter to this issue in addition to supplementary notes. The works of the Task Force on Educational Finances of the deucation commission (1966) are also worth noting. Misra (1959) dealt with the problem in a historical perspective ranging over a total period of 1698 to 1959. Shah (1969) studies the finances resources, allocation of funds to various levels and types of education, the financing by private and public sector and such other issues between 1950-51 and 1960-61. Mathur's (1968) study was in the same direction and for some years. The contribution of fees as related to overall educational expenditure has been studies by Panchamukhi (1970). Pandit (1972) also studied the financing or India education in the first three plan periods for its effectiveness. Nair and Pillai's plan (1962) study stood out of this treland. They studied the problem of finance in the same texture but only at the state level- Karala.The main problems of the study were the procedures of educational finance, source of financial responsibilities of central, state local and private agencies.

The second trend in this area is to deal with the problem of finance at different levels but in all India prospective. Nail and Lawler (1965) studied and financing of elementary education. The main objective of their study was to develop the procedures of financing on the principles of equalization. They came out with a formula for central aid per pupil. The second study, pertaining to primary education, has been done by Pathak (1967). Pathak's study has , however, been more of a theory testing, of the Naik Lawler formula to be applied in case of financing of Zilla Parishads in U.P. Except for the reports of the Commissions like secondary Education (1952) and Education Commission (1966), the financing secondary education has not been studied either at the doctoral or at the Insititutional levels separately. Problem of financing of higher education was studies by Razvi (1960) in less developed countries. Azad (1972) studies by Razvi (1960) in less developmed countries. Azad (1972) studied the financing of higher education in independent India rather critically. His main concern has been analysis of the patterns both aggregate as well as instititional in terms of central and state government roles and functions, and certainpolicy issues pertaining to financing of higher education. In a second study, Azad (1975) surdies the patterns, procedures and policies of government to institution of heigher education.

Third group of studies is the financing of universites sponsored by the ICSSR. In all there are six studies in this group. The six universities that have been studied are Bombay (Panchamukhi, 1974), Calcutta (Mukerji, 1974) Karnataka (Nanjudappa, 1975), Kerala (Mukerji, 1974), Patna (Jha, 1974) and Rajasthan (Nigam,1974). These studies have major focus on sources of finances, expenditure by heads, and the diffculties faced by the different universities due to financial indequancy. It may be noted that in these studies, affiliating unversities were selected expect for Patna. One major features of university financies is that while state government has been the biggest source for many universities, the fee, especially for examinations, have been the largest resource for Calcutta University and to a great extent for Kerala University.

Endowments play a considerable role on financing the universities of Bombay and Calcutta. So far as expenditure is concerned there has been a phenomenal rise; a special feature in this regard is the right expenditure on administration as compared to that on academic purpose. Another notable feature is that the trend of expenditure which was weighted more towards academic items than that on administration has been reversed (Mukerji, 1974).

A comparatively related problem to educational financing is the grant-in-aid system. Since 1854, when the grant-in-aid system was introduced, this has grown is size and complexity. In independent India, this has been the main procedure of financing at all stages. Naik (1965) made a comparative study of rules relating to grant-in-aid to colleges of arts and science, and secondary schools. The problem of grant-in-aid in higher education was further studied by Azad (1975) with special reference to patterns, procedures and policies.

The studies on financing have been mostly of historical and descriptive nature. Document analysis has been the common method of data collection except for a few where other methods of social seiences research have been utilized. Questionnaires as an instrument was used by Nair and Pillai (1962), Shah (1969),Panchamukhi (1970), Azad (1972, 1975), and Jha (1974). Nailk and Lawyers (1965) study was rather akin to modeling and Patnak's (1967) was of theory testing . While most of the studies have been either historical or descriptive, the works of the commission on education have made efforts to the project the future expenditure on education. The methods of analyses and presentation of the data have been mainly in terms of total expenditure at currents prices is the comparability of effective amounting over the years for the purpose of studying the growth of educational expenditures.

Financing of education has been the major area of research in economics of education. But the above review indicates the inadequency in certain respects. If the purpose of research of financing can be considered for financial planning also, the quoted researches are far inadequate. Morever, the treatment has usually been at global level. In that case, the finance has been mainly shown on the basis of plan outlays. The non plan budget, which is much larger at state levels needs to be studied. Further, whether at macro or micro levels the behaviors of revenue sources and expenditure heads need to be studies in depth.

Education has been the most vulnerable sector so far as the budget allocation is concerned, so much so that the five year plan budgeting has been only national in character. Education growth and efficiency needs to be studies. Last, but not the least important, is the near absence of research on programmer modeling which is essential for a sound educational planning. Kothari and Panchamukhi (1975) reviewed three such models. But the absence of such an important area for doctoral research is rather conspicuous.

Expenditure and educational growth are not only interrelated but rather interdependent phenomena.Educational growth depends upon the availbility of certain minimum facilities of resources. Simultaneously the growth of expenditure depends upon the need arising out of the growth of the educational sector. Considering the interdependence, the expenditure on education can well be considering as an investment.This investment concept brings in the question of efficiency both in terms of quantitative and qualitative growth. A few studies have been conducted on these problems. These are by Karnik (1967), Panchamukhi (1679), Pandit (1972), Sharma (1973), and the Shina (1967).

Sharma (1978) considered the following objectives; (i) to examine the amount of resources were allocated to education as a percentage of national gross product and, within education to various levels (ii) to study the pattern of allocation of resources to education by State Governments, (iii) to study this compared with State income, (iv) to examine whether allocation of resources on education by India were commensurate with the returns from investment in education, and (v) to study the ways the resources were allocated to education.

The statistical series of Minist y of Education of the Government of India and of international bodies like UNESCO provided data. Data were analysed in descriptive forms and through the application of the regression equation technique.

The findings of the study were: (1) In 1971, the proportion of GNP spent of education by India was 2.5 per cent, in US 6.7 per cent, the USSR 7.3 per cent. The number of persons in educational institutions in India were 79.8 million compared with 63.2 million in the USA and 62.3 million in the USSR. In terms of total population, India, the USA and USSR had 14.2 25.68 and 30.9 per cent respectively (2) During 1971-72, Manipur spent 10.71 per cent of its total SNDP, the highest among the state is. It was followed by HP and Kerala with 5.63 and 5.31 per cent respectively. The smallest proportion (0.36 per cent) was spent by Jammu and Kashmir (3) Seven states had lower per capital income but there expenditure per student was comparatively higher. (4) Manipur spent the highest proportion of its SNDP 5.77 (per cent) and Haryana the least (0.48 per cent) on primary education. More states spent more than one per cent of their SNDP on this level of education. (5) HP was proportionately the highter spender (3.20 per cent) on highter secondary education. The average of all the states worked out at 0.78 per cent. (6) Manipur spent the highes (0.79 per cent) on highter on education. The average for all the states was 0.25 per cent. (7) Bihar spent 0.20 per cent of its SNDP on grants to universities and college. The average proportion of grantas to there SNDP was 0.08 per cent. (8) The majority of states allocated 20-25 per cent of their total state budgets to education but Bihar, Nagaland, Orissa, Haryana and J&K allocated less than 20 percent (9) the proportion of funds to total budget allocated by state governments had little relevance to per capital income. (10) In 1971-72 Dehli was the only Union tertitory increased to 43.2 per cent. The average of all territories increased to 28.7 per cent from 24.3 in 1971-72. (11) The share of higher education to total expenditure on education was around 10 to 14 per cent. the patern changed slightly between 1971 and 1975. (12) The states which were economically backward paid a little more attention to higher education compared to the economically developed states. (13) The pay scales of teachers varioed from state to state. In some states they varied between private and government managed institutions. (14) No systematic planning in allocation of funds appeared to have been followed by the state governments. (15) four variables, viz, state total income, and enrollment in higher education explained 62 per cent of the variation in the allocations of grants. The relationship between the enrollment variable and grants was found to be poor. No relating on ship was found between the enrollment variable and grant from the UGC. (16) The method of grants adopted by the state governments differed from state to state. In some states it differed from university to university.

Panchamukhi (1967) studied that effect of public expenditure on public education and health during the period 1948-49 to 1960-61. This study was carried out on an all India Basis. Pandit (1972) studied the effectiveness of educational financing in India during the first three five year plan periods. In this study, the effectiveness was measured in terms of growth in educational expenditure, and private and social rates of return. Kanik (1967), Sharma (1973) and Sinha (1967) studied the educational expenditure vis-a-vis educational growth during the five year plan periods in Gujrat, Madhya Pradesh and Bihar respectively.In Gujrat, the educational devlopments was remarkable during the first three plan periods. The educational devlopments at all stages were far too short of mark in Bihar in spite of overall increase in the expenditure to a considerbale extent. Sharma's (1973) study was also in the same line except for an added dimension of studying the regional inqualities within the state of Madhya Pradesh.

These studies depended mainly on documents as the source of data. These documents are mainly the report available with the government department. The finding of these atudies would be valid to the extend of the reliability and validity of the data presented in the source material utilized for the purpose. Opinion survery was, however, used to supplement the data has been usually in the form of percentage calculations or presenting the data in raw numerical froms. The growth of expenditure has been presented in absolute terms rather than in relative terms. Panchamukhi (1967) study adopted multiple data analysis techniques, which included the use to regression analysis, factor analysis and input-output model.Pandit's (1972) study was based on three hypotheses. But, by its nature, it could not be hypothesis testing in strict sense of the term.

Relating educational growth to expenditure in cause and effect relationship seems to be rather over simplification of the issue. Educational development in the countries, which shook off their bonds of slavery recently, has border social base. It has to reekon with centrally old social stratification and political oppression which had resulted into complete denial of educational facilities to large segments of population. The plan outlays as well as non-plan budgets are far too adequate to explain fully the pace of educational development in the country or, for that matter, in any state. The issue becomes rather complicated under the present conditions, where private enterprise in education has assumed in prominent place in the development of education in certain sectors like secondary schools and colleges of arts, science and commerece. Research on effect on public expenditure on educational growth is an important dimension. It should be preferable to conduct such research at micro levels of smaller education units. Further, the research design in this case ought to identify other variables that may also actual contribute to the educational development. Funding the actual contribution of public expenditure on educational growth may have to involve appropriate research designs using factor analysis and covariance. Simultaneously, the qualitative aspect of research has to focus on the local conditions and forces that are responsible for the educational development.

Historical data on educational development finance for all levels and types of education clearly bring out the increasing predominant role that the sector is playing in education over the years. Does this historical trend imply that education is emerging more as public goods than private goods? To what extent has the increasing role of public financing for the purpose of distributional considerations come in conflict with the objective of allocative efficiency ? To what extent does public financing of education replace private financing ? The behaviours of private financing was analysed in depth by Shah (1968). Panchamukhi (1969) brings out the complementary effect of public educational expenditures of private educational expenditure in India during the fifties and sixties.

Sharma (1975) investigated the role that the private enterprise played in the promotion of education in Punjab during 1984 and 1966 . The private enterprise in education in Punjab, according to the author, was motivated mainly by the religious considerations of checking the progress of Christian missionaries in Punjab. During the post-independence period the State's dominating role has weakened this motive force for the private enterprises. Razvi (1960) viewed the state participation in education in India as desirable and considered it more as a socio-political necessity. The State participation, according to him, has to be strictly on an individual rather than tnstitutional basis for catering to the economic to the economic needs of the society.

The study by Azad (1972) was undertaken (i) to analyse the patterns of higher education finance aggregative as well as institutional, (ii) to study the patterns and procedures of financing of higher education adopted by the central and the state governments, and (iii) to discuss certain basic policy relating to the subject under reference.

The study was mainly limited to higher education during 1947 to 1966. The data were obtained from various ministries of the Government of India and other concerned organisations as well as the State governments. A questionnaire, relating to the patterns and procedures of state grant-in-aid, including certain policy issues relating to financing principals of affiliated colleges and experts. In all, response of 180 persons were analysed.

The Major Findings are as Follows

(i) The annual rate of growth of expenditure over the years under study (at constant prices) is the highest (twelve per cent) in the case of higher education as compared to 9.1 per cent in the case of overall education and 3,4 per cent in the case of national income. (ii) Both as per centage of whole, the expenditure of higher education expenditure has indicated a much higher rate of growth. (iii) At consiant price, the increases in the per student expenditure is insignificant both in the case of education as well as higher education (iv) If one considers the educational expenditure as a percentage of the educational income. (converted of Asia like Burma, Jordan, Pakistan and Vietnam), (v) In terms of per capita expenditure on education as a proportion of the per capita net national product, there have been material changes in the position of states, over the years under study. It is, however found that the differences among the states. With regard to effort (as represented by the per capita expenditure on education as a prportion of the per capita net nation product), have indicated a tendency to narrow down. It is also found thar educational expenditure has been a social overhead and has an element of inevitability which must be incured regardless of the states financing capacity. The study has also revealed states which spend which spend more on education also spent more on higher education. (vi) An analysis of the inter institutional priorities revealed that the state have been mixing large outlays on higher education than another educational programmes. Further, the disparities amongst the states, as reflected in their proportionate expenditure on higher education, have narrowed down over the years. This is revealed by the decline in the coefficient of variation in respect of different states, over the years (vii) The Universities have been planning larger outlays on 'consumption' i.e. Staff salaries, scholarship and conduct of examinations than of investment like buildings equipment and libraries. (viii) The concentration of expenditure is more on universities than on colleges; further, the UGC has unduly spread its scope far too wide, with the result that its assistance has indicated a tendency to get diffused over a larger number of items. (ix) The main sources of finance for highter education have been the central and the state government the fees are the second largest sources of university finance. Their appropriate contribution has however been going down. Same is the case with endowments. Considered institution wise, the bulk of central assistance (86.13 per cent) in 1963-64 was confined to universities, research insitutions and professional colleges and the bulk of the state assistance was for professional colleges (41.9 per cent) followed by colleges for general education (33.9 per cent) and in unversities (21.5 per cent). (x) These has been no clear-cut demarcation between the central and the state governments in the matter of financing of institution of higher education and the systems of financing by the government have not always been based on rationally devised criteria for providing requisite financing assistance; they seem to be the result of a policy of 'adhocism' born mainly out of the exigencies of the financial situation prevailing at the central and the state levels. (xi) There is a multiplicity of organisations concerned with the financial and academic management of higher education; the UGC, which is the main instrument of central government for the co-ordination and determination of standards, has an extremely trusted responsibility. (xii) The state government grants for various types of institutions of higher education are based widely varying patterns and procedures the system lacks specificity and dynamism and is largely attuned to a ragged institutional pattern which makes innovation and experimentation difficult, and the 'deficit' grant system, which is generally is vogue, dampens the enthusians of the private bodies to raise resources.

Misra (1959) undertook a study on educational finances in India during 1698 to 1959 the objectives of the study were; (i) to survey the evolution of educational finance in India during the modern period, (ii) to evaluate existing trends and administrative practices in financing education; and (ii) to make suggestions to place educational finance on an adequate and sung footing to develop education, rapidly.

The historical research method was used. The data were collected from reports, reviews and documents of the central and state government of India and other primary and secondary sources dealing with education. The historical survey sources dealing with education. The historical servey on educational finance in the country was divided into six dealing with finances under the East India Company (1698-1833), Centralised Government (1833-70), Decentralised Administration (1871-47) and in independent India

(1947-37), Provincial Autonomy (1937-47) and in Independent India (1947-56). Financial policy in education was examined and the extent of the government contribution to education, its relation to total expenditure, the country's budget and the population, and its allocation to various of expenditure were assessed and evaluated. The educational balance sheet provided interesting criteria for comparing the efforts to different provinces or states. The evaluation of existing trends and practices in financing education was made by examining the roles of the central and state governments, local bodies and private, agencies during this long period.

The results have revealed some problems due to the increase in population peasant society, sparsely populated and tribal areas, the needs of the country education for the masses and the handicapped and the demand for technical personnel. On the basis of the finding, it has been made out the education to decentralise administration and co-ordinate various efforts for education. Each state should survey its educational needs and allocate twenty per cent or more of its revenue to education. The local bodies should be recognised and given more power and resources by levying an educational cess and they should spend atleast forty per cent of their revenue of education. The grain-in-aid rules should be periodically revised to suit changing conditions, and buildings and furniture should be provided with the help of the local community. Universities should meet their expenditure mainly from the fee receipts and endowments. Incentives grants should be given to private which should be encouraged to shoulder the greater part of the responsibility in secondary education. In order to achieve the constitutional directive for fee and compulsory education, measures to shorten school hours, review the indigenous community co-operation and higher allotment of finances for primary education should be undertaken. The requirements of buildings, furniture and equipment should be surveyed and loans be advanced to schools, by the state by borrowing from the Life Insurance Coperation of India and encouraging local aid. The miscellaneous expenditure should be checked by eliminating unimportant items. The heavy wastage and ineffectiveness in educational expenditure should be eliminated. Priorities should be carefully decided and quality should not be sacrificed for quantity.

Nair and Pillai (1962) made a study of the history and problems of education finances in Kerala. The purpose of the study was to throw light on problems like (i) the increase in expenditure on items on which it can be cut and items on which it can be increased; (ii) procedures of educational finance's (iii) stages role in educational finance; (iv) sources from which finances can be tapped; and (v) responsilbilities of different administrations central, state, local and private agencies.

The study was based on records, in state manuals, administration records, educational codes and budgets, comparative studies of several countries and of some Indian states with respect to sharing responsibilities for educational finance by different agencies were done. A questionnaire was administered to collect opinions on questions like contribution from state revenue. The questionnaire was administered to 4000 people including MLAS, member of local bodies, municipal commissioners, advocates, political leaders, press representatives, government officers, headmasters, colleges lecturers, school teachers and managers.

The study revealed that (i) expenditure on education in Kerala has been growing very rapidly in recent years because of the rise in salaries of teachers due to the increased cost of living and also because of increase in population and increase in cost of school material; (ii) the low standard attained by pupils at the poor quality of educational services, namely, overcrowding in classes, absence of satisfactory working conditions, lack of sincerity and lack of proper supervision and guidance; and (iii) tremendous increase in expenditure on school building, equipments, salaries of teachers, teacher training, refresher course, health inspection and extension was considered necessary. To reduce overall expenditure, it was suggested that (i) unaided, fee taking schools be allowed on conditions that they maintain the standard and follow the rules; (ii) the shift system be introduced with two sets of teachers; (iii) start more schools with cheap building and minimum necessary equipment; (iv) centre and state should contribute more; (v) local educational tax be levied; and (vi) states should raised public loans for education.

Panchamukhi (1970) conducted a study on "Fee Financing of education in India". The purpose of the study was to examine the importance of the total education finances in India in the context of different types and levels of educations.

Study is divided into several sections. Section (i) discuss the importance of the fee income in overall education in the country. In section (ii) ans analysis of the role of fees with different levels of disaggregation is made. Section (iii) discusses the importance of fees in meeting indirect expenditure. Section (iv) presents states of the country. In section (v), an attempt is made to assess the significance of different factors in determining the fee rate and fee income. Section (vi) discusses some major policy issues in fee financing of education. In the final section, the conclusion of the study are given. Data collected for the study included information from Report of the Education Commission, Vol. II, Government of India, replies received from the state, Governments to the questionnaire issued and the replies to the questionnaire sent to fifty five colleges throughout the country to collect information on fee rates, income of the parents of the students, scholarships granted, etc. The data about the parents income were collected for 224 students in different higher educational courses in Maharashtra from their application forms for different scholarship. Fees as the source of income for educational institutions, were classified according to a management the sex of students, types and levels of education offered. The incidence of fees on students was analysed as the income effect of fees and the substitution effect of fees. Since personal income and enrollment are considered as two important determinants of fees rate, the enrollment elasticities of fee income and the extent of regressivity in the fee rate structure in different types of education were assessed. Two regression models were tried -(i) Y= A+bX and (ii) Log Y = Log a+b Log X - consideration to professional education (Y) as a function of the proportion of average rate of (Y) as a function of the proportion of average rate of fees in general education to professional of average rate offers in general education to professional education (X). According to model (i) b is the marginal effect of fee rate on enrollment ratio with a variable elasticient of substitution. In model (ii) b is the co-efficient of elasticity of substitution with a variable marginal effect co-efficient.

Some of the important findings are (i) fees are declining in importance as a source of income for the educational system; (ii) fee function as an effective device for allocation; (iii) the effectiveness of the rate increases with the rate divergence between different types of higher education determined in relation to the private benefit and supply costs of education: and (iv) a case for abolition of fee at all levels of education appears to be weak. The study recommended that all states in India should bring special educational cess as a surcharge on property tax or land revenue.

Sha's (1969) study was on outlay on education and its financing in India between 1950-51 to 1960-61. The main issues examined in this study were ; (i) financial resources entering education in India (ii) the allocation of funds between various levels and types of education, (iii) the performance of various types of education (iv) the finding of education by the public and private sectors, the growth of educational expenditure over the period 1950-51 to 1960-61, and (vi) in the financing of education according to level and type of educations as well as according to institution, by management.

The indices selected for the purpose were: (i) growing of educational expenditure inconstant prices; (ii) increase in expenditure per pupil, in real irems; (iii) Proporton of school going population and children actually enrolled; and (iv)teacher-pupil ratio. Data were collected from government publications and from a small survey undertaken by the investigator.

The following are the main finding of the study. (i) The public sector has spent 2.9 per cent of the national income on education in 1965-66 and including private personal expenditure, the proportion comes upto 4.5 per cent. (ii) Total recorded educational expenditure in India increased by 204 per cent in current prices, over the decade 1950-60. In terms of composite index which includes constant salary, per teacher, contant cost of building, the increase in the educational expenditure works out to 116.3 per cent or should eight per cent on an average per annum. (iii) The share of elementary education declined, whereas that of secondary and higher education increased over the decade and a half. On the basis of international comparison it appears that all allocation of the direct expenditure in India has been more in favour of higher levels of education. (iv)The direct expenditure, per pupil, of elementary schools declined by about eight per cent in real tearms, whereras that of secondary schools remained more or less unchanged and that of the college level showed more or less unchanged and that of the college level showed an increases of 7.3 per cent. (v) Both the distribution of students between two types of schools and allocations of direct expenditure between general and professional education shoe that the educational system in India is heavily based in favour of general education. (vi) In 1965-66, the government share in the recorded educational expenditure was as high as 77.5 per cent. Government financed fifty three per cent of the recorded direct expenditure incurred on general education schools in 1960-61.The same holds true for the third level also. (vii) The recorded direct expenditure per pupil in government schools, general and professional, and in government professional colleges, is higher than similar private aided institutions, though the average number of pupils per institutions is larger scope for the increase in enrollment capacity without providing for education and for at the second and their stages of education and for vocationalising education by shifting the emphasis from general education to professional education. (xi) of the two broad types of private constitution and non-tuition, the latter seems to be reasonable for the non-egalitarian trends we observe today in our education system. Tuition fees are mostly covered by aided received from various sources and its contribution comes almost to zero.

Azad (1975) made a study on government grants to higher education. The objectives of the present, the procedures and the policies of financing of the institutions of higher education in India; (ii) to assess the adequacy or otherwise of the system of financial administration with a view to identifying its bottlenecks; and (iii) to study certain basis issues of financial policylike purpose of central and state grants, fee policy, mechanism of student aid programmer, respective responsibilities of the central and the state governments etc.

The study was conducted in two stages. In the first stages, information about the patterns and procedures of grant-in-aid to institute of higher education were collected from the state governments, tabulated and sent back for checking up updating. In the second stages two questionnaires - one on patterns and procedures of state grant-in-aid and second on some policy issues on financing of institutions of higher education in India-were developed. Th first Questiooaire was mainly commerce, education, and engineering and technology representing the percent of the private colleges. The second questionnaire was mailed to 356 principals of affiliated college of arts, science, commerce, education and engineering and technology representing ten percent of the private colleges in each state with some weightage given to women's colleges. The second questionnaire was mailed to vice-chancellors of eighty nine universities and to fifty four economists and educationists . However, the questionnaire was responded by 144 college principals, while the second questionnaire was responded by twenty five vice-chancellors and eleven experts only.

The study revealed that; (i) there were large variations in the type and quantum of state grants - the maintenance and grants ranged between 33 to 100 per cent of the approved expenditure, (ii)The system of deficit grant and the concept of approved expenditure, were disfavoured by the respondents; (iii) a majority of the respondents felt the need to streamline the UGC, extending its establish regional centers or state UGCs; (iv) the establishment of an informal committee of vice-chancellors to advise the state government in formulation of grant-in-aid rules and annual allocation of grants was favored; (v) the affiliation should, according to the respondents, be the concern of the state government in affiliating institutions and releasing grants; (vi) it was opined that the objectives of central and state grants were to equalise the level of facilities for higher education, regulate the spread of educational facilities, locate and help talent, and persude enterprise in education to help achieve nationally determined goals; (vii) it was felt by a majority of respondents that the central governments should concentrate on qualitative improvement, and postgraduate education and research. While the responsibilities of the governments should include undergraduate education maintenance and development of collegiate institutions, encouragement of spread of education in backward areas and the development of the regional languages (ix) half of the respondents thought it desirable to raise fees but only on third support it at this atage; (x) a large majority supported the idea of fixing standard fees with option to private institutions; (xi) private contribution was not much encouraged by the institutions instead the proposal of enactment that private enterprise requiring technically trained manpower should contribute a portion of their profits for education development was supported; amd (xii) a combination of grant and loan to students to prosecute a studies for higher education was faroured by respondents.

The purpose of the study conducted by Malaiya (1977) were (i) to study the financing of secondary schools and their organizations in Madhya Pradesh; (ii) to study the control and administration of secondary school finances in Madhya Pradesh; (iii) to examine the sources and objects of expenditure in secondary schools of Madhya Pradesh; (iv) to identify the existing school trends and problems in financing of secondary schools; and (v) to make suggestions for putting secondary school finances on sound basis. The study was limited to the following aspects only.

(i) study of total expenditure of their higher secondary schools; (ii) comparative study of different sources of income, such as grant-in-aid, fees, donations and subscriptions and other sources; (iii) comparative study of the various items of expenditure in different region and in different types of secondary schools, and (vi)financial powers of the principals and the managing committee or superior controlling officers of secondary schools.

The population of the study consisted of 348 boy's and 72 girls higher secondary schools in Madhya Pradesh in 1960. A systemic random sample of 176 boy's and 37 girls higher secondary schools was chosen for the study. Out of these schools 57 boy's and 13 girl's higher secondary schools responded.

This was the final sample on which the study was conducted. The data were collected through school records publications of government of Madhya Pradesh, meetings with schools principals, and through a questionnaire sent to school principals. The questionnaire consisted of sixty five questions respresenting six aspects, namely, (i) factual information about the nature of school, (ii) total expenditure during the years 1957 to 1961, (iii) total source of income, (iv) item wise expenditure during the years mentioned, (v) income and expenditure on hostel, playgrounds and creche and (vi) financial powers of the school principal and other authorities. The descriptive statistical techniques like mean, standard deviation, percentage, and chi-square were employed to analyse the data.

The following were the major findings of the study; (i) the socio-economic status and the geographical conditions demanded more inputs in the school education, (ii) the trend in financing secondary schools had been towards shifting local burden on the state government allowing more fee concessions and scholarships., by taking over more non-government schools,a nd by allowing increased grant-in-aid. (iii) the principals of privately managed schools and government schools enjoyed different tyes and levels of financial power. (v) the per capital cost in local bodies and privately managed higher secondary schools. (vi) The increase of totalexpenditure was 49.8 per cent during thr five years for all types of schools but it was still more when only girl's schools were taken into consideration. (vii) There was a trend of increased central aid for schools of Madhya Pradesh and there was a tendency of centralisation of Finances. (viii) expenditure on rents, taxes and insurance was more inono-government higher secondary schools than their counterparts. (ix) (ix) The schools of Madhya Pradesh has spent very less money on purchase of books, maps, equipments tranportation and holiday camps. (x) fee formed the main sources of income: the other sources of income such as endowments, contributions from managing committee, donations,etc., were not properly tapped.

The major aims of the study conducted by Mathew (1974) were; (i) to find out the main sources of income in terms of their relative importance (ii) to examine whether the income derived was steady and adequate, and (iii) to ascertain whether the university was subject to any financial stresses and strain which adversely affected its operational efficiency.

The period under study was 1974-48 to 1970-71, and within this period financies in 1970-71 were subjected to detailed study. The data were collected from the budget and audit reports, records of meetings of the various bodies of the university and the university handbooks and notifications. Analyses were done in terms of main trends in financing .

The study revealed that (i) the unversity derived revenues from university departments, grants from the state government, the UGC, the government of India and from other sources; (ii) the conducting of examination happened to be the single largest source and lately become a major concern for heavy outlay; (iii) till 1954 -55, the state government was the main financier of the university, afterwards government of India came into picture and the UGC stared financing from 1957-58; (iv) there had been a rapid expansion of expenditure in the university, frequent pay revision and fast expansion of number of employees being the suggested reasons (v) more money was spent on examination than teaching and research; (vi) the expenditure in study and research in science department was nearly the double of the funds spent in humanities; (vii) the overall expenditure of the university increased by seventeen per cent per year; (viii)the expenditure on general administration increased from seven percent in 1947-48 to nineteen percent in 1970-71; (ix) the teaching and research department ranked somewhat low on expenditure pattern of the university; (x) the budget estimates largely remained the same over the period 1970-71 to 1973 -74;

and (xi) in terms of finances, the university was entering a period of stringency.

Mukherji (1974) conducted a study with the ICSSR's financial assistance on Calcutta University Finances.The present investigation aimed at (i) studying importancs on each source (ii) examining the relationships between the state and the central authorities and the university regarding university finances; and (iii) ascertaining if the university had been under financial stresses and strains with the consequences thereof.

Methodological, it was a descriptive and analytical servey, while the detailed study was restricted only to the year 1970-71, the total period of study was from the budget and audit records, annual reports, minutes of the finances committee meetings and various notifications. Analysis of the data was categories and subsequently breaking them down into subsidiary categories.

The study revealed that (i) the undergraduate examination fees by themselves, of the total examination fees, constituted the largest single resource of receipt for the universty; the next in order were grants from the state government, and individual small items like other fees, income from capital funds, etc., (ii) the adminstrative expenditure remained stable around thirty three per cent between 1948-49 and 1969-70, but the salaries of teachers after reaching a peak of 33.12 per cent in 1951-52 fell gradually to 18.76 percent in 1969-70, and miscellaneous expenditure remained stable around eighteen percent, though there were large fluctuations during the intervening years; (iii) the financial arrangements under which the university operated did not provide for any procedure by which a physical programmer was considered and translated into financial terms, (iv) expenditure on ecademic aspects was often delayed due to redtapism (v) there was found no departmental working plans with a reasonable synthesis between teaching, non-teaching and materials inputs; (vi) the university did not have any formnal legal support from the government in respect of financial liabilitities althouugh the institutional grent was becoming increasinsly more important; and (viii) the trusts and endowments funds went a long way in the past to sustain the finances of the University of Calcutta.

The major objectives of the study done by Nigam (1974) were; (i) to find out the sources of income of the university of Rajasthan (iii) to examine the steadiness and adequacy of the income; and (iv) to as certain whether the unversity was subjected to financial stress that affected its operational efficiency and independence.

Out of the twenty five years of its existence a slice of eleven years from 1960-61 to 1970-71 was selected for the study from finances. The data were collected from the following sources, namely, (i) published annual budgets of the universities, (ii) annual reports of the university (iii) the minutes of meetings of the various bodies of the unversity published from time to time and university handbooks and notifications. The financial position of the unversity was analysed in the context of autonomy, adequacy and flexibility.

The study revealed that (i) the different sources were the fees from students, the grant receives from the state governmental and the UGC, (ii) due to the phenomen development of the university since 1962, there has been huge and recurring deficit in the budget of the university, the government grant was found - to be inadequate; (iii) the method of adhoc grants to cover deficit was found to be unsatisfactory; and (iv) the fixing of non-plan maintenance grant was a welcome measure, but the accompanying conditions the university autonomy of maneuvering of the fund to reallocate for their optional use. It was pointed that (a) a state level body in the pattern of UGC would help in setting the financial issues better; (b) within the university, selective allocation of funds to different department would promote better settlement; and (c) the per capita material and educational facilities should be stabilised.

Aher , H. (1986) has done a critical analysis of university finances in Maharashtra. The study was an attempt to investigate the causes underlying poor financial conditions of non-agricultural universities in Maharashtra and to examine whether the grants received from different sources were adequate and whether the expenditure made was proper or other wise. Some of the specific objectives were, (i) to study the financial administration of the universities of the state. (ii) to analysis their financial working in relation to income from various sources, including fees, grants from state and central governments, endowments, and (iii) to analyse the expenditure pattern.

Some of the major conclusions were: 1.The Maharashtra State Government has been paying block grants to the universities of Bombay, Nagpur, Poona and the SNDT university with 6 percent increase over the previous grant each year to meet the maintenance expenditure. From the year 1962-63 onwards, this growth was reduced from 6 to 3 percent. The rate of 6 percent was restored from the financial year 1976-77. It was interesting that for Maharashtra's universities, Aurangabad, and Shivaji, University, Kolhapur, were paid maintenance grants on 100 percent deficit basis. 2. In1980-81, the total recurring annual income of the Maharshtra Universities was Rs. 17.52 crore.. Bombay University was at the top and Poona University at the bottom of the income scale. The main sources of income of the income scale. The main sources of the universities of Maharashtra were government grants followed by fees, examinations fees, hostel fees, publications, printing, endowments and miscellaneous. 3. Recurring annual expenditure of university of Maharashtra was Rs. 1930 crore. The expenditure of Bombay University was the highest at Rs.5.25 crore, the lowest being that of Shivaji university, Rs. 2.97 crore. 4. Unit cost per student on the items of non-teaching staff, teaching staff, teaching department, equipment, books and jounals was calculated. Unit cost per student on non-teaching saff was the highest at Rs.5083 in Nagpur University in the year 1980-81 and he lowest was at Rs. 2,388 in Poona University. Unit cost on teaching was highest at Rs.4,557 in Poona universiy and the lowest was at Rs.1472 in 1980-81. The average unit cost of equipment and furniture in the year 1880-81 was Rs.596.90, which was the highest among the universities of Maharashtra and the lowest was at Rs.50.56 in Marathwada University. Unit cost of books and journals was highest in the year 1980-81 at Rs. 780 in SNDT Universities, Bombay, and lowest in the Nagpur Univrsity at Rs. 17.89 in 1980-81. 5. The major financial problems faced by the universities in Maharastra were (a) Stringency of funds, (b) wasteful expenditure, (c) the state government's of funds (b) wasteful expenditure, (c) the state government's policies and (d) problems of financial administration.

Jena. S.L.,(1983) has done a case study on University finances of M.S.University, Baroda. The major objectives of the study were (i) to examine the sources of revenue for the university, (ii) to syudy the operating expenditure of the university, and (iii) to examine possibilities of augmenting the resources of the universities in terms conventional sources and supplemental sources.

The major finding of the study were: 1. The average share of state grants, students fees and receipts from the university's activities constitutioned around 58,32 and 10 per cent respectively of the university's income. 2. A trend of increasing reliance on grants from the state government was seen as t he internal receipts decreased from 50 per cent in 1970-71 to 27 per cent in 1978-79. 3. The grant-in-aid system was evolved through a process of confrontation, collision and persistent persuasion, which was in dissonance with the parameters of adequacy, efficiency, equity, elasticity and specificity, 4. The residual in the total income, which repesented the university's own contribution around ten percent was experiencing a downward drift. This was because of the non-progressive attitude of the university in mobilising up its own internal sources through an efficient management of its own activities. 5. The proportionate share of different heads of expenditure were faculties and institutions (71 per cent), students'welfare (10 per cent), and examination (3 per cent), 6. The personnel costs under the heads of faculties and institutions consisted of 83 percent.

There was increasing trend of this cost over the years. 7.There seemed to prevail an iniquitous allocation of resources among various faculties and institutions. 9. Contrary to the expectation that activities such as halls of residence, examinations and auxiliary services would be self-financed, their operational inefficiency's largely due to the unversity, had made them dependent on public subsidy.10. Though the expenditure on student's walfare increased, the expenditure on university library did not receive any priority attention. 11. The university has had deficit budgets throughout its existence. 12. The factors contributing to the recurrent incidence of deficits were found to be, (i) inadequacy of state grants, (ii) the mechanics of fixation of grants, (iii) inordinate delay in the fixation and release of grant, (iv) conflicting perceptions of the state government and the university on usual expenditures and (v) the high income elasticity of expenditure.13. The per capita expenditure of the university ascended the scale from Rs.1,251 in 1970-71 to Rs.2,855 in 1978-79. Classroom based courses; special education courses were the costliest of all. 14. The university needed to explore the possibilities of supplementing its resources by institution a consultancy unit, starting new enterprises in unconventional areas, organizing extension programs, and fund-raising drives.

Pandit (1972) made a study on the effectiveness and financing of investment in Indian Education. The aim of the persent investigation was to study the financing and effectiveness of Indian education during the first three year plans (1951-56). It also envisaged to test the investment hypotheses formulated were; (i) the private and public sources would be going hand in hand in the financing of education; (iii) investment with education would be optimally allocated between different stages and types of education; and (iv) there would be no divergence between private and social rates of return from education.

To test the above stated hypotheses different types of data were collected. There were; (i) national income and related data from series data on national income, national consumption expenditure, etc. (ii) educational and budgetary expenditure from the central and state sources; (iii) education age-earing data from annual earnings classified by age and educational level; and (iv) data from official surveys. After clarifying the theoretical framework of cost benefits analysis as applied to the study of inverment effectiveness and financing of education, hypothesise (i) and (ii) were tested on the basis of budgetary expenditure on education and real expenditure data. These two hypotheses were also tested on the basis of cost estimates prepared for the periods of 1905-51 to 1065-66, cost and earning profiles by thirteen levels of education were estimated for 1964-65. There cost and earning profiles by levels and types of education were utilised to test the hypotheses (iii) to (iv).

The study revealed that (i) the education expenditure in relation to the total resources of the economy did not hold in spite of slow growth of domestic product; (ii) despite, decentralization of administrative set up of education and state control in the financing of education (iii) overtime burden of financing education was being shifted to the state and private participation was on the decline; (iv) education was found to be taking on increasing share of the total resources of the economy; (v) adjustment due to stagnation raised the private unit cost of different levels of education from sixteen to twenty seven per cent (vi) adjustment due to wastage led to an increase in social unit cost of different levels of education from 19.6 to 38.4 percentage; (vii) the secondry and higher stages of education appeared decidedly unprofitable; (viii) these were poor returns for vocational skills developed through formal educatio.ı; (ix) the rate of return for an illiterate to become literate was 18.8 per cent; (x) social and private rates of return diminised with an increase in the level of education (xi) the returns of middle education were the highest followed by primary education and those for the higher education were the least (xii) within the higher education, professional and techincal education had an edge over the general education in science and arts; and (xiii) higher education had reached a stage where both students and society did not find it a profitable are to invest.

Ramachandran (1981) had the following major objectives (i) to identify vital problem area in higher education such as enrollment, expenditure, financing and planning (ii) to assess the total cost in higher education classified under relevant institutional categories, (iii) to compare cost for different agencies of higher education like the State Government, the UGC etc.

This was a normative historical study. Necessary data were collected for primary sources like documents and reports of the state government, universities the UGC, and the planning commission. The secondary sources of data were mainly published books, research papers, reports of conferences and seminars on higher education.

The major findings of the study were (i) There was a phenomenal growth of institutions of higher education in Kerala during the period under review. There was only one university in 1956 and the number increased to four, and the number of arts and science colleges increases from 46 to 128 by 1975-76. The establishment of colleges was done without much forethought and planning.The district-wise distribution of arts and science colleges and the population served by each college showed, in certain districts like Qulion,Palghat, Cannonore, the number of colleges were, on an averages less in relation to their population (ii) More than 82 per cent arts and science colleges in the State were under private management (iii) The average annual rate of growth of enrollment for on general education courses was about 11.8 per cent during the period under study (iv) Public expenditure on education has been growing very rapidly in the State of Kerala. A sum of Rs. 1,037 lakhs about 31.5 percent of the total revenue expenditure, was spent on general education in 1957-58 but the total expenditure increasesd to Rs. 13,226 lakhs by 1975-76 i.e. 37.3 percent of the total expenditure of the state. Though the percentage of annual increase was not high in absolute terms the increase was to the tune of 11.76 times. The index of growth during the period under review was 1275. The average annual expenditure on education during the period of study was about 34 per cent of the state's total budget. (v) where as the total public expenditure on general education was increasing year after year, the corresponding return to the revenue of the state Government was very low. The receipt under education was about 3.6 per cent of the total revenue receipts of the state in 1975-76, whereas total public expenditure on general education during this year was to the tune of Rs. 13,226 lahks (vi) the expenditure on University education showed phenomenal increase. When the total expenditure increased by 11.76 times the amount spent in 1957-58 the share to higher education increased by 28.61 times over the 1956-57 amount. The total expenditure was only Rs. 1.568.79 lakhs by 1957-76 showing an increase to 29.61 times. The expenditure on higher education as only 6 per cent of the overall expenditure on education 1957-58 but it constituted 11.9 percent in 1975-76. (vii) The bulk of the publics expenditure on higher education was spent for the development and maintenance of arts and science colleges in Kerala. The total direct expenditure on these colleges in 1957-58 was Rs. 22.22 lakhs and formed about 41.9 per cent of the overall expenditure on higher education. An amount of Rs. 1,262.93 lakhs was the direct expenditure on arts and science colleges in 1975-76 and constitutioned 80.5 per cent of the total expenditure on higher education showed tremendous growth both as percentage on the total expenditure on higher education as well as in absolute.

Riziovi (1960) made a study on the financing of higher education in less developed countries. The major objective of the study was to investigate the question of financing education educational facilities in less-developed countries, with special reference to higher education. The following specific research question were raised to investment in the provision of education services ? (ii) was there any special from of investment that could be considered desirable for less developed countries with respect to higher education ? (iv) What was the historical retrospect of education finance in

India ? (v) In the light of the statistical data, was the size of the educational expenditure consistent with socioeconomic policy of the country expressed through its official channels ? (vi) Was the expenditure on universities and college in India, and its distribution between the different types of education of a size and character that reflected optimum level of investment ? If not, were the main obstacles and what reforms could remove these obstacles and bring them adequate resources but without their autonomy or free choice of individual (vii) If the appraisal showed that the need for additional resources was imperative, who should acquire them and how ?

The investigator has gathered materials from a large variety of sources, offical and non-offical, Indian and those of other national and the international organizations ranging from purely educational to those relevant to economic theory.

The findings were: (i) The problem or resource allocation was real and almost universal and there was no universally acceptable formula that could serve as an easy, mechanical and full-proof device for determining the size of the economic resources which tended to bring optimum investment in the provision of educational services. (ii) There was disgreement as to who or which institutions should perform the purpose of valuation. Different communities belonging to different political creed approached problem differently and, consequently, their emphasis on the role of the state in this respect also showed radical differences (iii) The lesson for less-developed countries was that state participation in education was necessary particularly given the kinds of objectives commonly supported in such countries. However, state participation would have to strictly on an individual rather than an institutional basis, if it was desired to, encourage education which could be in tune with the economic and social needs of the country. (iv) In view of the actual economic backwardness, the right policy for less-developed countries would be to develop all types of education but to facilitate economic development and to banish disease, poverty, hunger, and ignorance, they should invest more in scientific and technical education. (v) Creation of new universities expansion of arts and science colleges, professional, teachnical education. (vi) Creation of new universities expansion of arts and science college, professional, technical, and special educational colleges and a subitantional increase in enrollment were the highlights of the post independence era. However, the complexion of educational structured and its problems were more or less the same as they were pre-independence period. The only difference was that the outlook has become rather more expansionist. (vii) There had been a countinous rise in educational expenditure. Notable as this increase appeared to be, proportions of the outlays diverted to education and higher education of NDP (Net Domestic Product) were 2 per cent for general education and 0.37 per cent incurred by private bodies was 65.9 per cent, whereas on government maintained institutions imparting professional and technical education. Income from public funds and fees countinued to be the mainstay of the higher education finance. The bulk of the public expenditure on education was incurred on primary education, secondary education was given second priority. Higher education accounted for 11.4 per cent of the total public expenditure of education.(viii) The expenditure on higher education in India and its distribution between the different education in India and its distribution between the different types of education was of size and character that was well below the optimum level of investment, with reference to criteria of both the democratization of education opportunities an higher education's effectiveness to serve as a sound and dynamic basis of the solution of the nation's socio-economic problems, there existed a vast disparity between thin community's honest professions and a record of its actual achievements. This situations could be attributed to thin low level of investment but primarily to the system of finance by which the already inadequate resources were actually more available to the institutions of higher education.

Kumar, I., (1983), has made study on A study of Economic Aspects of Higher Secondary Education in Delhi. The objectives of the study were (i) to find out the school outputs, namely, academic achievement of students, motivational level of students, educational expectation of parents and educational attitudes of teachers, (ii) to find out the school inputs, namely, student input, school achievement, teacher input, cost input, etc., (iii) to find out the relation between school inputs and outputs, (vi) to find out the financial classification cf school expenditure, (v) to find out the efficiency of education in higher secondary schools under study, (vi) to find out the relationship between efficiency of education, and the functional classification of school expenditure, (vii) to find out the economics of scale in the case of the selected sample of Delhi schools, and (viii) to find out the optimum size of higher secondary schools in Delhi. The researcher formulated the following hypotheses: (a) There are no significant effect of school inputs on school outputs. (2) At the existing level of costing no relationship existed between efficiency in school education and functional classification of school expenditure. (3) The economics of scale do not work in the case of schools. (4) There is no relationship between size and cost of an educational institution.

The study was conducted in 20 selected higher secondary schools. These schools were of four types: public schols, government schools, kendriya vidyalayas, and government-aided schools. The study was divided into two parts, In the first part, the effectiveness of school was analysed with the help of a " School Effectiveness Model ", in the second part , the efficiency in relation to cost and size was analysed with the help of a " Cost Efficiency Model ", The tools used were Jenkin's Non-verbal Intelligence Test adapted to test the general mental ability, students, teachers and schools by the investigator. These schedules covered various aspects, viz., initial ability of students, motivational level of students, socio-economic background of students, teachers; attitudes towards students, school environment and educational, influence of school environment of students, parents expectations about their children, and performance of students in the final examination. Multiple regression and step-wise regression analysis. For analysing the process of schooling which produced several ouputs, Two Stage Least Square (2 SLS) was used.

The major findings of the study were,1. Socio-economic status and per capita income had a significant effect on achievement. 2. Mother's education was a significant factor for the achievement of student while father's education contributed motivation. 3. A unclear family contributed more to the motivation than a joint family. 4. Laboratory facilities available in Delhi schools promoted healthy educational attitudes on teachers. But they were negatively correlated with achievement of students. 5. There was inverse relationship between school buildings and motivation of students and same reeducational attitudes of teachers. 6. Compared to experienced teachers, less-experienced teachers contributed more to the achievement of students. Misra. G., (1984), made a study on Educational Finance and Primary Education in India after independence. The study was designed to get an idea about provision of finanees for primary education from different sources and an analysis of expenditure on different items. It also aimed at calculation of per student cost of primary education in different types of schools. An attempt was also made to compare to the expenditure on primary education in different states.

The relevant figures were collected from reports published by the Government of India and state governments.

The main finding of the study were: 1. The main sources of finance for primary education are grants from the state, grants from local bodies, fees and endowments, etc. 2. The main sources of finances for primary education is aid from the government. The income from fees and other sources accounts for two to give per cent of the total income. 3. About 93 to 97 per cent of the total expenditure on primary education is spent on salary and allowances of the teachers. 4. In 1950-51, 10.4 per cent and 9.6 per cent of the total expenditure was on primary education of boys and girls respectively. 5. In 1975, per student expenditure on primary education was twice the per student expenditure in 1965. 6. Progress of primary education in states of Kerala, Tamil Nadu, Uttar Prdesh and Maharashtra was the best. It was slowest in Jammu and Kashmir and Bihar and Orissa.

NIEPA, (1986), conducted a study on Education Financing and Equity; : A comparative study of Haryana and Kerala. The study was undertaken by the financial assistance of UNESCO.

The objectives of the study were (i) to analyse the financial flows in the given two years, (ii) to examine the allocations by levels-objects, etc. to infer possible implications for equity and, specially, to see changes in allocations were related to changes in equity, and (iii) to examine the policies and procedures of government assistance in the field of education, either for establishment of institution or by way of scholarship or compensatory finance.

The study was based on the analysis of the available secondary data collected from various official and semi official publications.

The major findings of the study were: 1. Both Kerala and Haryana presented a picture of educational growth. There was also marked reducation in inequalities between a groups. 2. The share of expenditure of hostels and scholarships declined as a part of overall decline in indirect expenditure. This affected inequality adversely. 3. Non- teaching expenditure was very low, indicating that schools were going without needed equipment. 4. Private initiative in education was declining, thus drying up an important source of financing, which would affect expansion of education. 5. The share of elementary education in allocation and expenditure needed to be considerably increased in Harana. 6. Grant-in-aid rules needed to be liberalized, particularly in respect of backward areas. 7. Capital grant were needed on the basis of assessment of needs. 8. Free education would have limited impact on equity. A more substantial policy of compensatory finance was necessary for a breakthrough in equity. Attention to equality was equally necessary.

NIEPA, 1986, conducted a study on Financing of Education and Equality of Opportunity with reference to Uttar Pradesh and Kerala. Equality of opportunity in education and equity are areas of investigation which have received considerable amount of attention. Indeed the debates are by no means closed. But one important aspect and one very relevant for policy purposes is the system of financing education for achieving objectives like efficiency, equality or diversity and this has not received the attention due to it.

The main objectives of the investigation were (i) to study the system of financing education for achieving objectives like efficiency, equality or diversity, and (ii) to focus on problems arising out of inequalities in education in different districts.

The major findings of the study were: 1. There were inequalities of many kinds within Uttar Pradesh and Kerala, to a lesser extent in Kerala than in Uttar Pradesh. However, in both the states, to some extent, inequality was reduced as indicated by the fall in coefficient of variation from 69.7 to 50.6 in UP and from 27 to 14 in Kerala. 2. For the country as a whole, the per capita expenditure had gone up from 48.7 in 1979-80 to 81.00 in 1983-84. The coefficient of variation for Uttar Pradesh had gone down from 69.7 to 50.6 and for Kerala during the same period standard deviation had moved from 7.35 to 9.6. The coefficient of variation had gone down from 27 to 14. The per capita expenditure in Kerala had gone up from 26.81 in 1970 -71 to Rs. 63.38 in 1976-77, while foi UP it had limped from Rs.11.77 to 1970-71 to Rs. 29.82 in 1976-77. Uttar Pradesh still had the lowest per capita expenditure on education and had a great deal disparity in educational expenditure by districts. 3. In Kerala there was a tendency towards greater equality at all levels of education due to various reasons like the long tradition of free primary schooling, spread of literacy, extension of free schooling to high schools stage and beyond, supply of free meals to some categories of students, the broad base of the educational system and the structure of higher education. The pattern of expenditure in terms of sectorial composition as wall as by times for Kerala had been such that it had resulted in greater equality and the educational system was performing better. Consequently, the limit of achievement, at least in terms of ensuring a mimimum level of education to a greater majority of the population, thus appeared to have been reached in Kerala. 4. A comparative study of the pattern of expenditure and revenue both for UP and Kerala indicated that 1983-84, Kerala had the highest non-plan revenue expenditureof 35.1 percent and highest per capita expenditure of Rs. 110.15 while UP had 25.7 percent or Rs. 46.72 as the per capita expenditure. Kerala's expenditure in education as percentage of its own total tax revenue and sales tax were 57.6 and 91.4 per cent while for UP had not 52.2 and 94 per cent. A comparsion of the central assistance to the two states showed that UP had not come out over favourabe, thereby indicating need for greater equity consideration in central assistance to states. 5. As regards inter-district variations in educational expenditure in UP, in 1976-77, out of total expenditure on all recognized educational institution, the percentage share was the highest in Allahabad with 6.2 per cent followed by Varanasi with 5.8 per cent, Kanpur with 5.6 per cent and the lowest in Uttarkashi 3 per cent. Per capita expenditure in Uttra Pradesh in the same year was Rs. 27.60. The range of variation in all the district was between Rs. 11.70 in Unnaao to Rs.75.90 in Nainital. In 22 districts the per capita expenditure was more than the state average. In the other 34 districts, it had been than the stage average. 6. Cost per student in primary schools varied from Rs.306.70 in Uttarkashi to Rs. 40.80 in Deoria. For the state in 1976-77, it was Rs. 64.50 and in 30 districts it was more than the state average. The major policy conclusions of the study are to the effect that there is need for regionalization of financial policies of states in the matter of releasing grant and funds to the districts. There has to be greater concern with the need of the individual region at all levels and appropriate planning and financial procedure changes.

Parashar, G.S.,(1981), has made a study on The University Finances in Madhya Pradesh. The objectives of the study were (i) to provide a clear picture financial position of different universities in Madhya Pradesh (MP), (i) to discuss of income, their proportional contribution, limitations and trends in various universities in MP, (iii) to identify the highlights of expenditure and emerging trends therein, (iv) to estimate the unit cost in each university and its adequacy, and (v) to suggest measures to improve university finances in MP.

The study covered all universities of MP which were in existence between 1950-51 and 1975 -76, expect the Agriculture University, Jabalpur, and the Music University, Kairagarh. The study was limited to this period only (1950-51 to 1975-76). Following the techniques of the historical and descriptive method of research, the data were collected from primary sources like yearly statistical reports published by the Ministry of Education, Government of India, under the title Education in Universities in India, a special issue on education in states published under the title,The Education in Reorganized States in 1955-56, annual accounts of different universities of the states, and annual reports of various universities.Along with these data from secondary sources like reports of various commissions and views of various officials, vlz., vice-chancellors, educationists, and experts associated with direct financial administration of universities of MP were collected.

The major findings of the study were 1. Formerly, block grants were given to the universities for their maintenance and these were revised ever five years. With the coming into existence of the University Grant Commission (UGC), developmental grants began to be received from it, on the basis of sharing a part of the total expenditure by the state government. The state education department which was to give these grants could often take the burden of matching UGC grants. Hence, several developmental schemes could not be implemented. 2. In order to improve the organization and promotion of higher education, maintain standards teaching, research and examinations, and to advise the government in respect of higher education, the Uchha Shiksha Anudan Ayog was established in Bhopal in 1973. The major function in Uchha Shiksha Anudan Ayog was to give maintenance grants to examine the developmental plans of, and to provide funds for the universities. For any new plan which involved additional expenditure, the Ayog had to seek the permission of the state government. Section 51 of the MP Universities Act, 1973, authorized the state government to assume financial control of the universities. In case of financial mismanagement, it had to the power to remove the vice-chancellor on grounds of maladministration and appoint a successor and a committee of experts to help him. This showed that it was the state government, which had final authority on the universities, and not the ayog. The Ayog could not develop into an independent body like UGC. Its function was reduced to that of a post office. 3. The major source of recurring income of the universities was grant aids from the central and state governments. But this varied from university to university. It was 59 per cent in the case of Sagar University and 7 per cent in the case of Bhopal University during 1975-76.The variations were mainly in developmental grants, other sources of income were examination fees, which varied from 18.48 per cent (Vikram University) to 1 per cent (Indore University) miscellaneous receipts like donations, telephone charges, hostel fees, transportation charges, sale of publication, guest-guest rent etc. Which varied from 30.46 per cant (Bhopal Universty) to less than 1per cent (Indore University). The non-recurring income which was made up of UGC grants and state grants was always inhigher in the case of Sagar university and always lowest in case of Rewa University. The main items of expenditure were teaching departments, including the salaries and allowances of teachers, establishment expenses, expenditure on conducting examinations and miscellaneous expenses. The nonrecurring expenditure also was the highest in the case of Sagar University and lowest for Bhopal University. This expenditure was mainly on building construction, equipment and furniture. 5. All the unversities, expect those of Rewa, Bhopal and Raipur were running in deficit. The highest deficit was in case of Sagar University and the lowest for Jiwaji University. 6. The annual unit cost per student on teaching, establishment,books and journals, and equipment was highest in case of Vikram University (Rs.4034.27) and lowest in the case of Sagar University (Rs.129.80). 7. The major financial problems observed were the deficit financial position in most of the universities, availability of UGC grant for developmental schemes only and not for maintenance, inability of the state government to share the financial burden, uneconomic expenditures in the universities, advance increments to teachers and clerks, no uniformity in respect of salary revisions in different universities, special relaxations in the age of retirement to some employees, payments for invigilation work, losses due to non-observance of proper rules, unnecessary interference of state government in financial matters, conventional budgeting, no uniformity and updating of account, and non-availability of reserve funds or endowments in universities. 8. Different suggestions forwarded to improve the financial position of the universities were the provision of more grants to the universities from the state government making the Uchha Shiksha Anudan Ayog an independent body with adequate resources, deletion of the Section 51 of the MP Universities Act, 1973, revision and enhancement of government grants to the universities every second year, making provision of charging of reserve funds for the universities, limiting establishment expenditure to 10 per cent and miscellaneous expenditure to 20 per cent of the total expenditure, enrolment of more students to curtail the per student cost, appointment of employees of actual-retirement basis and ban on advaance increments, declaration of teaching as a non–vocational job, examination of losses by an agency with in the university and fixation of responsibility for it, checking of irregularities in accounts pointed out by auditors, etc.

Sharma, G.D., (1978), conducted a study on Resource Allocation on Education.The objectives of the study were (i) examine the ammount of resources were allocated to education as percentage of national gross product and, to within education various levels, (ii) to study the pattern of allocation of resources to education by state governments, (iii) to study how this compared with state income, (iv) to examine whether allocation of resources on India were commensurate with the return from investment in education, and (v) to study the ways the resources were allocated to education.

The statistcal series of Minister of Education of the Government of India and of international bodies llike UNESCO provided data. Data were analysed in descriptive forms and through the application of the regression equation technique.

The findings of the study were: 1. In1971, the proportion of GNP spent on education by India was 2.5 per cent in the US 6.7 per cent, the USSR 7.3 percent. The number of persons in education institution in India were 79.8 million compared with 63.2 million in the USA and 62.3 million in the USSR. In terms of total population, India the USA and USSR had 14.2, and 30.9 per cent respectively. 2. During 1971-72, Manipur spent 10.71 per cent of its total SNDP, the highest among the states. It was followed by HP and Kerala with 5.63 and 5.31 per cent respectively. The smallest proportion (0.36 per cent) was spent by Jammu and Kashmir. 3. Seven states had a lower per capita income but their expenditure per student was comparatively higher. 4. Manipur spend the highest proportion of its SNDP (5.77 per cent) and Haryana and least (0.48 per cent) on primary education. More states spent more than one percent of their SNDP on this level of education. 5. HP was proportionately the highest spender (3.30 per cent) on higher secondary education. The average of all the states worked out at 0.78 per cent. 6. Manipur spent the highest (0.79 per cent) on higher education. The average for all the states was 0.25 per cent. 7. Bilar spent 0.20 per cent of its SNDP on grant to universities and collages. The average proportion of grants to their SNDP was 0.08 per cent. 8. The majority of states allocated 20-25 per cent of their total states budgets to education, but Bihar, Nagaland, Orissa, Haryana and J&K allocated less than 20 percent. 9. The proportion of funds to total budget allocated by state governments had little relevance to per capita income. 10. In 1971-72 Delhi was the only Union territory to allocate 34.5 per cent of total budget for education.

During 1975-76 the allocation rate increased to 43.2 per cent. The average of all territories increased to 28.7 per cent from 24.3 in 1971-72. 11. The share of higher education total expenditure on education was around 10 to 14 per cent. This pattern changed slightly between 1971 and 1975. 12. The states which were economically backward paid a little more attention to higher education compared to the economically developed states. 13. The pay scales of teachers varied from state to state. In some states they varied between private and government managed institutions. 14. No systemtic planning in allocation of funds appeared to have been followed by the state governments. 15. Four variables, viz., state net domestic product (SNDP), state revenue income, state total income, and enrolment in higher education explained 62 per cent of the variation in the allocations of grants. The relationship between the enrolment and the grants from found variable to be poor. No relationship was found between enrolment data and the grants from the UGC. 16. The method of grants adopted by the state governments differed from state to state. Insome states it differed from University to University.

Tewari, M., (1986), has made A study of the Budget of Kumaun University. The investigation was designed to study the amount of grants received by the Kumaun University from various sources and its expenditure on different educational programmes. It also at aimed a critical examination of the suitability of expenditure on different faculties and it different levels.

Information about income from different sources and figures about expenditure on different faculties and at different levels within the faculties were collected from the university records. Information was collected about the number of students and teachers in the different faculties of the university.

The maintain findings of the study were : 1. There was no consistent and rational policy underlying fixation of priorities regarding expenditure under different headings. 2. There was lack of planned development of various programmes of education. 3. The number of teacher in the faculties of education and commerce had not increased in proportion to the increase in the number of students. 4.There was no qualitative improvement in education during the period under study. 5 . Per student expenditure in the faculty of science was the highest. 6. Per student expenditure in the faculties of commerce and law was quite low. 7. Comparatively more research work had been done at Nainital than at Almora. 8. Greater attention had been paid to development of the campus at Nainital than of the campus at Almora.

Yadav, R.S., 1985, has made A critical study of Financing of Secondary Education in Haryana. The objectives of the study were (1) to study the policies, patterns, procedures and quantum of financing of secondary education, (2) to study the priority accorded to secondary education vis-a-vis other sectors on five year plans, (3) to examine sources of income and items of expenditure in secondary schools of Haryana, and (4) to make suggestions for streamlining the patterns, procedures and policies of financing of secondary schools of Haryana.

The data for the study were collected from a variety of sources like 347 secondary schools, offices of District Education Officers, the Directorate of Public Instruction of Haryana, the Ministry of Education (Government of Haryana), the Economic and Statistical Organisation, Planning Department (Government of Haryana), surveys conducted by National Council of Educational Reasearch and Traning, The Planning Commission, the then Ministry of Education and Culture (Goverment of India). The Haryana Education code which included grants-in-aid rules, school recognition rules, pupil fund rules, building fund rules, the Punjab Primary Education Act, and the Haryana Aided Schools Rules were also examined critically. A questionnaire and a data schedule relating to patterns and procedures of government grants to institution of secondary education, including certain policy issues, were prepared and administered. The questionnaire and data schedule were mailed to 621 secondary schools of three districts of Haryana. In addition, 60 questionnaires (20 in each district) were sent to distinguished educationists, economists, administrators and authorities concerned with financing of secondary education. The responses of 347 secondary schools and 50 educationists, economists, administrators and experts were received and analysed.

The findings of the study were: 1. After the formation of the state, the government had made all possible efforts for the expansion of educationinal facilities, but the absence of well throught out state policy and experience in formation of educational plans had resulted in haphazard expansion, causing inter district imbalances in educational facilities at the secondary stage. 2. The contribution of private enterprise at secondary stage had been declining in quantitative terms. 3. The education of girls was a matter of great concern. 4. The education of scheduled casted was lagging behind. 5. The state was free from the backlog of trained teachers. 6. Haryana had been allocating lower proportion of its revenue budget on education as compared with other Indian states. 7. The state ranked tenth in 1966-67; its position deteriorated and it ranked 15th in 1979-80 in terms of budgetary allocation to education. 8. Haryana had been far behind other states in terms of educational expenditure as a proportion to the per capita net domestic product. The states with lower per capita net domestic product than Haryana had been spending more per capita on education. 9. The expenditure on total general education and secondary education increased faster than the state's net domestic product. The expenditure on secondary education in terms of state's net domestic product indicated far more accelerated progress than on education as a whole. 10. There had been wide variations in the per capita and per student (direct) expenditure on total education and secondary education in Haryana. The districts which were spending more per capita on general education, were also spending more per capita on general education. But the districts which had higher cost per student on overall education did not have the same position in respect of secondary education. 11. The ratio between recurring and non-recurring expenditure at secondary stage in 1966-67 was 88:12, by 1979-80 the ratio touched 98:2. 12. The proportion of expenditure on staff salaries and other items indicated that the state government had been providing increasingly higher outlay for teachers and other staff salaries in comparison with allotments for educational infrastructure like building,equipment and libraries. 13. The expenditure on scholarship and stipends had increased in absolute terms, but as a percentage to total recurring expenditure it had declined. 14. An analysis of the component of Non-recurring Expenditure had revealted that the expenditure on buildings had increased whereas than on equipment and libraries had been gradually declining. 15. The developmental expenditure on education had always exceeded the outlays provided in the plans, except during the period of interregnum. 16. The first priority was accorded to elementary education in the plans. With the expansion of the base at the elementary stage, second priority in plans was accorded to secondary education, except in the fifth plan (1974-79) in which due to the establishment of the Maharishi Dayanand university, Rohtak, and the starting of new colleges, more funds were allocated to university education. The third priority had been accorded to university education. The third priorty had been accorded to university education. The next in priority were social and adult education. teacher education, etc. 17.More than 90 per cent of the developmental expenditure had been spend on quantitative expansion and inadequate attention had been given to qualitative improvement of secondary education. The unit cost of expenditure in terms of per student expenditure had been higher on quantitative expansion than on qualitative improvement. 18. Ever since the formation of the state, considerable progress had been made in providing facilities and expending involvement at the secondary stage. But planning failed to vocationalize secondary education and to bring qualitative improvement to the desired extent. 19. The responsibility of the state government in regard to recurring income had gone up over the years while there has been a corresponding decline in the contribution from private sources like fees, endowments and other sources. In the case of non-recurring income, the share of government had declined, whereas that of endownments and other sources had increased considerably. 20. The long channels through which an application for grants had to pass delayed finacial assistance to institution of secondary education. 21. The deficit-grant system followed in the state dampened the enthusiasm of private bodies to raise their own resources. Further, the rules framed by the government lacked specificity.

Johnson, Janice Haydon, Ed.D.,1995, made a critical study on Alternative finance systems for funding Arizona Public school. The purpose of this study was to simulate and conduct an impact analysis to illustate the re-distributive effects of alternative finance systems for funding Arizona public schools as a result of the recent Arizona Supreme Court decision, Roosevelt, v.Bishop, 1994. Specifically six alternative methods were explored.

SIMULATION 1 : Update the current formula by revising the weights suggested for special education.

SIMULATION 2 : Change special education to a service delivery system, taking into consideration inclusion.

SIMULATION 3 : Change special education to a population-based funding program.

SIMULATION 4 : Create a two-tier equalization program using SIMULATION 2 as the first tier and equalizing maintenace and operation overrides in the second tier.

SIMULATION 5 : Develop a three-tier equalization program using SIMULATION 2 as the first tier, equalising maintence and operation overrides in the second tier, and equalizing a merged debt service third tier.

SIMULATION 6 : Use a guaranteed tax base formula to equalize debt service expenditures.

Each of the six alternatives investigated had potential for addressing some of the gross disparities as addressed in Roosevelt v. Bishop, 1994. If the legistators decide to focus on the inadequate educational opportunities for special needs students SIMULATION 2 provides the best option because it allows for the funding of inclusion. The legislators would not want to consider SIMULATION 3, because it does not account for variance in incidence of special needs students among Arizona districts.

If the legislators decide to focus on disparities in facilities and assessed valuations per pupil, SIMULATION 6 provides the best option because it equalises debt service expenditures. If the legislators decide to focus on the entire funding system, SIMULATION 5 provides the best opportunities for special needs students as well as the disparities in assessed valuations per pupil.

The court was not clear about what the goal of the new finance system should be or what adjustments needed to be made to the current system.The issues are complex and the focus will depend upon the legislative intent of the alternative finance system.

Reddy. K.N., (1995), conducted a study on Pattern of financing primary education in India. An attempt is made to analyse the pattern of financing primary education in India during 1974-75 to 1986-87, the period of which comparable and consistent data are available. Agencies providing 'primary' education are (1) by government and (2) Nongovernment agencies. The former includes central government, state governments, local bodies and their agencies, pupil sector enterprises, autonomous bodes which get support directly or indirectly from general revenues of the budget. The nongovernment agencies include private schools, private sector industries, charitable institutions, philanthropists and external agencies outside the country.

Pattern of Spending on Primary Education

(1) Primary Education, (2) Secondary Education, (3) Special Education (4) Pre-University Education (5) University Education and Higher Education, (6) Medical Education, (7) Sports and Welfare and (8) General.

Findings

(1) Both at the national level as well as the states level, according priority was given to primary education. (2) As a percentage of GDP, resources devoted to calculation in the country increased marginally. (3) There are disparties among the studies in the allocation of resources to primary education. (4) Bihar, Madhya Pradesh, Rajasthan and Uttar pradesh, the proverbial low income states - spent higher percentageof their GDPs on education than the so called high income states, e.g., Andhra pradesh and Karnataka. (5) In terms of priorties accorded to different categories of

education, as of 1986-87, Bihar, UP and Rajasthan allocated a little more than 50 per cent of education expenditure to primary education, (6) Punjab, Haryana, West Bengal, Andhra Pradesh, Karnataka, Orissa, Madhya Pradesh, Maharashtra, and Gujrat accorded relatively low priority to primary education in spite of their relatively higher fiscal capacity and lower level of literacy. (7) There are inapproriate allocations as between direction and administration on the one hand and Govt. Primary schools, Non-govt. primary schools, local bodies schools, teacher training, minimum needs programme, tribal area sub-plan and other item on the other.

Furquan Qamal, Ilyal Hussein (1995) conducted a study on budgetary practices in colleges of higher education in India. This study is based on a survey of colleges of higher education situated in 18 states, representing almost all categories of colleges found of the country. The sample covers 82 colleges under jurisdiction of as many as 44 universities. The paper discusses various aspects of the budgetary process. These include the type of budget prepared, availability of budget facilitating documents, and budget participation.

Objective

(1) Is to know the five year plans may provide certain schemes, programmes on projects like new courses, college buildings, laboratories, libraries etc. (2) To know whether allocations made for meeting the expenditure to implement such schemes are provided out the plant, (3) whether at the institutional level they constitute the plan budget, (4) to know the different budgets like salary budgets, recurring, non-recurring budgets.

Methodology

The present study draws its sample from these very colleges. Based on a random sampling, data schedules and questionnaires were sent to 172 colleges situated all over India.

Findings

(1) The most colleges prepared their budgets as a routine exercise and do not attach to them much significance. (2) More number of government colleges do so. (3) In case of salary budgets more than three-fourth of the government colleges prepare them while the proportions of private preparing such budgets is as high as 88 per cent. (4) Some of the state may not be insisting on a separate salary budget. (5) As far as the development budgets are concerned, they are prepared by around 63 per cent of the Government Colleges and 60 per cent of the private colleges 61 as 17 per cent of the colleges have revised their budget manuals during the last five years. Over 2 per cent of them have a definite policy of updating their budget manuals

at regular intervals. (7) Around 83 per cent of the Government colleges are78 per cent of the private colleges have budgets guidelines. (8) All of the Government and Private colleges submitted their budgets well within the stipulated data. (9) Private colleges do play a more democratic attitude in preparing their budgets, compared to the Government colleges. (10) 33 per cent of Government colleges was reported by 22 per cent. (11) The most of the colleges principles prepare budgets because of statutory compulsion.

Studies at International Level

Horn, Willem Sterrenberg,(1988), has made a study on Guidelines for the financing of education up to secondary level in the Republic of South Africa. The most important characteristics of South African education are the gross differences in the quantitative and qualitative provision of education to the different sections of the population. These differences among the various education systems are noticeable in the per capita spending, the availability of physical facilities,the average qualifications of teachers and the pupil/teacher ratio. Although the South African Government is committed to bringing about parity among the education systems for the different cultural groups, it must take cognizance of the following realities in South African society : (1) South Africa has a heterogenous society with educational goals which are Virginia school districts during the 1987-88 school year, became independent variables in multiple analysis with school finance data and student outputs data as the dependent variables.

Community Type, Fiscal Capacity, and Economic Composition of a District Population accounted for 61 per cent for of the variability in current expenditure per pupil and 63 per cent of the variability in the percentages of students planning to attend a four year college. Over 70 per cent of the variability in Achievement Test Scores was accounted for by Black Family Structure, Fiscal Capacity, Economic Composition of a District Population, and Community Type characteristics.

Barwick, Woody, Joe, (1990), has made study on The antecendants to the school financial crisis in Kentucky. In a class action suit brought to obtain a judgment declaring that the Kentucky system of financing public elementary and secondary education violated the Kentucky Constitution Judge Ray Corns rules the system unconstitutional on May 31,1988. He held that the system violated not only the state constitution but also the due process and equal protection clauses of the 14th Amendment of the United State Constitution.

The purpose of this study was twofold. First, the study traced the historical and legal development of the financial support system for public elementary and secondary education from 1830 to the present data. Second, the study analyzed the facts surrounding the ruling declaring the system unconstitutional.

The study was a historical review of the legislative documents, historical records and legislative acts which set the stage for the unconstitutional judgement. Judge Ray Corns, the circuit judge rendering the decision, and other key actors in the Council for Better Education v. Wilkinson were interviwed to analyze facts and events related to the ruling that the system was unconstitutional.

Arvin, Robert Leonard, (1989), has made a study on School finance equity, local financial effort, and student learning in Kentucky. This study's theoretical perspective was that high local involvement in school districts contributes to higher learning. Examination of the effect of the student learning from expenditures and local financial effort in Kentucky for 1984/85 to 1987/88 was the purpose of the study. The literature review confirmed that centralization was the predominant solution recommened to resolve school finance inequity and that higher expenditures had an inconsistent effect on student learning outputs.

The data analysis employed multiple regression/correlation analysis with four dependent learning variables: a dropout index, student attendance, American College Act (ACT) scores, and Kentucky Essential Skill Test (KEST) performance. The research questions, after removing the effect of proportion of economically deprived, per capita income, taxable wealth, district size, district status, district classification, pupil teacher ratio, and proportion of students tested were: (1)What was the effect of overall expenditures for current expenses on student learning outputs? (2) What unique effect did instructional expenditure have. Weidmann, Maja Brigitt, (1988), has made a study on expenditures in Wisconsin School Districts : A comparative analysis of zero-aid and positive districts. The purpose of this study was to examine the expenditures behaviour of zero-aid and positive-aid school districts in Wisconsin. Due to the absence of a recapture provision in the equalization aid formula, zero-aid districts have access to more fiscal resources that positive-aid districts. The fiscal advantage of many zero-aid districts is enchances by the payment of minimum aid.

Zero-aid districts can respond to their fiscal advantage in three ways, (1) they can increase their spending, (2) they can decrease their tax rates, or (3) they can institute a mix of the first two options. The nature of their response, as compares to the expenditures dehaviour of positive-aid districts, was the focus of this study.

The sample consisted of 15 pairs of K-12 zero-aid and positive-aid districts matched on the basis of average daily membership, median family income, and geographic location. Data over a three year period (1983-84, 1984-85 and 1985-86) were examined.

Descriptive statistics and correlations were employed to complete the data analysis. Small sample t-tests were used to determine if significant differences existed in the expenditures choices and tax rates of two groups of districts. Correlation coefficients determined the relationship between tax rates and pupil total and personal-only expenditures for major Fund 10 and 20 expenditure categories.

Noteworthy results included : (1) Zero-aid districts used a portion of their fiscal advantage to decrease tax rates and the remaining portion to increase spending. (2) The increased spending in zero-aid districts appeared to be spread relatively evenly across all school functions. (3) The increased spending in zero-aid districts appeared to be divided between personnel and non-personnel expenditures in about the same proportion. (4) Aberrations of a power equalization paradigm exit when the recapture of negative aid is not permitted. The implementation of the minimum aid provision accentuates this aberration. (5) The cancellation of negative aid recapture, along with the payment of mimimum aid, is counterproductive to the equalization of educational opportunities.

Pillainayagam, Manuelpillai George, has made a study on A Longitudinal Equity Study of Ohio's Public School Finance System. The purpose of this study was to examine the status of Ohio's school finance system on two dimensions of child/student equity: equal treatment of equals and equality of educational opportunity. This was accomplished by analyzing alternate year school finance data from fiscal year 1980/81 through 1988/89. Trends in equity, that occurred in three dollar based per pupil equity objects: (1) current (operating) expenditures, (2) instructional expenditures, and (3) local plus state revenues were estimated for all (615) school districts and monal school districts (excluding the top 2 per cent high expenditures districts). All school districts were placed into three classifications based on (a) state basis aid allocation methods, (b) administrative type, and (c) property wealth level and their subgroups were treated independently.

The conceptual framework for student equity, and associated six horizontal equity measures recommended by Berne and Stiefel (1984) and certain pupil weighted measures were used in the statistical anatysis. The School Price Index (SPI) was used to estimate 1983 constant dollar values of the equity objects for comparison over the ten-year period. The relationship statistics: simple regression, correlation, slope, and elasticity were used to measure the equal educational opprtunity dimension of equity in all school districts, modal districts, and the subgroup classifications.

For all school districts, it was concluded that Ohio's system of financing education was ineffectual in moving toward greater equity from 1980 to 1989. The foundation plan employed in Ohio to finance public schools improved horizontal equity and decreased equal educational opportunity simultaneously. The guarantee provision was found to exacerbate movement towards greater inequity and equal educational opportunity. Low wealth school districts and local school districts improved in equity and fiscal neutrally, but suffered from inadequate funding.

High wealth school districts and some exembted villages took advantage of their wealth which caused increased disparities in the funding system. Reforms are required in Ohio school system to provide " through and efficient" system of schooling.

Maclachlan, Malcolm, (1993), has made the study on Sustaining Human Resources Development in Africa : The influence of Expatriates. Negative attitudes and stereotypes of Africans by expatriate managers and trainers regard human resource development. Instead of importing "remedies", collaborative research on the indigenous contexts of African problems will lead to appropriate solutions.

Davis Larry Nolan, Mink, Oscar G.,(1992), conducted a study on Human Resources Development : An emerging purpose. Any organised activity centered on human development could legitimately6 be seen as huiman resources development (HRD). A more holistic view defines HRD as a wide range of integrating processes aimed at developing greater purpose and meaning, higher performance, and greater capacity to respond to change, leading to more effective individuals, terms, and organizations.

Anderson, Geoff.Gonczi, Andrew, (1992), made a study on Human Resources Development for the Global Economy. Human resource development is more than training; it fosters the ability to see the big picture - the organizations place in the global environment and the ability to change in response to environmental changes.

A critical study conducted by Spencer, Lyle, M., (1984), was How to Calculate the Costs and Benefits of an HRD Program. This study presents simple methods for calculating the costs and benefits of training, consulting, and other human resource development interventions in a variety of settings.

Jendlicka, Janet Sue., (1995), made a study on Financing Occupational Therapy Education in Mississippi.The costs of higher education have escalated in the last decade. Traditionally, students have financed their education through parental assistance and federal and state supported financial aid programs. In addition, there has been a shift in the funding patterns of these financial aid programs. This has increased the need for finding alternative resources for financing higher educatiopn. The preemployment contractual agreement is an alternative resources that is being used more frequentlly in financing occupational therapy program at the University of Mississippi Medical Center financed their education. Also addressed were the perceptions of alumni and employers regarding the use of preemployment contractual agreements in financing occupational therapy education.

Surveys were sent to 79 alumni. There was 68 surveys returned for response rate of 86 per cent. Twenty health agencies or employers in Mississippi were identified as offering preemployment contractual agreements for students enrolled in occupational therapy educational programs. Allof these facilities agreed to participate in a telephone interview.

Alumni from occupational therapy program used loans, grants, scholarships and parental aid in financing their education. In addition, 44 per cent of the graduates used preemployment contractual agreements. Alumni with higher loan debt were more likely to enter into preemployment contractual agreements. Similarities were found between alumni and employers regarding therate of fulfillment of employment commitment and overall satisfaction with the preemployment contractual agreement.

Descals-Tormo, Asensi., (1994), made a study on Financing Higher Education : A Students Direct Subsidies Model. This dissertation focuses on analyzing the problem of financing a service, higher education, from the double perspective of efficiency and equity. Our proposal defends a scheme which represents a change in the way that public subsidies are assigned, from higher education institutions to students. For the group of taxpayers, the proposed pattern of financing implies a great ability to differentiate among different students according to their personal characteristics. This is compared with the schemes of financing which are working nowadays in developed countries.

The results and consequences of the proposed model are found positive by the author for several reasons which are analysed in the last chapter. Many changes are expected in students and university behaviour.

As a first step, we connect the pattern of financing and the goals of higher education service.We also identify the groups at stake in the university student, parents, government or taxpayers and phillanthropy institutions and try to share the costs of higher education service among those groups, according to the benefits they receive. So we study the real sharing of costs in a group of developed countries, defining, first of all, the costs of higher education direct costs, maintenance costs and forgone income.

Then we use the economic analysis to justify proposal of sharing the costs of higher education and the way it should be made. So we have to decide between two extermely different models to transfer public resources to higher education. We study both of them and we choose a students direct subsidies model which is better both from the efficiency and from the equity point of view.

The last conclusion leads us to carefully study different ways of giving direct subsidies to students as users to the service. Special attention is paid to two of them : Grants and students loans schemes. We include the last one as a part of the proposed model of financing.

Finally, we study the consequences of the model and try to make an application to the Valencian University System.

Brackett, John and Others, (1983), made a study on The Legacy of Rational Budgeting Models in Education and a Proposal for the Future. This paper represents a backdrop from which to consider the development of planning and budgering model for local education agencies. The first part of the presentation describes the demands and external pressures that affect resource allocation decisions in schools districts. The ability of this local school officials to link the cost consequences and implications of these policy and environmental pressures provides the rational for designing the Local Planning and Budgeting model (LPBM). The second part examinses in detail the strengths, weaknesses, and performance of two well known, previous budget reforms, Planning, Programming and Budgeting System (PPBS) and Zero-Based (ZBB); and summarizes the lessons to be leared from these prior attempts to rationalize educational budgeting process. The chapter ends with a skeletal overview of the LPBM's conceptual framework and the implications from Part II for the development of a strategy for implementing the LPBM in local school districts.

Peterson, David.,(1991), made a study on School-based Budgeting. School-based budgeting decentralizes fiscal decisions and is usually adopted as a part of a comprehensive school-based management plan. The practice requires cooperation, particularly from the school board, superintendent, and principals.The purpose of school-based budgeting is not to reduce costs but to improve school productivity by altering authority relationships within the district.

Harman, Peggy L. Hartman, William T., (1982), made a study on Local Special Education Planning Model. To help school districts estimate the present and future needs and costs of their special education programs, this manual presents the Local Special Education Planning Model, an interactive computer program (with worksheets) that provdies a framework for using a district's own data to analyze its special education program. Part

1 of the manual discusses the model, its development, and its four oprating steps, which include filling out worksheets, entering the data into the computer, reviewing the output, and making alternative projections. Part 2 describes how to complete the eight worksheets, which cover basis district data, special education categories and instructional programs related district services, current and anticipated student placments in the instructional programs, personal ratios, and district support services. Entering the data into the computer is explained in part 3, while part 4 review 18 reports generated by the model that show the current and future costs, placement, personnel requirements, and program and services requirements, of a district's total special education program. Attached to the manual are copies of the model's computer program and blank copies to the manual are copies of the model's computer program and blank copies to the manual are copies of eight worksheets.

The report describes activities and results of the second year of the Special Education Planning Model (SEPM), designed to help planners and policymakers estimate special education program needed and costs. SEPM uses a computer simulation based on users assumptions and priorities in such areas as incidence rates, handicapping conditions to be served, services to be offered, program standards for the services, and costs of resources.The model was tested in 26 states. A users guide outline input steps and the data preparation procedures for six planning steps on the following topics; total student population, special education population, instructional programs, student placement patterns, and specific and nonspecific related services. Guidlines are further offered for understanding the reports and using the projections to make policy and planning decisions.

Bryers,Verne Rechard, (1988), made a study on a fiscal equity assessment on Indiana's public elementary and secondary school operating expenditurcs since the implementation of the local levy freeze. The purpose of this study was to examine and analyse the fiscal equity of Indiana's school operating expenditures. Specifically, the objective of this study was to answer the following research questions: (1) What is the current degree of fiscal equity in the Indiana public school operating expenditures, and (2) Science the enactment of the property tax levy freeze in 1973, has the degree of fiscal equity in terms of school operating expenditures changed?

Chosen for the study was the 1972-73 school year and the 1985-86 school year preceded the tax levy freeze and the 1985-86 school year contained the latest available data. Examination and analysis of the fiscal equity was conducted in two parts. : (1) horizontal and analysis of fiscal equity measurements on the school operating expenditures; and (2) fiscal neutrality measurements on the school operating expenditures, the adjusted tax rate, and the adjusted assessed valuation. The horizontal methods selected were (1) boxplot, (2) coefficient of variation, (3) federal range ratio, (4) Gini coefficient, (5) Lorenz Curve, (6) McLoone index, (7) range, (8) restriced range, (9) standard deviation, and (10) variance. The fiscal neutrality measurements selected were the (1) pupil-weighted Pearson Correlation and (2) data plot. Of the 305 school corporations chosen for examination and analysis included 309 taxing districts for the 1972-73 school year and 301 taxing districts for the 1985-86 school year.

The horizontal equity measurements revealed that the 1985-86 school year indicated an overall deterioration of fiscal equity. With the exception of the McLoone index, the measurments indicated that the 1972-73 school year was more equitable.

The fiscal neutrality measurements indicated that the 1972-73 school year had less of a linear relationship between the (1) school operating expenditures and adjusted tax rate and the (2) adjusted tax rate and adjusted assessed valuation. A decreased linear relationship between the school operating expenditures and assessed valuation was indicated for the 1985-86 school year.

Myers, Robert Cornelius, (1988), made a study on Predictors of local current expenditures for North Carolina public schools and community colleges.The purposes of this study were two fold : (1) to determine the predcitability of the amount of country current expenditure for the North Carolina Public School System by using nineteen county characteristics and (2) to determine the predictability of the amount of county current expenditures for the North Carolina Community College System by using these same nineteen county characteristics. All data were collected from the year 1985 with the exception of general population data, which were secured from the Census of 1980.

Factor analysis was performed on the nineteen predictor variables in order to remove multicollinearity between the variables and to reduce the data to a manageable size for subsequent multiple regression analysis. Stepwise regression was then utilized to determine which factors best predicted the amount of local revenues spent for educational current expenditures.

Factors 2, 3, and 5 were significant predictors for per pupil local current expenditure for the public schools. Factor 2 included median years of education completed by the general population, high employment and high income variables. Factor 3 described the relationship with per capital property value and per capita property tax. It also included the migration rate in the general population. Factor 5 included per pupil state current expenditure for the public schools, percent of high school junior passing the North

Carolina Competency Test, and percent of lab or force in new and expanded industry.

Factors 2 and 4 were significant predictors for per pupil local current expenditure for the community college. Factor 4 represented per pupil state expenditure for the community college and per cent of white pupils in the community college.

Yoon, Yong-Sik., (1991), conducted a study on Equity trends in Wisconsin school finance, from 1980-81 to 1988-89. The major objectives of this study were to determine input equity trends in and levels of Wiscons in school finance and to examine how the treatment of the Milwaukee School District has affected Wisconsin school finance equity. Two major data sets - fiscal resource data and human resource data - were used to examine input equity trends in all 373 Wiscosin K-12 school districts from 1980-81 through 1988-89.

Children were viewed as the recipients of equity by using a pupil unit of analysis. Six fiscal resource inputs and two human resource inputs and were used as proxy measures of equity. Two equity concepts-horizontal equity and equal opportunity - were applied in order to draw conclusions as to whether the eight input - equity objects were distributed fairly and to what degree the eight input - equity objects were realated with the independent variables. Four equity measures were used in the study to assess the input-equity objects; the coefficient of variation, the Gini coefficient for horizontal equity, the Pearson correlation, and the elasticity for equal opportunity.

All expenditure and revenue objects except local revenue per pupil showed a generally improving trend in horizontal equity. The six fiscal resourse objects showed a worsening trend in equal opportunity with respect to district wealth. The three expenditure objects exhibited an improving trend in equal oportunity with respect to percentage of minority students, while local revenue per pupil plus state revenue per pupil plus federal revenue per pupil object exhibited a worsening trend after 1985-86. The treatment of the Milwaukee School District generally contributed to greater equity with respect to horizontal equity opportunity with respect to dictrict wealth, while the treatment of the Milwaukee School District generally tended to reduce opportunity with respect to percentage of minority student.

The distribution of teacher per 1000 pupils was more equitable than instructional expenditures per pupil for both horizontal equity and equal opportunity measures.

Turner, D.R., (1982), made a study on The Financing of Universities. The means by which universities, particularly in the United Kindom, have been finances up to the present are examined. Chapter one looks at the historical background in outline, with special reference to Oxford and Cambridge and the comparatively rapid developments of the nineteenth century. There follows a more detailed review of events in the firest few decades of the twentieth century, and the changes which came about after the establishment of the University Grants Committee in 1919.

Evidence is produced regarding the vast increases in the amount of government financial support after the end of the Second World War in 1945. The way in which it became increasingly obvious that, if public money was to be poured into higher education, there would have to be an increased measure of accountability on the part of the recipient institutions, is outlined and the effect of even greater expansion as proposed by the Robbins Committee Report in 1963 is made clear. The changes resulting in the mid-1960s i.e., the DES assumption of responsibility for University finance, carried by the Treasury since 1919, and the granting of investigatory powers to the Comptroller and the Auditor General, are investigated in depth. An interpretation of the effects of these changes is made.

Finally, more recent events in an era of economic stringency are reviewed, and the ways in which their effects have been felt and may yet pose problems for universities are outlined. Some alternative or additional ways of financing are suggested. The concluding opinion is that a great measure of freedom remains to universities, in spite of the fact that increased accountability must be expected to accompany major financial support from public funds.

Taylor, Earlene Pankey, (1990), made a study on A comparative analysis of the budgeting process at three senior educational institutions in the university system of Georgia. Purpose :The allocation of limited financial resources is an essential function of college administrators. This study identified the current budgeting practices at three senior colleges in the University System of Georgia and compared their practices and procedures. The participation of faculty in budgeting process was investigated. The perceptions of the faculty and administrators were compared in an attempt to more fully examine the budgeting process and its role in the financial management of each college.

Methods : A pilot study was conducted to test the interview procedures and questions and the faculty Quetionnaire. At each of the three colleges, selected administrators were interviewed and faculty members were surveyed. Thirty-five administratiors participated in the study. Questionnaires were mailed to 425 faculty members. The average response was calculated for each statement of the questionnaire. Tables are provided summarising the data from the faculty.

Results : The administrators identified specific budgeting procedures, methods of budgeting used, and the role of budgeting in the financing management of each college. All colleges practice incremental budgeting and use the budget as a control factor in funding decision. However, one college is unique in its organizational structure as it relates to the budgeting function. Two hundred eighty-four faculty completed questionnaires for a response rate of 66.82 per cent. The faculty and the administrators disagree about the level of participation practiced and desired by the faculty in the budgeting percess.

Reimers, Fernando Miguel.,(1988), made study on the Trends of educational finance Latin America : The impact of the external debt. This thesis examined the impact of the Latin American external debt on education.

The association between series of aggregate national indicators of educational expenditures and levels of debt in 18 countries of Latin America was examined for the period 1970-1985. Additionally the results of the intra-country analysis for all the countries of the region were summarized and used to examine the impact of macroeconomic variables on the relationship between debt and educational expenditure. A detailed analysis of six countries further expanded the study to additional indicators of government finance, discussing the observed impact of the external debt on the structure of educational finance in the context of socio-political developments in each country.

It was found that the decreases in educational expenditure observed in recent years in Latin America are systematically related to the increases of the levels of publice external debt.

As debt increases education diminishes as a priority of government spending in most of the countries. In some of these countries the same is true of total educational expenditures. This association is characterised by a "threshold-effect" in some countries. Before the external debt reaches certain levels the association between debt and education was positive; beyond those levels the association flattened out or became negative.

Exploring the factors that may influence the variability of the association in 18 countries examined, it was observed that per capita GNP and enrollment levels were negatively related to the intensity of the impact of debt on education, while GNP, population, debt levels and change in debt levels seem to have had no effect on the association between debt and education.

The detailed analysis of six cases revealed the consistent impact of adjustment policies resulting. from external indebtedness on education expenditures. It was observed that the adjustment policies in recent years consistency resulted in reductions in educational expenditures, both in absolute and relative terms.

The thesis concludes discussing the implications of the impact of the debt on educational expenditures and reviewing policy to respond to the crisis.

Studies at State Level

Nanjundappa (1975) conducted a study for his Ph.D. with the ICSSR's financial assistance on university finances.

The main objective of the investigation was to study the working of university financies with reference to (a) growth of revenue and behaviours of components of revenue; (b) growth of expenditure and behaviours of components of expenditure; (c) allocation of available funds among the different activities and discipline; and (d) financial relations between the university and the UGC and that between the government and the University. The finances of Karnataka University since its inception in 1949-73 were studied. The data were collected from the university records.

The major findings were; (i) the total revenue increased from Rs. 1.45 lakhs (1949-50) to Rs. 177.85 lakhs (1972-73) showing an average annual growth of forty two per cent (ii) the state government financed upto fifty four per cent, the income from fees shared thirty five per cent and the UGC shared four to five per cent; (iv) there were a decline in the per capita greants indicating the comparative decline of unversity finances when comoared to increased enrollment; (v) the total expenditure increased from Rs. 33,036 in 1949-50 to 2.23 crores of Rupees in 1972-73; (vi) the changes in the per capita expenditure increased from Rs. 33,036 in 1949-50 to 2.23 crores of Rupees in 1972-73; (vi) the changes in the per capita expenditure was from Rs. 80,000 (1949-50) to Rs.5401 (1958-59) Rs.3306 (1972-73) to (vii) the rises in the per capita expenditure between 1949-50 and 1972-73 were from Rs. 261 to 275 in case of library Rs. 1 to Rs.8 in student facilities Rs. 46 to Rs.70 in case of fellowships, Rs. 28 to 92 for hostels, Rs. 4 to Rs.103 in case of examinations, Rs. 74 to Rs. 1500 for academic departments and Rs. 6 to 58 for administration; (viii) the cost of education of an individual amounted to Rs. 5372 of which net academic cost cane to Rs. 3242 and private cost to Rs. 2130 (ix) the physical facilities available during 1961-62 declined in the later years; (x) the establishment of UGC and its introduction of four tier pattern of grants was a boon and a life saver to the university the large share of UGC grants in approved schemes helped the unversity to reduce reliance on the state government; (xi) over the four plan period the proportion of grants; for teaching staff was only thirteen per cent and (xii) the economic-cum-functional classification showed that there was a non-optimal allocation of funds among the different items of expenditure indicating the utmost economy of expenditure to be imposed on general services.

Manvikar, S., (1983), conducted a study on A Critical Study of the Relationship between Expenditure Pattern and Efficiency Levels of the Secondary schools of Bangalore District. The major objectives of the study were (i) to compare the expenditure patterns of different types of secondary schools of Bangalore District, (ii) to compare the efficiency of Banglore District rural and city secondary schools, (iii) to find out the relationship between components of expenditure and components of efficiency of the secondary schools of Bangalore district, and (iv) to find out the relationship of school factors like strength, age of the school, teacher's age, qualifications and experience with school efficiency and expenditure.

The sample consisted of ten secondary schools of eighteen educational districts (expect Bangalore district) of the Karnataka State for reliable tool to measure school efficiency. The expenditure efficiency relationship was studies only in 110 schools of Bangalore district rural and city. A tool was developed to obtain information on expenditure pattern. A School Efficiency Index Scale was also developed by the researcher. Information about expenditure was obtained for three academic years - 1977-78, 1978-79 and 1979-80. The investigator visited 25 schools for cross-checking the information. For data analysis conclusions, mean, standard deviation, t-test , correlation, and simple linear and multiple linear regression analyses were used.

The major findings were : 1. Bangalore city and rural secondary schools differed in respect of expenditure pattern and efficiency. City schools spent significantly more on some items of expenditure than rural schools. Again city schools were significantly more efficient than rural schools in terms of their total efficiency and certain components of efficiency . 2. Total efficiency and total expenditure on furniture and equipment, contingency and cocurricular activities was associated with total efficiency, whereas in the case of rural schools, only expenditure on contingency was significantly associated with total efficiency, personnel and organizational efficiency and school-community relationship efficiency were significantly related to expenditure on furniture and equipment in city schools. In case of rural schools, school plant and equipment- efficiency were related to expenditure on building and financial management efficiency was related to expenditure on non- teaching staff salary. 4. None of the important components of school efficieny like personnel and organizational efficieny and outcome efficiency was found related to expenditure on salary. 5. In the case of city schools, larger schools were more efficient in terms of their total efficiency and outcome efficiency than smaller ones. In the case of rural schools, large schools has better utilization of resources. 6. All expenditure variables together could explain only about 21 per cent of the variance in the total efficiency in the case of rural schools and about 29 per cent in the case of urban schools.

The findings imply that there is a need for a differential urban-rural grant-in-aid code policy for granting permission to start new secondary schools and for better plans for allocation of resources. The study has also underlined the need for consolidating non-viable secondary schools in rural areas. Dr. A.S. Seetharamu has made a longer study on educational expenditure made by Karnataka state (1987). The study, among other things beings equal, revealed the following aspects. It emphasised that Karnataka was spending 2.6 per cent (2.5 all-India) of its SDP in 1960-61. It rose upto 3.66 per cent (3.2 all-India) in 1976-77 and remained steady there after. The per capita expenditure during the reference period went up Rs.9 (Rs.8.8) to Rs. 35 (Rs.all-India) on education in state. Cost per pupil went up from Rs. 46.7 (Rs.53.7 all-India) to Rs.187 (Rs.211 all-India). Budget expenditure as percentage of total (revenue) budget went up from 21.2 per cent (22.5 per cent) in 1960-61 to 23.5 per cent (24.3 per cent) in 1982-83.

In 1960-61, of the total educational expenditure in the state, 72 per cent came from Government 3 per cent from local bodies, 12 per cent from fees and 12 per centfrom other sources. But in 1976-77 the picture was that Government paid 79 per cent, local bodies proportion was negligible, fees constitutioned hardly 6 percent (enrolment went up and fees came down), and other sources only 15 per cent.

The general picture is that, of the total educational expenditure efforts in the states, only 9.3 per cent is paid by the Centre and 90.7 per cent is paid by the state governments (1978-79) (Education is in the concurrent list, i.e.. a joint responsibility of the Centre as well as the State).

Incidentally Karnataka spends the highest proportion on higher education among all the states in India. Secondary education has been much neglected.

Of the total costs on education, 94.8 per cent is of recurring type: salaries of teachers (71.6 per cent), salaries of non-teaching staff (9.5 per cent), Totalling 81.1 per cent on salaries, and the rest on stipends, fee concessions (2.7per cent) maintenance of buildings, equipment and furniture, chemicals and apparatus, libraries, games and sports, hostels etc.Non-recurring cost is hardly 5.2 per cent of the total (1976-77 data) which is spent on buildings, libraries, equipment, furniture, etc.

Social cost per pupil is very high for some cources like Public Health; Business Management; Venterinary Science; Agriculture and Forestry;

Medicine; Physical Education; Engineering; Technology and Architecture, as compared to general education courses.

In the fifties and the early sixties, non-plan expenditure and plan expenditure were in 60:40 ratio. Now it is 86:14(1980-81), 84:16 (178-79). While non-plan expenditure has grown by 14.8 per cent plan expenditure has grown only by 11.5 per cent over the years 1950-51 to 1980-81.

The above review gives a clear picture that, studies on financial aspect of educational planning are not comprehensive in nature. Although some studies have attempted to find out relationship between investment in education and progress of education, but they could not establish a principle based on scientic procedure. Not a singly study was able to workout per capita expenditure for various stages of education like primary, secondary, higher etc.

As far as studies in Karnataka are concerned no study is found to attempt to construct an index to show total educational allocations and expenditure during plan periods. There is also an urgent need to find out compound growth rate of allocations and expenditure for all sectors in Karnataka. Therefore, the present study is a sincere attempt to cover uncovered area of educational research with special reference to financial dimension in Karnataka.

3

Methodology of the Study

This chapter describes broad objectives, specific objectives, statement of the problem, assumptions of the study, definitions of the terms and concepts used in the study, methodology employed, sources of data, statistical techniques for the analysis of the data and delimitations of the study.

Broad Objectives of the Study

The present study was undertaken with the following broad objectives in view.

1. To analysis financial allocations and expenditure for education in the state of Karnataka at different levels and type from Ist five year plan to VIIIth five year plan.
2. To compare budget allocations for different sectors of education in Karnataka with neighbouring states of AP, Kerala, Maharasstra and Tamil Nadu from 1951-52 to 1995-96.
3. To findout the order of priority given for various sectors of education in the plan and non-plan allocations and expenditure in the state of Karnataka.

Specific Objectives of the Study

1. To examine and compare the total financial allocations to all sectors with total allocations on education sector in Karnataka.
2. To find out compound growth rate of allocations to all sectors and total (plan + non-plan) educational allocations in Karnataka.
3. To examine and compare the total financial expenditure to all sector with total expenditure on education in Karnataka.
4. To find out and compare the total financial expenditure to all sector with total expenditure on education in Karnataka.

5. To compare the total state expenditure budget and expenditure on education with percentage, and SDP in the neighbouring states of Andhra Paredesh, Kerala, Maharastra and Tamil Nadu with that of Karnataka.
6. To analyse sectorwise expenditure percentages in the neighbouring states of Andhra Pardesh, Kerala, Maharashtra and Tamil Nadu.
7. To find out the increase, if any, in the plan allocation for education from 1951-52 to 1996-97 in Karnataka.
8. To know the extent of disparities in the plan allocation for education in different sectors.
9. To compare the compound growth rate of plan allocations for education from 1951-52 to 1996-97 in Karnataka.
10. To find out the percentage of plan allocations for different sectors of education from 1951-52 to 1996-1997 in Karnataka.
11. To find out plan (period-wise) allocations and percentage of allocations for different sectors of education in different plans from 1951-52 to 1996-97 in Karnataka.
12. To find out the increase, if any, in the non-plan allocation for education from 1973-74 to 1996-97 in Karnataka.
13. To know the extent of disparities in the non-plan alocation for education in different sectors.
14. To compare the compound growth rate of non-plan allocations for education from 1973-74 to 1996-97 in Karnataka.
15. To find out the percentage of non-plan allocations for different sectors of education from 1973-74 to 1996-97 in Karnataka.
16. To find out non-plan (period-wise) allocations and percentage of allocations for different sectors of education in different plans from 1951-52 to 1996-97 in Karnataka.
17. To find out the increase, if any, in the plan expenditure for education from 1973-74 to 1996-97 in Karnataka.
18. To know the extent of disparities in the plan expenditure for education in different sectors.
19. To compare the compound growth rate of plan expenditure for education from 1951-52 to 1994-95 in Karnataka.
20. To find out the percentage of plan expenditure for different sectors of education from 1951-52 to 1996-97 in Karnataka.
21. To find out plan (period-wise) expenditure and percentage of expenditure for different sector of education in different plans from 1951-52 to 1996-97 in Karnataka.

22. To find out the increase, if any, in the non-plan expenditure for education from 1972-73 to 1994-95 in Karnataka.
23. To know the extent of disparities in the non-plan expenditure for education in different secotrs in Karnataka.
24. To compare the compound growth rate of non-plan expenditure for education from 1972-73 to 1994-95 in Karnataka.
25. To find out the percentage of non-plan expenditure for different sectors of education from 1972-73 to 1994-95 in Karnataka.
26. To find out non-plan (period-wise) expenditure and percentage of expenditure for different sector of education in different plans from 1972-73 to 1996-97 in Karnataka.
27. To examine the growth of total educational allocations as compared to the other sectors of economy in the successive Five Year Plans from 1951-52 to 1996-97 in Karnataka.
28. To examine the growth of total educational expenditure as compared to other sectors of the economy in the successive Five Year Plans from 1951-52 to 1994-95 in Karnataka.
29. To examine the growth of total allocations and total expenditure for education and to find out the percentage of total educational expenditure to total allocations for education from 1951-52 to 1996-97.
30. To examine the growth of plan expenditure for education as current and constant prices with base years (1960-61 to 1980-81) from 1960-61 to 1994-95 in Karnataka.
31. To examine the growth of non-plan expenditure for education at current and constant prices with base years (1960-61 and 1980-81) from 1972-73 to 1994-95 in Karnataka.
32. To examine the plan and non-plan allocation and expenditure for education (Rs. in lakhs) at current and constant prices with base years (1960-61 and 1980-81) from 1960-61 to 1994-95 in Karnataka.
33. To find out per capita expenditure on primary education in Karnataka.
34. To find out percentage of variation in primary per capita educational expenditure.
35. To construct an index for showing total educational allocations and expenditure from 1960-61 to 1995-96 in Karnataka.
36. To find out percentange change in variable in expenditure on education and in NSDP in Karnataka.
37. To find out the elastricity of educational expenditure in Karnataka.
38. To find out correlation between educational allocations and expenditure with GSDP and NSDP at current and constant prices in Karnataka.

39. To recomend the strategies for restructuring of the allocations and expenditure on education on the findings of the study in Karnataka; and
40. To depict these trends, graphically, to make them more lucid.

Statement of the Problem

A critical study of allocations and expenditure for education in State of Karnataka during the plan periods.

Assumptions of the Study

The investigator has made the following assumptions based on economic trend in the field of education, views expressed by both educationists and economists, research reviews and the personal experience of investigator himself:

1. Although there is increase in plan and non-plan allocation for education in Karnataka from 1951-52 to 1996-97, there exists disparity in the allocations for different sectors of education.

2. Although there is increase in plan and non-plan expenditure for education in Karnataka from 1951-52 to 1994-95. There exists disparities in the expenditure for different sectors of education.

3. The percentage of variation of per capita expenditure for primary education in Karnataka from 1951-52 to 1994-95 more or less remained constant.

4. The percentage of variation of per capita expenditure for all sectors of education in Karnataka from 1951-52 to 1994-95 more or less remained constant five year plan periods in Karnataka.

5. There is fluctuation in the growth of educational expenditure during the successive

6. Value differences do not appear whem current prices of educational allocations and expenditure are converted into constant prices.

7. As GSDP and NSDP at current and constant prices increases the allocations and expenditure for education would also increase.

8. Budget allocation and expenditure for education in Karnataka is less when compared to the sectors of economy.

9. The relative magnitude of the budgeted allocations and expenditure on education in Karnataka over a period of time is less than neighbouring states like AP, Kerala, Maharashtra and Tamil Nadu.

10. Priority in the allocations and expenditure for Elementary, Secondary, University/Higher, Special and General Education in Karnataka over a period of time more or less remain unchanged.

Definitions of the Terms and Concepts

(a) G.N.P.: Gross National Product (GNP): It is gross domestic product plus the income accuring to domestic residents resulting from investment abroad less income earned in the domestic market by foreigners from abroad.

(b) Plan Allocations: Allocations are the amounts earmarked for educational sector in the beginning of each plan. These amounts are likely to be revised on the plan procedures and all that allocated need not be spent and thus expenditure will generally be lesser than allocations.

(c) Plan Expenditure: Plan expenditure means the expenditure incurred on the new developments projects. The plan expenditure on education is nothing but the expenditure incurred on the new developments evisaged in respect of education in the plan. Such expenditure is incurred on the construction of new buildings, recruitments of new teachers, provision of facilities for new enrolments innovations etc plan expenditure on educational sets direction for future development of education.

(d) Non-plan Expenditure: Non-plan Expenditure on Education Educational infrastructure incurred on the existing on the schemes undertaken in previons plans. Committed expenditure or non-plan expenditure is recurring expenditure. Plan expenditure on educational gets translated into non-plan expenditure at the end plan and it is called normal expenditure. The non-plan expenditure on education is needed for maintenance of the existing schemes of education.

(e) Revenue Expenditure : This is not the expenditure that is spent on equipment and buildings. but, this is the expenditure intended for revenue items such as teachers salaries, etc.

(f) S.D.P.(State Domestic Product): This is state income in common perlance and is measured as the total value at factor cost of all goods and services produced within the state in a year of reference, counted without duplication. The estimates of SDP at output in the economy of the state over a period of time. SDP in per capita terms is also used as measure of the level of development of the economy of the state.

(g) Per Capita Expenditure : Per capita expenditure for education is obtained by dividing the expenditure allocated for educational by the number of the prices of a base year. Accordingly we have to concepts of constant prices. When the prices are assumed to remain unchanged when compared with a base year and the national income is value at that price of the base year, it is called income at constant prices.

The prices paid for goods and services may also include taxes like sale tax paid to the Government or subsidies given by the Government.

When taxes are deducted or subsidies added to the national income, the sum is called gross national income or national income at factor cost. When depreciation for the capital also is deducted, it become net national income at factor cost. Thus we have the following identity:

GNP =GNI at Factor Cost

GNP = GNI at Market Prices

NNP = NNI at Market Prices

National Income at Factor Cost

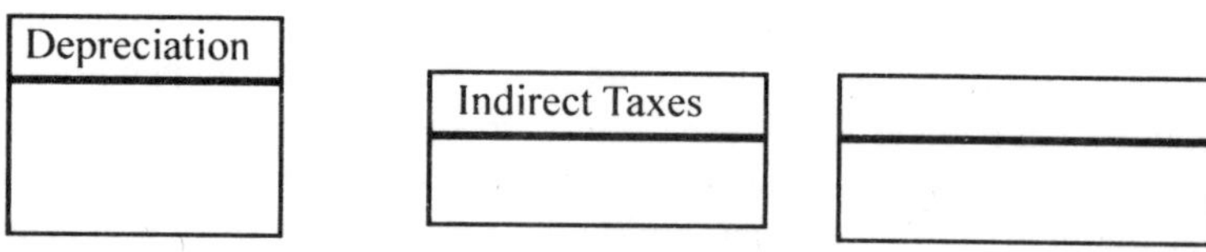

(i) Elasticity of Educational Expenditure. It is defined as the percentage of change in a Educational Expenditure due to a percentage change in NSDP.

(j) GDP (Gross Domestic Product). It is the market value of all the goods and services produced with the geographical of the state.

(k) Price Index : The price index attempts to compare the price level at one time with that of another period, or to compare relative prices in two different places. It is thus always measures relative to a base level.

(l) Planning: In common usage planning can means either 'control' or forecasting.

(m) Ex-ante and Ex-post: Ex-ante refers to what was expected before certain events took place and ex-post to the actual situation which arises.

Methodology Employed in the Study

The present study is trend study in nature. Such studies are generally classified as developmental research. Persuance of socio-economic or political data and corresponding prediction of a trend which is likely to take place in future. Descriptive method is found to be more adequate. Research workers engaged in the type of work either repeat the same status study at intervals over a period of years, or gather information from documentary sources that describe present events or conditions on those that occur different times in the past after comparing the data, studying the rate and direction of change, they predict that conditions may prevail in future. This type of study should combine Historical, Documentary and survey technique. As rightly prescribed by Fowler and Fowler (1975) trend is the general direction, or tendency or drift.

Therefore, the investigator employed 'descriptive resarch method' as a procedure in order to carryout the present research study.

Sources of Data

The required data on the allocations and expenditure for education during the plan periods has been collected from the commissions reports, bulletins, journals, the plan documents and also from Government reports.. These all come under primary sources of data. In other words, the investigator has made use of primary as well as secondary sources of data. The following classification further shows details of sources of data.

(1) Primary Sources of Data

(i) *Official Documents :*

(a) Governments of Mysore Budget Estimates for the year 1951-52 to 1973-74.

(b) Detailed estimaters of the expenditure - Volume - II for the year 1974-75 to 1991-92

(c) Detailed estimates of the expenditure Volume III for the year 1992-93.

(d) Governments of Mysore, the progress of the First Five year plan of Mysore, 1951-56.

(e) Eighth Five Year plan draft - 1990-95 Volume-I, Planning Department, Government of Karnataka.

(f) Government of Karnataka- Economic Survey 1993-94.

(g) Governments - interstate economic indicators.

(h) Eighth Plan document - Goverment of india - 1992-93.

(i) Report of the Karnataka Universities Review Commission - 1993 (Prof. T. Navaneeth Rao Committee Report).

(j) First, Second, Third, Fourth, Fifth, Sixth, Seventh Five Year Plan documents, Government of Mysore/Karnataka.

(2) Secondary sources of Data

Books and Journals

(a) Padmanabhan - *Economics of educational Panning in India,* New Delhi ; Arya Book Depot. 1971.

(b) Parlokars J.S., (Pardesi) "Education of Young Farmers and its Impact on Agriculture Production" *Literacy Work* - Volume-I (6) May- 1972.

(c) Thimmaiah G., "Growth of Public Expenditure in Karnataka" *Southern Economist*, No. 1-1997.

(d) Tilak Jandyala, " Education and Economic growth in India between 1950-51 abd 1967-70 - An Empirical Investigation" *Indian Educational Review*, Volume - 10, No. 1, 1975.

Statistical Techiniques used for the Analysis of Data

In persuance of specific objectives of the study and assumptions made earlier the following statistical techniques for the analysis data have been used.

The allocations and expenditure given in absolate figures is transformed into percentage for all the years and also plan - period wise to draw conclusions. The growth of allocations and expenditure is depicted graphically using bar graphs and line graphs. The statistical technique along with their formula are given below.

1.NSDP at Deflator

Net State Domestic Product (NSDP) at current prices converted to state Income at Deflator. The formula is

$$\text{NSDP} = \frac{\text{Assessment Year}}{\text{Base Year}} \times 100$$

The researcher has used two Base year values, that are 1960-61, 1980-81, to compare the trends.

2. Educational Expenditure at Constant Prices

Educational Expenditure was converted into Constant Prices using the formula

$$\text{EXCP} = \frac{\text{Educational Expenditure at Current Prices}}{\text{CPI/SI/Average}}$$

Where CPI / SI / Average is calculated as

$$\text{Average} = \frac{\text{CPI} + \text{SI}}{2}$$

3. Consumer Price Index

Consumer Price Index has calculated the CPI (Consumer Price Index) of a year

$$\text{CPI} = \frac{\text{Whole Sale Price Index}}{\text{12 Months}} \times 4.93$$

4. Annual Average Rate of Growth

To Calculate the Annual Average Rate of Growth of Increase. The formula is

$$AARG = \frac{\text{Assessment Year - Base Year}}{\text{Base Year}} \times 100$$

in this calculation the Researcher has used two Base Year Value, 1960-61 and 1980-81.

5. Primary Educational Per Capita Expenditure

This was calculated by the formula

$$PECE = \frac{P_1}{P_0} \times 100$$

P_1 = Primary Educational Expenditure for Assessment Year.
P_0 = Primary Enrollment for an Assessment Year.

6. Percentage of Variation in Per Capita Educational Expenditure

Percentage of variation in Per Capita Educational Expenditure was calculated by the formula

$$PAPCEE = \frac{A_1}{A_0} \times 100$$

A_1 =The Per Capita Educational Expenditure of assessment year
A_0 = Previous year's value.

7. Index of Total Educational Allocations and Expenditure

This was calculated at current and constant prices taking total educational expenditure and NSDP respectively, the formula is

$$ITEAE = \frac{\text{Assessment Year Value}}{\text{Base Year Value}} \times 100$$

8. Elasticity of Educational Expenditure

To calculate the Elasticity of Educational Expenditure with the NSDP at current and constant prices with Base Year 1960-61, 1980-81 the formula is

$$EEE = \frac{\text{\% of Change in Expenditure on Education}}{\text{\% of Change in NSDP}}$$

9. Percentage Change in Variables

The technique to calculate % of Change in Expenditure on education and % change in NSDP is

$$\frac{\text{Assessment Year - Base Year}}{\text{---------}} \times 100/N$$

10. Relationship Among Different Variables

To analyse the relation between educational expenditure, educational allocations, and NSDP at current and constant prices as well as GSDP at current and constant prices. Karl Pearson's coefficient of correlation is calculated. The formula is

$$r = \frac{\Sigma xy - (\Sigma c\ \Sigma y) / N}{\sqrt{\left[\Sigma x^2 - \frac{(\Sigma x)^2}{2}\right]\left[\Sigma y^2 - \frac{(\Sigma y)^2}{2}\right]}}$$

The significance of the correlation coefficient is tested by t test. The formula for t test is and the significance $t = \frac{\sqrt{n-2}}{\sqrt{1-r^2}}$

In addition to these the special techniques likepersentage, ratios, avrage have been calculated to provide conculsions.

11. Compound Growth Rate

$Y = a b^t$

((10^ex + Co-efficient) - 1) x 100

Delimitations of the Study

Any research is bound to be done under several limitations. These limitations arise in two respects:

1. Limitations due to topic chosen for research itself.
2. Limitations due to time constraints as well as nonavailability of accurate and objective information on which generally conclusions are drawn.

The present study has both the delimitations as shown below:

1. The present study analysis the allocations made by the

Government of Karnataka from 1951-52 to 1996-97. The study attempts to identify only the trends of allocations. Consequently the study has no justification beyond this.

2. The present study analysis the expenditure incurred by Government of Karnataka from 1951-52 to 1994-95. The study attempts to identify only the trends of expenditure.

3. The present study attempts to know financial allocations and expenditure of the state Government only. But the central allocations, financial schemes, constituency development grants through Members of Parliament (MPs), allocations of Zilla Panchayat, Taluk Panchayat, Municipal Corporation, Town Municipalities for educational development in their respective localities has not been taken into consideration.

4. The study has not attempted to make a relative comparison of allocations and expenditures with progress of education achieved in the state of Karnataka.

4

Analysis of Data and Results

Research data collected from the authentic records regarding financial allocations and expenditure in the state of Karnataka constituted raw data for the present study. In pursuance of objecives - Broad and Specific - as well as assumptions of the study the data were subjected to organisation, tabulation and statistical analysis. This chapter describes in detail the procedure followed in the analysis of data.

Table 4.1 reveals that the allocation for all sectors of the economy have been fluctuating showing decrease or increase. However, total allocations for all sectors have increased from Rs. 15930.41 during 1951-52 to Rs. 2456000.77 during 1996-97. During 1956-57 there is a sudden increase in a total allocation followed by immediate decrease up to the year 1969-70. From 1970-71to 1971-72 it is shown a steadily stagnation of total allocation Rs. 1003348.56 and 105707.36 respectively. Especially 1990-91 onwards in the total allocation for all sectors has been increased steadily.

As compared to total allocations for all sectors to plan allocations for education there found fluctuations of decrease or increase trend with of Rs. 308.96 during 1951-52 and Rs. 43471.48 during 1996-97. The trend compares between total allocations for all sectors and plan allocations for education that an increasing trend is shown in some years comparatively followed by decreasing trends only in plan allocation for education during 1973-74, 1974-75 and 1975-76 with of Rs. 671.65, 545.25 and 537.33 respectively. Whereas in the case of non-plan allocation for education is increasing consistently from Rs. 612023 during 1973-74 to Rs. 153897.16 during 1996-97. This is because of commitment in non-plan allocations for education in the state, whereas plan and non-plan allocations has a trend of incresing from Rs. 308.96 during 1951-52 to Rs. 197368.64 during 1996-97 expect 1959-60 in which year the plan and non-plan allocation is decreased to Rs. 1132.43.

Table 4.1

Total Allocation for All Sectors and Plan Plus Non - Plan Allocations for Education in the State and Percentage of Total Allocation for Education to Total Allocations for all Sectors in the State

(Rs. in Lakhs at Current Prices)

Sl. No.	*Year*	*Total Allocations for All Sectors*	*Allocations for Education*			
			Plan	*Non-Plan*	*Plan and Non-Plan*	*Plan and Non-Plan Allocations as % age of Total Allocations All Sectors.*
1	2	3	4	5	6	7
1.	1951-52	15930.41	308.96	-	308.96	1.94
2.	1952-53	14447.04	330.26	-	330.26	2.28
3.	1953-54	14854.14	357.46	-	357.46	2.41
4.	1954-55	19033.25	377.90	-	377.90	1.98
5.	1955-56	15156.34	446.48	-	446.48	2.94
6.	1956-57	187199.45	487.53	-	487.53	0.26
7.	1957-58	28862.68	1046.86	-	1046.86	3.63
8.	1958-59	31855.82	1378.36	-	1378.36	4.33
9.	1959-60	47461.54	1132.43	-	1132.43	2.38
10.	1960-61	55606.40	1321.27	-	1321.27	2.38
11.	1961-62	65780.73	1575.00	-	1575.00	2.39
12.	1962-63	65801.12	1775.03	-	1775.03	2.70
13.	1963-64	65623.22	1875.75	-	1875.75	2.86
14.	1964-65	72857.21	2191.50	-	2191.50	3.01
15.	1965-66	75543.40	2498.79	-	2498.79	3.31
16.	1966-67	77039.86	2971.50	-	2971.50	3.86
17.	1967-68	86476.26	3347.98	-	3347.98	3.87
18.	1968-69	85371.81	3608.12	-	3608.12	4.23
19.	1969-70	89138.64	4606.47	-	4606.47	5.17
20.	1970-71	100348.56	4888.75	-	4888.75	4.87
21.	1971-72	105707.36	5670.88	-	5670.88	5.36
22.	1972-73	71387.78	5967.00	-	5967.00	8.36

Contd.

1	2	3	4	5	6	7
23.	1973-74	83782.68	671.65	6120.23	6791.88	8.10
24.	1974-75	113056.43	545.25	7426.65	7971.90	7.05
25.	1975-76	113068.52	537.33	8714.67	9252.00	8.18
26.	1976-77	139472.00	851.96	10303.04	11155.00	7.75
27.	1977-78	152840.49	1408.21	11701.79	13110.00	7.75
28.	1978-79	172936.19	1626.31	12648.69	14275.00	7.33
29.	1979-80	193234.37	1031.60	13712.40	14744.00	7.63
30.	1980-81	233476.87	1021.64	15028.36	16056.00	6.88
31.	1981-82	261253.07	1443.51	17389.49	18833.00	7.21
32.	1982-83	316447.78	1370.16	22568.84	23939.00	7.57
33.	1983-84	393434.49	1964.16	24642.84	26607.00	6.76
34.	1984-85	469326.94	3225.56	28656.44	31882.00	6.79
35.	1985-86	514381.68	1986.21	35007.89	36994.10	7.19
36.	1986-87	622324.13	2284.23	41365.42	43919.65	7.05
37.	1987-88	689259.43	3018.48	50604.12	53622.60	7.78
38.	1988-89	801156.50	3417.84	58384.76	61802.60	7.72
39.	1989-90	922702.63	6809.32	72287.04	79096.36	8.57
40.	1990-91	1005907.03	9772.39	78087.42	87859.81	8.73
41.	1991-92	1290978.00	12622.70	86579.64	99202.36	7.68
42.	1992-93	1484051.28	24724.60	97116.07	121840.67	8.21
43.	1993-94	1765655.89	35806.89	109145.12	144952.01	8.21
44.	1994-95	2053375.90	42634.84	121699.21	164334.05	8.00
45.	1995-96	2271682.77	40678.33	136482.22	177160.55	7.79
46.	1996-97	2456000.77	43471.48	153897.16	197368.64	8.03

It is observed that the educational allocations as the percentage of total allocations for all sectors have ranged between Rs. 0.26 per cent to 8.73 per cent during 1951-52 and 1990-91 respectively, during 1951-52 the percentage is Rs. 1.94 per cent and in 1996-97 it is Rs. 8.03 per cent during 1951-52 to 1963-64. The percentage of educational allocations to total allocations have been around Rs. 2 per cent to 3 per cent expect during 1958-59 when they have crossed 4.33 per cent during 1968-69 to 1971-72. But the booM period appears to be between 1972-73 to 1975-76 when they have ranged between Rs. 7 per cent to 8 per cent also after 1991-92 between 1976-77 to 1982-83 they have been around Rs. 6.88 per cent during the period from 1983-84 to 1985-86.

On the basis of above analysis it can be opined that, the total allocations for all sectors are increasing. Plan, non-plan allocations for educations are also increasing. The percentage of plan and non-plan allocations as compared to total allocations is increasing. However the share of education has still remained below 10 per cent in all these years. In a developing economy, where manpower shortages are common, more and more allocations are required to fill the gaps.

Table 4.2
Compound Growth Rate of Total Allocations for all Sectors and Allocations for Education (Plan and Non-plan) in Karnataka from 1951-52 to 1996-97

Sl No.	*Period*	*Total Allocatios for all Sectors*	*Total Allocations for Education*
1.	1951-52 to 1960-61	17.89	21.10
2.	1961-62 to 1970-71	6.45	13.98
3.	1971-72 to 1980-81	12.09	13.64
4.	1981-82 to 1990-91	16.02	18.62
5.	1991-92 to 1996-97	14.19	14.33
6.	1951-52 to 1996-97	11.01	15.10

The Table 4.2 reveals the compound growth rate of allocations for all sectors and allocation for education.

Interestingly, when it is compared between allocations for all sectors and the education sector all the decadel growth rates show that, true allocation to education sector is higher. Between 1961-62 to 1970-71 the allocation for all sectors showed just 6.45 per cent growth rate per annum. Whereas it was not reduced to the education sector which remained 13.98 per cent of growth rate per annum. Even for the entire period the growth rate for all sectors is lower, i.e., 11.01 per cent whereas the education sector showed 15.10 per cent which is higher.

The trends observed in Table 4.2 are depicted in graph 1.

Graph -(1) Compound growth rate of total allocations for all sectors and allocations for education in Karnataka

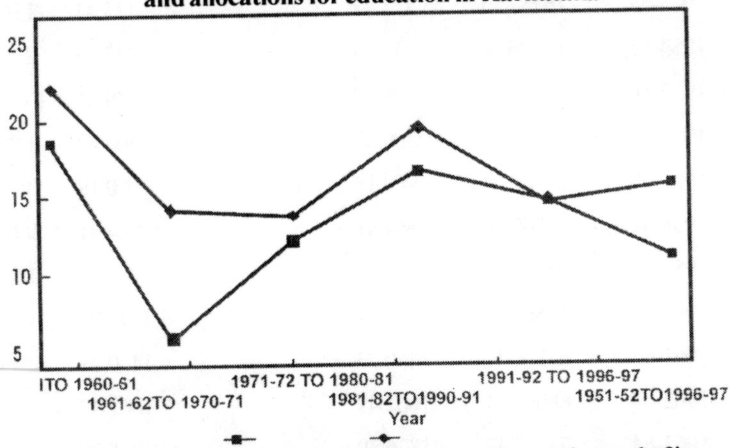

Table 4.3 shows that, from 1972-73 onwards a steady trend of increase in expenditure on education is maintained. This is due to the consistent increase in non-plan expenditure on education which is able to compensate the fluctuations in plan expenditure during this period. In the total expenditure on education the share of non-plan expenditure is very high. The share is above average in all the years between the period 1972-73 to 1994-95. Further it is observed that the share of education in total expenditure on all the sectors is below 8 per cent.

Table 4.3

Total Expenditure for all Sectors and Plan and Non-plan Expenditure for Education in the State and Percentage of Total Expenditures for Education to Total Expenditure for all Sectors in the State

(Rs. in Lakhs at Current prises)

Sl No.	*Year*	*Total Expenditure for all Sectors*	*Expenditure for Education*			
			Plan	*Non-plan*	*Plan and Non-plan*	*Plan & Non -Plan Educational Expenditure as % age of All Sectors*
1.	1951-52	15902.07	285.03	—	285.03	1.79
2.	1952-53	16380.23	316.80	—	316.88	1.93

1	2	3	4	5	6	7
3.	1953-54	16782.17	323.44	—	323.44	1.93
4.	1954-55	16329.26	342.65	—	342.65	2.10
5.	1955-56	365.47	39.27	—	39.27	10.74
6.	1956-57	15177.55	300.87	—	300.87	1.98
7.	1957-58	27988.54	900.19	—	900.19	3.22
8.	1958-59	49809.76	964.41	—	964.41	0.12
9.	1959-60	58691.88	1085.31	—	1085.31	1.85
10.	1960-61	71860.10	1247.27	—	1247.27	1.73
11.	1961-62	63866.13	1440.23	—	1440.23	2.55
12.	1962-63	68090.71	1662.47	—	1662.47	2.44
13.	1963-64	71213.12	1826.39	—	1826.39	2.56
14.	1964-65	74194.11	2066.91	—	2066.91	2.78
15.	1965-66	76457.69	2460.27	—	2460.27	3.22
16.	1966-67	89809.60	2838.21	—	2838.21	3.16
17.	1967-68	82793.80	3152.93	—	3152.93	3.80
18.	1968-69	101695.67	3856.19	—	3856.19	3.79
19.	1969-70	108321.92	4257.53	—	4257.53	3.93
20.	1970-71	69914.69	5378.70	—	5378.70	7.69
21.	1971-72	76117.61	5240.27	—	5240.27	7.12
22.	1972-73	167047.41	446.10	5912.95	6359.05	3.81
23.	1973-74	162280.34	563.56	6357.37	6920.93	4.26
24.	1974-75	110468.40	386.81	7826.29	8213.10	7.43
25.	1975-76	133047.45	496.75	8803.37	9300.12	6.99
26.	1976-77	150252.91	789.26	9694.37	10483.63	6.97
27.	1977-78	173952.51	1021.20	10932.14	11953.34	6.87
28.	1978-79	197587.50	1478.83	11916.50	13395.33	6.78
29.	1979-80	231513.63	796.34	13973.34	14769.68	6.37
30.	1980-81	271453.96	1047.36	16134.86	17182.22	6.32

Contd.

1	2	3	4	5	6	7
31.	1981-82	299781.12	1330.49	18461.75	19792.24	6.60
32.	1982-83	346997.04	2067.09	22416.94	24484.03	7.05
33.	1983-84	428076.66	3016.17	24248.82	27264.99	6.40
34.	1984-85	524167.62	4304.83	28615.49	32920.32	6.28
35.	1985-86	619510.78	2214.64	35842.19	38056.83	6.14
36.	1986-87	614825.47	2129.47	41622.28	43751.75	7.12
37.	1987-88	749957.34	3311.35	53921.03	57232.38	7.63
38.	1988-89	861724.03	4517.23	59420.50	63937.73	7.41
39.	1989-90	1025250.31	5276.26	66656.61	71932.87	7.01
40.	1990-91	105306.54	8587.90	71621.50	80209.40	7.26
41.	1991-92	1898390.36	10620.48	85518.23	96138.71	5.06
42.	1992-93	2191160.49	14662.24	95113.57	109775.81	5.01
43.	1993-94	2628426.67	20961.15	106851.09	127812.24	4.86
44.	1994-95	2908172.03	25062.01	119751.29	144813.30	4.98

Table 4.4

Compound Growth Rate of Total Expenditure for All Sectors and Expenditure for Education (Plan and Non-plan) in Karnataka from 1951-52 to 1994-95

Sl No.	*Period*	*Total Expenditure for all sectors*	*Total Expenditure for Education*
1.	1951-52 to 1960-61	22.33	21.62
2.	1961-62 to 1970-71	3.91	15.37
3.	1971-72 to 1980-81	10.31	13.45
4.	1981-82 to 1990-91	15.58	17.21
5.	1991-92 to 1994-95	15.74	14.81
6.	1951-52 to 1994-95	12.83	16.26

The above table reveals that unlike Plan allocations and plan-expenditure for education sector the total expenditure for education sector compared to all sectors is higher, expect 1951-52 to 1960-61 and 1991-92 and 1994-95 periods. These two decadal growth rate shows that expenditure on all sectors marginally higher compared to education sector. Otherwise education sector's expenditure is higher for all the periods.

One can make out the importance of education and the due importance given to this sector when compared to all other sectors. However with all efforts the government and the department could make major attempt in the development which is already reflected in the literacy level of our population in the state.

The trends observed in Table 4 are depicted in graph 2.

Graph -(2) Compound Growth Rate of Total Expenditure for All Sectors and Expenditure for Education in Karnataka

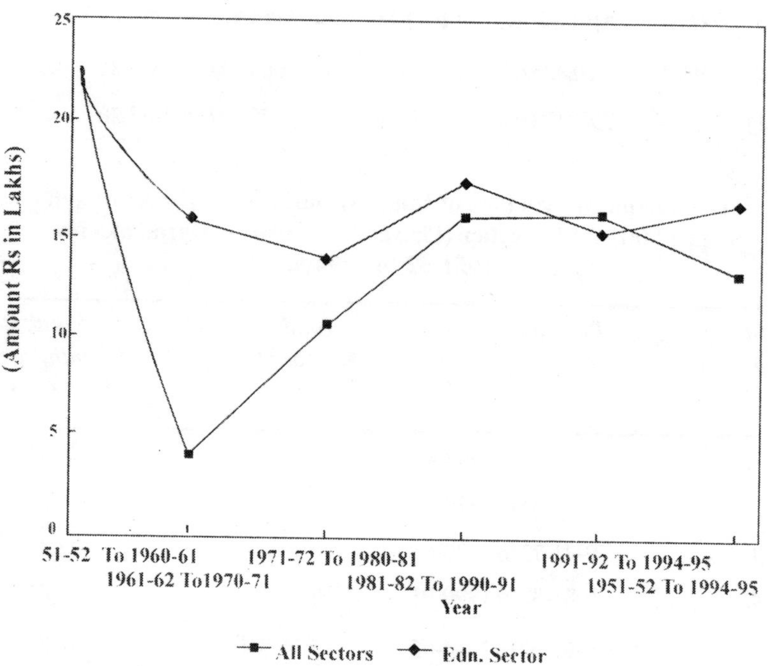

Table 4.5

Plan Allocation for Education in Karnataka from 1951-52 to 1996-97 and the Allocations for Different Sectors of Education

(Rs. in Lakhs)

			Sector Wise Allocations				
Sl. No.	*Year*	*Plan Allocation For Edu.*	*Primary*	*Secondary*	*Higher/ Univ.*	*Special*	*General*
1	2	3	4	5	6	7	8
1.	1951-52	308.96	77.81	48.06	25.00	9.34	148.73
2.	1952-53	330.26	142.85	70.43	45.82	9.91	61.72
3.	1953-54	357.46	180.78	72.09	46.79	10.38	7.40
4.	1954-55	377.90	156.80	79.38	43.40	13.37	84.94
5.	1955-56	446.48	187.28	87.25	54.01	16.79	101.13
6.	1956-57	487.53	246.82	59.24	75.46	17.76	88.23
7.	1957-58	1046.85	540.65	115.87	104.47	45.93	239.92
8.	1958-59	1378.26	63.64	131.64	106.04	46.89	457.24
9.	1959-60	1132.43	628.66	136.39	124.91	52.22	190.24
10.	1960-61	1321.27	650.76	140.92	137.43	169.62	222.52
11.	1961-62	1575.00	816.33	220.41	155.60	130.00	252.65
12.	1962-63	1775.03	924.47	228.89	175.95	141.93	303.77
13.	1963-64	1875.75	985.61	273.26	173.26	139.25	304.13
14.	1964-65	2191.50	1039.74	329.05	296.54	74.45	451.70
15.	1965-66	2498.79	1233.49	364.39	323.90	78.48	498.51
16.	1966-67	2971.50	1488.18	428.74	288.54	81.42	684.59
17.	1967-68	3347.98	1744.73	537.93	327.71	105.31	632.28
18.	1968-69	3608.12	1851.13	639.48	392.75	104.96	619.79
19.	1969-70	4606.47	2306.19	936.11	489.08	116.44	759.62
20.	1970-71	4888.75	2338.01	1023.91	538.38	140.40	848.02
21.	1971-72	5670.88	2620.60	1196.1	629.57	190.33	1034.52
22.	1972-73	5967.00	2756.17	1160.61	735.07	208.93	1106.22
23.	1973-74	671.65	185.50	430.01	380.77	29.57	59.80
24.	1974-75	545.25	194.65	528.20	174.55	32.93	90.30

1	2	3	4	5	6	7	8
25.	1975-76	537.33	203.95	599.00	155.80	17.23	100.45
26.	1976-77	851.96	456.05	708.00	190.55	21.76	112.80
27.	1977-78	1408.21	922.00	106.00	234.85	31.40	113.65
28.	1978-79	1626.31	917.65	142.00	260.69	60.11	245.65
29.	1979-80	1031.60	440.42	247.00	274.51	107.30	184.64
30.	1980-81	1021.60	375.77	128.18	304.00	118.91	94.78
31.	1981-82	1443.50	578.10	163.00	427.05	122.73	152.63
32.	1982-83	1370.16	531.00	136.50	461.55	138.81	102.30
33.	1983-84	1964.16	920.00	246.00	420.55	161.11	217.00
34.	1984-85	3225.56	1563.00	350.50	697.55	308.41	306.10
35.	1985-86	1986.21	930.33	145.50	114.25	322.79	473.34
36.	1986-87	2284.23	916.04	117.82	445.57	420.90	383.90
37.	1987-88	3018.48	1132.00	507.00	496.78	432.10	450.60
38.	1988-89	3417.84	1107.54	857.24	545.81	487.65	419.60
39.	1989-90	6809.32	2150.44	1854.20	990.55	676.68	1137.45
40.	1990-91	9772.39	4206.08	2249.34	2032..30	621.55	663.12
41.	1991-92	12622.72	6482.71	2495.14	1859.60	798.10	987.17
42.	1992-93	2472.60	14743.40	4584.17	1965.91	479.87	2951.24
43.	1993-94	35806.89	20207.40	6687.77	2955.19	940.25	5016.20
44.	1994-95	42634.84	21383.46	6200.74	789.30	975.62	6235.72
45.	1995-96	40678.33	20262.56	8222.38	3905.00	790.88	7497.51
46.	1996-97	43471.48	22257.56	10659.54	4406.90	659.35	5488.13

The Table 4.5 reveals the total plan allocation for the educational development in Karnataka. The data has been gathered from 1951-52 to 1996-97 from various sources of state, central government publications. Among the five important factors of education primary, secondary, higher (university), special and general education most of the funds are being spent for the development of primary and secondary education. Whereas the allocation on general education taking third position followed by the university education and lastly for special education. Even though there are minor difference are found between the years and different sectors the above trend prevails in general.

Education plays an important rule for the development of people and the country without the progress of this sector economy will be under depression ultimately. The Table 4.6 reveals the growth rate of plan allocation from 1951-52 to 1991-92 to 1996-97. The decadel figure shows 1991-92 to 1996-97 was the peak which is 52.45 per cent, whereas the growth rate was negative (– 11.41) from 1971-72 to 1980-81. The over all plan allocation shows the growth rate of 6.98 per cent per annum. This type of extream situation in the education sector which is importance sector for the our all development of the economy is an answerable question to think seriously.

Table 4. 6
Compound Growth Rate of Plan Allocation for Education in Karnataka from 1951-52 to 1996-97

Sl. No.	Year	Plan Allocation for Edu.	Sector Wise Allocations				
			Primary	*Secondary*	*Higher/ Univ.*	*Special*	*General*
1.	1951-52 to 1960-61	21.11	19.34	11.62	10.60	10.60	15.25
2.	1961-62 to 1970-71	13.98	13.41	19.63	-0.62	-0.62	14.40
3.	1971-72 to 1980-81	11.41	-9.71	-9.71	-20.95	-3.14	-14.67
4.	1981-82 to 1990-91	20.78	18.20	34.59	21.77	21.77	23.13
5.	1991-92 to 1996-97	52.45	22.76	29.09	1.67	1.67	39.26
6.	1951-52 to 1996-97	6.98	8.07	7.57	7.09	8.51	5.70

Out of the different sector in education itself, variation is found. Primary and special education got utmost importance which shows 8.07 and 8.51 per cent respectively. The least importance is given to 5.70 per cent growth rate per annum. Even the subsector in education show the negative growth rate in the 1971-72 to 1980-81 decide. It is difficult to predict by the growth rate is not uniform throughout from 1951-52 to 1991-92 to 1996-97.

The trends observed in Table 6 are depicted in Graph 3.

Graph - (3) Compound Growth Rate of Plan Allocations for Education in Karnataka.

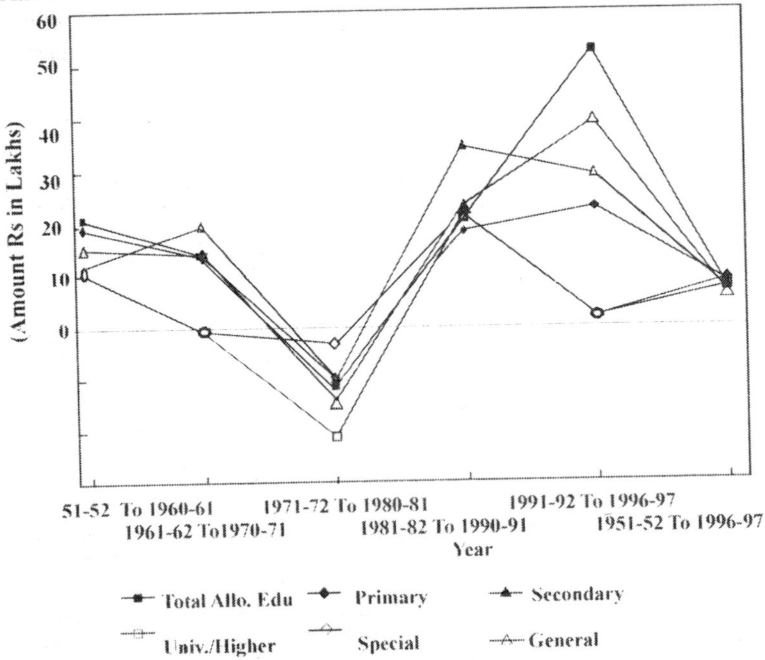

Table 4.7

Plan Allocations for Education in Karnataka from 1951-52 to 1996-97 and the Percentage of Allocations for Different Sectors of Education

(Rs. in Lakhs at Current)

				Sectorwise Allocations as Percentage to Total Plan Allocations					
Sl. No.	*Year*	*Plan Allocation for Edu.*		*Primary*	*Sec.*	*Higher/ Univ.*	*Special*	*General*	
1	2	3	4	5	6		7		8
1.	1951-52	308.96	(100)	25.18	15.56	8.09	3.02	48.15	100.00

Contd.

1	2	3	4	5	6	7			8
2.	1952-53	330.26	(100)	43.17	21.32	13.87	3.09	18.55	100.00
3.	1953-54	357.46	(100)	42.18	20.17	13.10	2.90	21.65	100.00
4.	1954-55	377.90	(100)	41.50	21.00	11.48	3.54	22.48	100.00
5.	1955-56	446.48	(100)	41.95	19.54	12.10	3.76	22.65	100.00
6.	1956-57	487.53	(100)	50.63	12.15	15.48	3.64	18.10	100.00
7.	1957-58	1046.85	(100)	51.65	11.07	9.98	4.38	22.92	100.00
8.	1958-59	1378.26	(100)	46.19	9.55	7.69	3.40	33.17	100.00
9.	1959-60	1132.43	(100)	55.51	12.04	11.03	4.61	16.81	100.00
10.	1960-61	1321.27	(100)	49.25	10.68	10.40	12.83	16.84	100.00
11.	1961-62	1575.00	(100)	51.83	13.99	9.89	8.25	16.04	100.00
12.	1962-63	1775.03	(100)	52.08	12.89	9.91	8.01	17.11	100.00
13.	1963-64	1875.75	(100)	52.55	14.57	9.25	7.42	16.21	100.00
14.	1964-65	2191.50	(100)	47.44	15.02	13.53	3.40	20.61	100.00
15.	1965-66	2498.79	(100)	49.37	14.58	12.96	3.14	19.95	100.00
16.	1966-67	2971.50	(100)	50.08	14.44	9.71	2.74	23.03	100.00
17.	1967-68	3347.98	(100)	52.11	16.07	9.79	3.15	18.88	100.00
18.	1968-69	3608.12	(100)	51.30	17.72	10.89	2.91	17.18	100.00
19.	1969-70	4606.47	(100)	50.06	20.32	10.61	2.52	16.49	100.00
20.	1970-71	4888.75	(100)	47.82	20.94	11.01	2.87	17.35	100.00
21.	1971-72	5670.88	(100)	46.21	21.09	11.10	3.36	18.24	100.00
22.	1972-73	5967.00	(100)	46.19	19.45	12.33	3.50	18.53	100.00
23.	1973-74	671.65	(100)	23.61	6.40	56.69	4.40	8.90	100.00
24.	1974-75	545.25	(100)	35.70	9.69	32.01	6.04	16.56	100.00
25.	1975-76	537.33	(100)	37.96	11.15	29.00	3.20	18.69	100.00
26.	1976-77	851.96	(100)	53.53	8.31	22.37	2.55	13.24	100.00
27.	1977-78	1626.31	(100)	56.43	8.75	16.02	3.70	15.10	100.00
29.	1979-80	1031.60	(100)	42.70	2.39	26.61	10.40	17.90	100.00
30.	1980-81	1021.64	(100)	36.78	12.55	29.76	11.64	9.27	100.00
31.	1981-82	1443.51	(100)	40.05	11.29	29.59	8.50	10.57	100.00

(Contd.)

1	2	3	4	5	6		7		8
32.	1982-83	1370.16	(100)	38.77	9.96	33.68	10.13	7.46	100.00
33.	1983-84	1964.16	(100)	46.86	12.52	21.38	8.20	11.04	100.00
34.	1984-85	3225.56	(100)	48.46	10.87	21.63	9.56	9.48	100.00
35.	1985-86	1986.21	(100)	46.84	7.33	5.75	16.25	23.83	100.00
36.	1986-87	2284.23	(100)	40.10	5.16	18.58	19.36	16.80	100.00
37.	1987-88	3018.48	(100)	37.50	16.80	16.46	14.32	14.92	100.00
38.	1988-89	3417.84	(100)	32.40	25.08	15.97	14.27	12.28	100.00
39.	1989-90	6809.32	(100)	31.58	27.23	12.31	12.18	16.70	100.00
40.	1990-91	9772.39	(100)	43.04	23.01	18.68	8.48	6.79	100.00
41.	1991-92	12622.72	(100)	51.37	19.77	12.74	8.30	7.82	100.00
42.	1992-93	24724.60	(100)	59.63	18.50	7.95	1.94	11.98	100.00
43.	1993-94	35806.89	(100)	56.44	18.69	7.20	3.66	14.01	100.00
44.	1994-95	42634.84	(100)	50.16	14.54	8.27	12.40	14.63	100.00
45.	1995-96	40678.33	(100)	49.81	20.21	9.61	1.94	18.43	100.00
46.	1996-97	43471.48	(100)	51.20	24.52	10.14	1.52	12.62	100.00

Plan Allocations for education have increased from Rs. 308.96 during 1951-52 to Rs. 43471.48 during 1996-97. But the plan allocations do not indicate a consistent trend, increased trend may be observed between 1951-52 to 1972-73 from Rs. 308.96 to 5967.00 after this period the expenditure has suddenly decreased to Rs. 671.65. Further increasing and decreasing trend may be found from 1972-73 to 1985-86. Generally plan allocations should exhibit a consistent increasing trend as they reflect the aspirations associated with the development of education which results in human development. This has not been evidended between 1972-73 to 1985-86. The internal disturbances instability in the centre and emergency and other factors might have caused the low allocations for education in these years. From 1985-86 to 1996-97 the trend in plan allocations for education has increased from Rs. 1986.21 to 43471.48. This was possible as the Government of India had given more emphasis on education, science and technological development and also for the youth services.

As literacy is the main goal, importance was given to primary education, the sectoral allocations as percentage to total allocations clearly show the increasing trend in primary sector the lowest allocations are

23.68 per cent and the highest 65.47 per cent. However we may find a trend of fluctuations in 1951-52 from 25.18 per cent and in 1996-97 Rs. 51.20 per cent in between decreasing and also increasing trend in existing. The primary sector followed by secondary sector of allocations indicates fluctuations from 2.39 per cent to 25.08 per cent. The allocations in secondary sector have also increased from 1951-52 15.56 per cent and in 1996-97 24.52 per cent. The secondary sector followed by university/Higher Education is also indicating fluctuating trend from 5.75 per cent to 56.69 per cent. But this sector has given only less importance compared to primary, secondary sectors. Because from 1951-52 the plan allocation was Rs. 8.09 per cent and in 1996-97 is Rs. 1.14 per cent special education is exisiting with several fluctuating trends from 1.52 per cent to 19.36 per cent in 1996-97 in 1986-87 the plan allocation for special education was 3.02 per cent in 1951-52 and as low as 1.52 per cent in 1996-97. General education that started with 48.15 per cent of allocation during 1951-52 dipped to 6.79 per cent duribg 1990-91 and decresed from 48.15 per cent during 1951-52 to 12.62 per cent during 1996-67. With fluctuations in the trend over the years.

Plan allocation for education are increasing. The emphasis is more on primary education followed by secondary education, special, university/ higher education.

Table 4.8

Plan (Period-wise) Allocations for Education in Karnataka and Percentage of Allocations for Different Sectors of Educations in Different Plans

(Rs. in Lakhs at Current Prices)

Plan	*Plan Allocation for Education*	*Sectorwise Allocations as Percentage to Total Plan Allocations*					
		Primary	*Sec.*	*High./ Univ.*	*Spec.*	*Gen.*	*Total*
1	2	3	4	5	6	7	8
First Plan 1951-52 to 1955-56	1821.06	39.28	19.61	11.81	3.30	26.00	100
Second Plan 1956-57 to 1960-61	5366.34	50.38	10.88	10.22	6.19	22.33	100

1	2	3	4	5	6	7	8
Third Plan 1961-62 to 1965-66	9916.07	50.42	14.28	11.35	5.69	18.26	100
Annual Plan 1966-67 to 1968-69	9927.60	51.21	16.18	10.16	2.94	19.51	100
Fourth Plan 1969-70 to 1973-74	21804.75	46.69	19.99	12.72	3.14	17.46	100
First Plan 1974-75 to 1977-78	3342.75	53.14	8.67	22.62	3.09	12.48	100
Janata Period 1978-79 to 1979-80	2657.19	51.09	6.28	20.14	6.30	16.19	100
Sixth Plan 1980-81 to 1984-85	9025.03	43.97	11.35	25.0	9.41	9.67	100
Seventh Plan 1985-86 to 1989-90	17516.08	35.60	19.88	14.80	13.36	16.36	100
Late Period 1990-91 to 1991-92	22395.11	47.72	21.19	17.38	6.34	7.37	100
Eighth Plan 1992-93 to 1996-97	187316.14	52.77	19.43	11.24	2.05	14.51	100

Notes:

1. From 1964-65 University Education includes Technicals Education.
2. From 1972-73 University Education includes PUC Education.
3. From 1972-73 General Education includes Sports, Youth Welfare, Art and Cultural Education.
4. From 1984-85 Higher Education includes PUC and Language Development Education.
5. From 1984-85 Special Education includes Adults Education.

The data given in Table 4.8 is abstracted in Table 16. Table 16 gives plan period wise plan allocations for education in Karnataka and the percentage of allocations for different sectors of education in the state as it can be seen from the table.

Plan period-wise-allocations for education do not show any consistent trend in the sense that there have been so many fluctuations in the allocations. Plan allocation that started in first plan Rs. 1821.06 has increased to Rs. 21804.75 during fourth plan during Janatha period plan dipped to Rs. 2657.19 and increased to Rs. 187316.14 during VIII plan. With fluctuating trends to Rs. 3342.75 during V plan.And Rs. 9025.03 during VI plan.

Sectorwise allocations as percentage to total plan allocations, for primary education has ranged from 39.28 per cent during I plan to 52.71 per cent during VIII plan. With fluctuations trends of 35.60 per cent during VII plan and 53.14 per cent during V plan. Similarly, in the case of secondary education with the percentage as low as 6.28 per cent during Janata Government period to 19.99 per cent during IV plan. During I plan the percentage was 19.61 per cent with unstable trends of 19.43 per cent during VIII plan with fluctuating trends (between the various plans). Allocations for Higher/university education is ranged between 10.16 per cent during annual plan to 25.60 per cent during VI plan. With decreasing and increasing trends during I plan. The percentage was 11.81 per cent and VIII plan percentage was Rs. 11.24 per cent. The higher education was given less importance during annual plan. From I plan to III third plan the emphasis is more or less are equal. Between IV plan to VI plan increasing emphasis is given. Further from VII to VIII plan the importance on higher education has been decreasing. The special education ranged between 2.05 per cent during VIII plan to Rs. 13.36 per cent during VI plan. With increasing and decreasing trends of 3.30 per cent during I plan to Rs. 5.69 per cent during III plan and 2.94 per cent during annual plan period. In case of general education. The percentage has decreased trend of 26.00 per cent during I plan 29.67 per cent during VI plan period, which again increased to 14.51 per cent during VIII plan period.

- The allocations to education sector during the plan period indicate that :

  (a) The total allocations in terms of monetary investment has shown an increasing trend up to Fourth plan period. The allocations were low during fifth and sixth plan but have increased substantially during 8th plan.

  (b) Investments across the various levels of education clearly exhibit the fact that, to attain the goal of universal primary education, primary education has been given added importance. The allocations in this sector are between 40 to 50 per cent in all the plan periods. Secondary education falls next. However during fifth plan period higher education was given much importance.

The trends observed in Table 4.8 are depicted in graph 4.

Graph -(4) Plan (period-wise) Allocations for Education and Percentage of Allocations for Different Sectors of Education in Karnataka

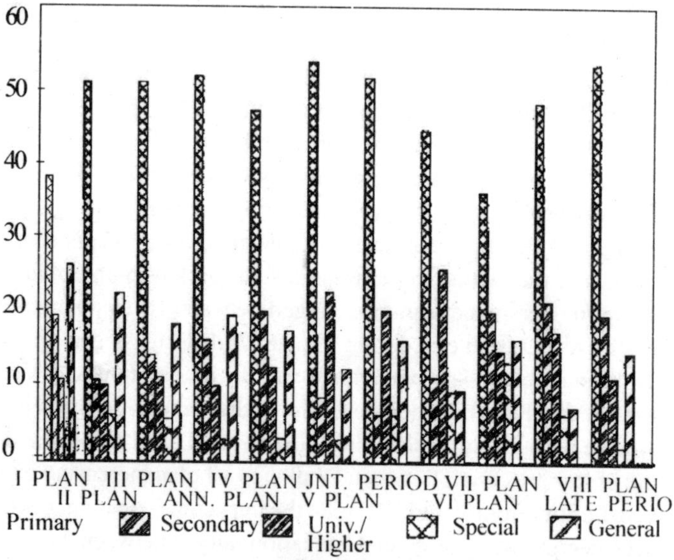

Table 4.9

Non- Plan Allocations for Education in Karnataka from 1973-74 to 1996-97 and the Allocations for Different Sectors of Education

(Rs. in Lakhs)

Sl. No.	*Year*	*Plan Allocation for Edu.*	*Sectorwise Allocations as Percentage to Total Plan Allocations*				
			Primary	*Sec.*	*Higher/ Univ.*	*Special*	*General*
1	2	3	4	5	6	7	8
1.	1973-74	6120.23	3278.20	1525.33	921.66	33.41	362.32
2.	1974-75	7426.65	4095.11	1789.56	122.95	70.40	242.08
3.	1975-76	8714.67	4750.94	2102.27	1534.67	47.55	279.44
4.	1976-77	1030.04	5657.61	2531.16	1744.38	53.30	316.59
5.	1977-78	11701.79	6442.38	2774.05	2030.55	59.68	395.13
6.	1978-79	12648.69	6826.62	2939.74	2400.22	60.11	422.00

Contd.

1	2	3	4	5	6	7	8
7.	1979-80	13712.40	7478.91	3031.47	2613.06	83.38	505.58
8.	1980-81	1508.36	8224.06	3270.90	2890.02	107.47	535.11
9.	1981-82	17389.49	9441.31	3882.52	3383.63	108.04	569.04
10.	1982-83	22568.84	12375.16	4947.20	4320.22	154.15	792.11
11.	1983-84	24642.84	13647.56	5377.16	4699.28	181.31	737.31
12.	1984-85	28565.44	15942.13	5988.26	5490.39	210.65	1048.35
13.	1985-86	35007.89	19060.83	5730.36	7076.35	44.00	1129.70
14.	1986-87	41635.42	22380.92	11463.66	6338.99	43.00	1409.47
15.	1987-88	50604.12	27436.14	14129.84	7500.17	76.50	1494.94
16.	1988-89	58384.76	31711.45	15896.31	9010.54	35.16	1689.96
17.	1989-90	72287.04	37089.79	18323.20	15061.11	41.32	1777.78
18.	1990-91	78087.42	38686.67	20664.65	16947.49	46.32	1747.29
19.	1991-92	86579.64	41250.19	25327.59	17986.03	48.32	1969.51
20.	1992-93	97116.07	47847.34	30114.67	16677.22	56.32	2428.52
21.	1993-94	109145.12	55164.15	33203.00	18216.24	86.32	2505.41
22.	1994-95	121699.21	61204.86	37087.91	20544.81	86.32	2775.31
23.	1995-96	136482.22	68265.76	41642.45	23406.44	86.64	3081.25
24.	1996-97	153897.16	77196.49	47424.61	25930.53	86.64	3258.89

The Table 4.9 reveals that non-plan allocation always higher from the plan allocation. Because non-plan allocation includes salary of the employees and other administrative costs. As has been explained already primary and secondary education takes the major share of non-plan allocations since the primary is the top most priority in Karnataka and also elsewhere.

Table 4.10

Compound Growth Rate of Non-Plan Allocation for Education in Karnataka from 1973-74 to 1996-97

			Sectorwise Allocations as Percentage to Total Plan Allocations				
Sl. No.	*Year*	*Plan Allocation for Edu.*	*Primary*	*Sec.*	*Higher/ Univ.*	*Special*	*General*
1	2	3	4	5	6	7	8
1.	1973-74 to 1982-83	13.42	13.88	12.09	5.85	14.39	11.36

1	2	3	4	5	6	7	8
2.	1983-84 to 1992-93	17.82	15.66	22.54	3.47	-16.59	11.62
3.	1993-94 to 1996-97	12.14	11.82	12.58	12.63	13.84	9.34
4.	1973-74 to 1996-97	15.42	14.83	17.00	12.77	0.05	12.32

The Table 4.10 reveals the growth rate for non-plan allocation and also expenditure. Data was collected from 1973-74 to 1996-97. Except the special education which showed positive growth rates eventhough we find primary and secondary education sectors were given top priority under non-plan allocation. Oniy five special education got least importance which shown just 0.05 per cent of growth rate per annum.

The trends observed in Table 10 are dipicted in graph 5.

Graph -(5) Compound Growth Rate of Non-plan Allocations for Education in Karnataka

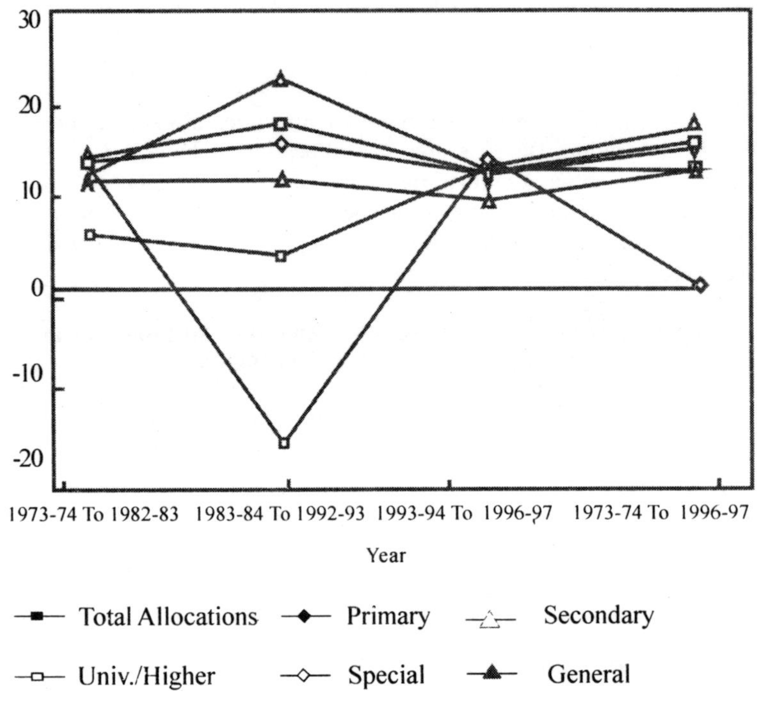

Table 4.11

Non-plan Allocation for Education in Karnataka from 1973-74 to 1996-97 and the Percentage of Allocations for Different Sectors of Education

(Rs. in Lakhs at Current Prices)

			Sectorwise Allocations as Percentage to Total Non-plan Allocations					
Sl. No.	*Year*	*Total Non-Plan Allocation for Edu. Universities*	*Primary*	*Sec.*	*High. Univ.*	*Spe-cial*	*Gen-eral*	*Total*
1	2	3	4	5	6	7	8	9
1.	1973-74	6120.23(100)	53.57	24.91	15.06	0.54	5.92	100.00
2.	1974-75	7426.65(100)	55.14	24.11	16.56	0.94	3.25	100.00
3.	1975-76	8714.67(100)	54.52	24.12	17.61	0.55	3.20	100.00
4.	1976-77	10303.04(100)	54.91	24.57	16.93	0.52	3.07	100.00
5.	1977-78	11701.79(100)	55.05	23.71	17.35	0.51	3.38	100.00
6.	1978-79	12648.69(100)	53.97	23.24	18.98	0.48	3.33	100.00
7.	1979-80	13712.40(100)	54.54	22.11	19.05	0.61	3.69	100.00
8.	1980-81	15028.36(100)	54.72	21.76	19.23	0.72	3.57	100.00
9.	1981-82	17389.49(100)	54.29	22.33	19.48	0.62	3.28	100.00
10.	1982-83	22568.84(100)	54.83	21.92	19.05	0.68	3.52	100.00
11.	1983-84	24642.84(100)	55.38	21.82	19.07	0.74	2.99	100.00
12.	1984-85	28656.44(100)	55.63	20.91	19.16	0.65	3.65	100.00
13.	1985-86	35007.89(100)	54.45	21.51	20.21	0.60	3.23	100.00
14.	1986-87	41635.42(100)	53.76	27.53	14.73	0.59	3.39	100.00
15.	1987-88	50604.12(100)	54.22	27.92	14.32	0.58	2.96	100.00
16.	1988-89	58384.76(100)	54.32	27.24	14.98	0.57	2.89	100.00
17.	1989-90	72287.04(100)	51.30	25.35	20.41	0.48	2.46	100.00
18.	1990-91	78087.42(100)	49.54	26.46	21.70	0.05	2.25	100.00
19.	1991-92	86579.64(100)	47.64	29.25	20.77	0.05	2.29	100.00

1	2	3	4	5	6	7	8	9
20.	1992-93	97116.07(100)	49.28	31.00	16.79	0.43	2.50	100.00
21.	1993-94	109145.12(100)	50.54	30.42	16.70	0.05	2.29	100.00
22.	1994-95	21699.21(100)	50.29	30.48	16.88	0.07	2.88	100.00
23.	1995-96	6482.22(100)	50.02	30.51	17.15	0.06	2.26	100.00
24.	1996-97	53897.16(100)	50.02	30.52	17.15	0.06	2.26	100.00

Notes:

1. From 1972-73 University Education includes PUC Education.
2. From 1972-73 General Education includes Sports, youth welfare, Art and Cultural Education.
3. From 1984-85 Higher Education includes PUC and Language Development Education.
4. From 1984-85 Special Education includes Adult Education.

It is evident from Table 4.11 that non-plan allocation which are presented for the last two decades or so far education have been increasing from Rs. 6120.23 in 1973-74 to Rs. 153897.16 in 1996-97. There has been a study impressed in non-plan allocations. This trends on conformity with the allocation for education at the centre and at the different states.

In terms of percentage there is a more of less stability in respect of these allocations for primary,secondary,higher/universing, special and general education. For primary education non-plan allocation has increasing trend from Rs. 50.54 per cent, 50.29 per cent, 50.02 per cent and 50.02 per cent during 1993-94, 1994-95, 1995-96 and 1996-97 respectively. Non-plan allocations for secondary education have a decreased trend from 24.91 per cent in 1973-74 to 20.91 per cent in 1984-85. It has been around 30 per cent or more since 1991-92.In case of higher/university education non-plan allocations have increased with of 15.06 per cent in 1973-74 to 20.21 per cent in 1985-86. There is a stagnation between 1986-87,1987-88 and 1988-89 with 14.73 per cent, 14.32 per cent and 14.98 per cent respectively. Since 1992-93 the percentage is constant around 16 per cent to 17 per cent. For special education the range is between 0.54 per cent in 1972-73 to 0.06 per cent in 1996-97. It has been declined much after 1990-91 falling to a low figure of 0.06 per cent in 1996-97.

It may be concluded that when, compared to plan allocations and expenditure, there is stability in the non-plan allocation for different sectors of education.

Non-plan allocation for education are increasing with stability. The emphasis is more on primary followed by University/Higher education and less emphasis is given to special and general education.

Table 4.12

Non-plan (Period-wise) Allocation for Education in Karnataka During 1973-74 to 1996-97 and the Percentage of Non-plan Allocations for Different Sectors of Education

(Rs. in Lakhs at Current Prices)

Plan	*Plan Allocation for Education*	*Sectorwise Allocations as Percentage to Total Plan Allocations*					
		Primary	*Sec.*	*High./ Univ.*	*Spec.*	*Gen.*	*Total*
Fourth Plan 1973-74	6120.23	53.56	24.91	15.06	0.56	5.92	100
First Plan 1974-75 to 1977-78	38146.13	54.91	24.11	17.14	0.61	3.23	100
Janata Period 1978-79 to 1979-80	26361.09	54.27	22.65	19.02	0.54	3.52	100
Sixth Plan 1980-81 to 1984-85	108285.97	55.07	21.67	19.18	0.68	3.40	100
Seventh Plan 1985-86 to 1989-90	250397.03	54.98	23.89	17.97	0.16	3.00	100
Late Period 1990-91 to 1991-92	164667.06	48.54	27.93	21.22	0.05	2.26	100
Eighth Plan 1992-93 to 1996-97	618339.78	50.08	30.64	16.95	0.06	2.27	100

Notes:

1. From 1972-73 University Education includes PUC Education.
2. From 1972-73 General Education includes Sports, youth welfare, Art and Cultural Education.
3. From 1984-85 Higher Education includes PUC and Language Development Education.
4. From 1984-85 Special Education includes Adult Education.

Table 4.12 indicates plan period-wise non-plan allocations for education in Karnataka. It indicates that the fluctuation with decreasing and increasing trends ranging between Rs. 612023 during IV plan period to Rs. 618339.78 during VIII plan period. It is dipped to Rs. 26361.09 and

164667.06 during 78-79 and later periods respectively. The percentage of non-plan allocation for primary education ranged about 48.54 per cent in late period to Rs. 55.07 per cent in VI plan. With the fluctuations and 53.56 per cent during IV plan to 50.08 per cent during VIII plan followed by secondary education with a stagnation for two plans namely IV and V plan and steadily decreasing trends from 78-79 period to VII plan and onwards with increasing trends from late period to VIII plan ranged between with of Rs. 21.67 per cent during VI plan to Rs. 30.64 per cent during VIII plan period. The higher/university education also has the fluctuations with 15.06 per cent during IV plan to 16.95 per cent during VIII plan. And with an increase to 21.22 per cent during the late period plan. In case of special education non-plan allocation is ranged between Rs. 1.05 per cent during the late plan period to 0.68 per cent during VII plan. With the fluctuations of 0.56 per cent during IV plan T 0.06 per cent during VIII plan period. The non-plan allocation for general education is steadily decreased from Rs. 5.92 per cent in IV plan to Rs. 2.27 per cent in VIII plan.

Plan periodwise non-plan allocation for education has less fluctuations. This demonstrates that more emphasis is on primary education. Secondary education received an increasing priority including higher education when compared to special and general education.

The trends observed in the Table 12 are depicted in graph 6.

Graph-(6) Non-plan (period-wise) Allocations for Education and Percentage of Non-plan Allocations for Different Sectors of Education in Karanataka

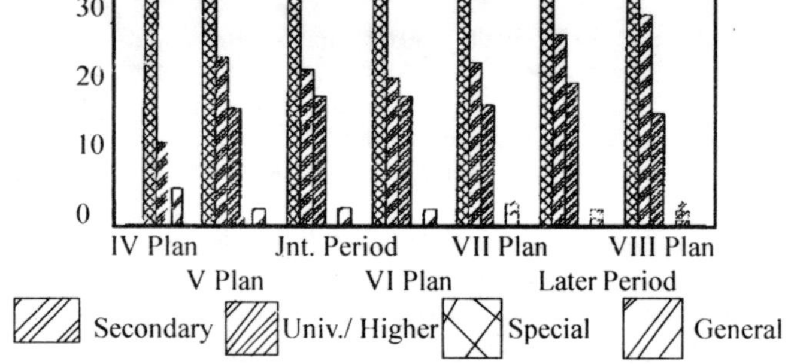

The Table 4.17 reveals that the plan expenditure on the same sectors for educational development. It is interesting to notice that, of all the sectors the plan expenditure is always lower than the plan allocation. This shows the gap between just allocation and actual expenditure. Under these circumstances, it is difficult to realise the target of human development.

Table 4.13

Plan Expenditure for Education in Karnataka from 1951-52 to 1994-95 and Expenditure for Different Sectors of Education

(Rs. in Lakhs)

			Sectorwise Allocations as Percentage to Total Plan Allocations				
Sl. No.	*Year*	*Plan Allocation for Edu.*	*Primary*	*Sec.*	*Higher/ Univ.*	*Special*	*General*
1	2	3	4	5	6	7	8
1.	1951-52	285.03	82.27	49.22	25.00	9.80	118.72
2.	1952-53	316.88	138.79	66.24	48.21	9.54	540.72
3.	1953-54	324.44	152.90	70.01	48.03	13.43	38.71
4.	1954-55	324.65	162.01	73.58	44.70	13.36	48.99
5.	1955-56	39.27	13.04	1.87	14.09	3.97	6.30
6.	1956-57	300.87	169.56	43.22	33.39	13.08	41.60
7.	1957-58	900.19	542.56	99.12	96.72	36.02	125.75
8.	1958-59	964.41	597.79	109.49	98.01	37.50	121.60
9.	1959-60	1085.31	645.18	119.09	117.20	41.05	162.76
10.	1960-61	1247.27	710.51	143.64	114.08	94.94	183.34
11.	1961-62	1440.23	801.21	196.75	146.01	106.35	189.88
12.	1962-63	1662.47	919.09	241.27	179.97	97.71	224.41
13.	1963-64	1826.39	1022.26	281.99	169.47	103.89	248.77
14.	1964-65	2066.91	1146.63	310.08	257.69	57.61	294.87
15.	1965-66	2460.27	1361.26	374.44	299.13	62.40	362.96
16.	1966-67	2838.10	1573.77	415.45	318.64	60.79	469.54
17	1967-68	3152.93	1708.82	549.74	332.09	75.78	486.59
18	1968-69	3856.19	1934.06	812.01	394.13	96.50	619.47

Contd.

1	2	3	4	5	6	7	8
19.	1969-70	4257.53	2140.47	8497.61	472.88	139.88	654.78
20.	1970-71	5379.30	2709.08	1048.02	612.22	175.71	833.65
21.	1971-72	5420.27	2646.68	1088.43	657.44	172.18	855.52
22.	1972-73	446.10	211.53	39.08	123.40	24.54	47.53
23.	1973-74	563.56	154.92	69.33	252.85	24.97	61.47
24.	1974-75	386.81	132.12	37.84	157.42	6.79	52.36
25.	1975-76	496.75	167.21	35.08	197.87	17.08	79.47
26.	1976-77	789.26	377.46	81.82	207.11	22.39	100.45
27.	1977-78	1021.20	449.41	128.66	297.73	26.83	118.56
28.	1978-79	1478.83	670.09	245.03	306.13	42.58	214.97
29.	1979-80	796.34	198.00	110.02	261.97	37.82	189.04
30.	1980-81	1047.36	277.27	167.67	412.71	116.27	73.41
31.	1981-82	1330.49	373.23	223.94	497.04	128.17	111.09
32.	1982-83	2067.09	684.64	361.16	735.50	106.78	178.99
33.	1983-84	3016.17	116.13	585.98	907.34	233.27	173.43
34.	1984-85	4304.83	1588.61	929.30	1230.28	291.27	265.24
35.	1985-86	2214.64	889.57	20.35	653.70	322.04	328.96
36.	1986-87	2129.47	701.37	167.89	510.76	374.43	375.00
37.	1987-88	3311.35	1686.23	377.74	572.93	278.73	396.19
38.	1988-89	4517.23	1326.80	1146.85	789.40	540.06	714.10
39.	1989-90	5276.26	1893.43	1492.79	851.43	567.90	470.69
40.	1990-91	8587.90	3335.77	2510.12	1306.69	902.73	532.59
41.	1991-92	10620.48	5787.80	2136.67	1298.48	619.57	777.96
42.	1992-93	14662.24	7068.08	3557.15	1605.69	720.63	1710.69
43.	1993-94	20961.15	12392.38	3777.83	2248.26	776.80	1765.88
44.	1994-95	25062.01	12444.30	6178.13	2940.59	892.47	2606.52

The plan allocation is not commensurate with the plan expenditure. The plan allocation growth at the rate of 6.98 per cent whereas plan expenditure growth at the rate of 6.50 per cent throughout the period

(Table 22). Expenditure shows the negative growth which is 32.80 from 1991-92 to 1993-94 whereas plan allocation was 52.45 per cent per annum. This clearly reveals that the development itself could not utilise the alloted funds for the development. The primary education sector is the worst in utilising the funds which shows the negative growth of 33.30 per cent per annum whereas all other sectors showing positive growth rate. The foundation has to be stronger for any sector but it is missing in case of primary sector which is lower when compeared to any of the sector except general education sector which is still worst. The growth rate reveals that most importance should be given to primary education in Karnataka state because the expected utilisation of funds is not satisfactory.

Table 4.14
Compound Growth Rate of Plan Expenditure for Education in Karnataka from 1951-52 to 1996-97

			Sectorwise Allocations as Percentage to Total Plan Allocations				
Sl. No.	*Year*	*Plan Allocation for Edu.*	*Primary*	*Sec.*	*Higher/ Univ.*	*Special*	*General*
1.	1951-52 to 1960-61	21.62	29.90	12.90	17.55	27.40	3.67
2.	1961-62 to 1970-71	15.37	13.90	20.65	16.15	4.62	17.87
3.	1971-72 to 1980-81	−1.53	−5.28	0.75	2.45	3.99	-2.09
4.	1981-82 to 1990-91	16.03	26.63	23.22	4.05	22.65	19.42
5.	1991-92 to 1993-94	−32.80	−33.30	38.34	32.17	11.97	44.18
6.	1951-52 to 1994-95	6.50	5.49	7.67	8.79	8.98	4.90

The trend observed in Table 14 are depicted in graph 7.

Graph -(7) Compound Growth Rate of Plan Expenditure for Education in Karnataka.

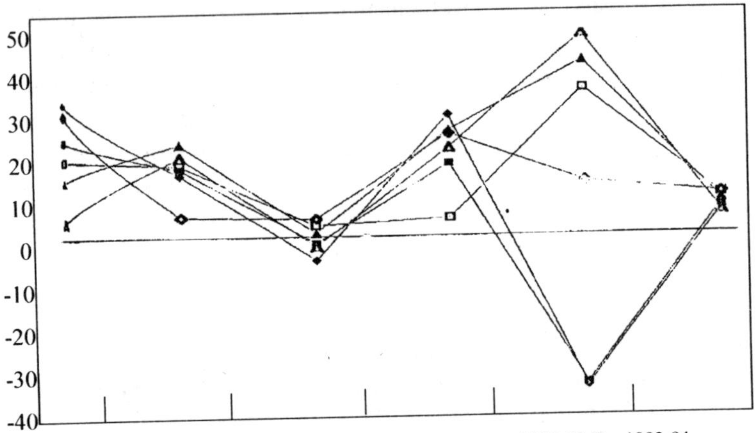

Table 4.15

Plan Expenditure for Education in Karnataka from 1951-52 to 1994-95 and the Percentage of Expenditure for Different Sectors of Education

(Rs. in Lakhs at Current Prices)

Sl. No.	*Year*	*Plan Expenditure for Edu.*	*Sectorwise Allocations as Percentage to Total Non-plan Allocations*					
			Primary	*Sec.*	*High. Univ.*	*Spe-cial*	*Gen-eral*	*Total*
1	2	3	4	5	6	7	8	9
1.	1951-52	285.03(100)	28.86	17.27	8.77	3.44	41.66	100.00
2.	1952-53	316.88(100)	43.81	20.90	3.01	15.21	17.07	100.00

Contd.

1	2	3	4	5	6	7	8	9
3.	1953-54	323.44(100)	47.28	21.65	14.92	4.15	12.00	100.00
4.	1954-55	342.65(100)	47.28	21.47	13.05	3.90	14.30	100.00
5.	1955-56	39.27(100)	33.21	4.76	35.88	10.11	16.04	100.00
6.	1956-57	300.87(100)	56.35	14.37	11.10	4.35	13.83	100.00
7.	1957-58	900.19(100)	60.27	11.01	10.74	4.00	13.96	100.00
8.	1958-59	964.41(100)	61.99	11.35	10.16	3.89	12.61	100.00
9.	1959-60	1085.31(100)	59.45	10.97	10.80	3.78	15.00	100.00
10.	1960-61	1247.27(100)	56.97	11.53	9.20	7.61	14.69	100.00
11.	1961-62	1440.23(100)	55.63	13.66	10.18	7.35	13.18	100.00
12.	1962-63	1662.47(100)	55.28	14.51	10.84	5.87	13.49	100.00
13.	1963-64	1826.39(100)	55.97	15.44	9.28	5.69	13.62	100.00
14.	1964-65	2066.91(100)	55.48	15.00	12.47	2.79	14.26	100.00
15.	1965-66	2460.27(100)	55.34	15.22	12.15	2.54	14.75	100.00
16.	1966-67	2838.21(100)	55.46	14.64	11.22	2.14	16.54	100.00
17.	1967-68	3152.93(100)	54.20	17.44	10.53	2.40	15.43	100.00
18.	1968-69	3856.19(100)	50.16	21.06	10.22	2.50	16.06	100.00
19.	1969-70	4257.53(100)	50.27	19.95	11.12	3.28	15.38	100.00
20.	1970-71	5379.30(100)	50.36	19.48	11.38	3.28	15.50	100.00
21.	1971-72	5420.27(100)	48.83	20.08	12.13	3.18	15.78	100.00
22.	1972-73	446.10(100)	47.42	8.76	27.66	5.50	10.66	100.00
23.	1973-74	563.56(100)	27.50	12.30	44.86	4.43	10.91	100.00
24.	1974-75	386.81(100)	34.16	9.78	40.70	1.76	13.60	100.00
25.	1975-76	496.75(100)	33.66	7.06	39.83	3.44	15.99	100.00
26.	1976-77	789.26(100)	47.82	10.37	26.24	2.84	12.73	100.00
27.	1977-78	1021.20(100)	44.00	12.60	29.16	2.63	11.61	100.00
28.	1978-79	1478.83(100)	45.31	16.57	20.70	2.88	14.54	100.00
29.	1979-80	796.34(100)	24.86	13.82	32.90	4.68	23.74	100.00
30.	1980-81	1047.36(100)	26.47	16.02	39.41	11.10	7.00	100.00
31.	1981-82	1330.49(100)	28.05	16.83	37.36	9.41	8.35	100.00
32.	1982-83	2067.09(100)	33.12	17.47	35.59	5.16	8.66	100.00

1	2	3	4	5	6	7	8	9
33.	1983-84	3016.17(100)	37.01	19.43	30.08	7.73	5.75	100.00
34.	1984-85	4304.83(100)	36.91	21.59	28.57	6.77	6.16	100.00
35.	1985-86	2214.64(100)	40.17	0.92	28.97	15.09	14.85	100.00
36.	1986-87	2129.47(100)	32.95	7.88	23.97	17.60	17.60	100.00
37.	1987-88	3311.35(100)	50.92	11.41	16.82	8.89	11.96	100.00
38.	1988-89	4517.23(100)	29.37	25.39	16.92	12.51	15.81	100.00
39.	1989-90	5276.26(100)	35.89	28.30	16.13	10.76	8.92	100.00
40.	1990-91	8587.90(100)	38.85	29.23	14.64	11.08	6.20	100.00
41.	1991-92	10620.48(100)	54.51	20.12	11.89	6.16	7.32	100.00
42.	1992-93	14662.24(100)	48.21	24.26	10.78	5.08	11.67	100.00
43.	1993-94	20961.15(100)	59.12	18.02	10.73	3.71	8.42	100.00
44.	1994-95	25062.01(100)	49.65	24.65	10.74	3.56	10.40	100.00

Notes:

1. From 1964-65 University Education includes Technical Education.
2. From 1972-73 University Education includes PUC Education.
3. From 1972-73 General Education includes Sports, Youth Welfare, Art and Cultural Education.
4. From 1984-85 Higher Education includes PUC and Language Development Education.
5. From 1984-85 Special Education includes Adults Education.

Table 4.15 deals about plan expenditure for education in Karnataka. The Expenditure is the actual amount spent for the development of education in the state. In the state the literacy rate is low and poverty is more, resulted in unemployment. At the same time government is keen to achieve social justice through various plans. The administrators, policy makers, political leaders and intellectuals might have realised the fact and prepared to spend more on education.

Plan expenditure for education rose from Rs. 285.03 lakhs in 1951-52 to Rs. 25062.01 in 1994-95. However, there has been unstable trend of increase or decrease during the period. The plan expenditure is always as Rs. 39.27 lakhs in 1995-56 and Rs. 386.81 lakhs in 1974-75. There has been a spurt in this expenditure during 1991-92, 1992-93, 1993-94 and 1994-95 with Rs. 10620.48, 14662.24, Rs. 20961.15 and Rs.25062.01 lakhs respectively.

Totally the plan expenditure has been fluctuating with increase in some years and decrease in some other years.

Similarly, the allocations in the percentage of expenditure for primary sector has increased with of Rs. 28.86 per cent during 1951-52 to Rs. 49.65 per cent during 1994-95. With decreasing and increasing trends of Rs. 24.86 per cent during 1979-80 to Rs. 61.99 during 1958-59. This was due to the policy of the state in order to provide universalisation of primary education to all citizens in the state. Followed by secondary education, the percentage plan educational expenditure is in the range between 0.92 per cent in 1985-86 to 29.33 per cent in 1990-91. With increasing and decreasing trends of Rs. 17.27 per cent in 1951-52 to Rs. 24.65 per cent in 1994-95. In the case of University/Higher eduaction, disproportionately attracted more percentage of education. Particularly duing 1973-74 44.86 per cent followed by 40.70 per cent during 1974-75, 39.83 per cent during 1975-76 and 35.88 per cent during 1955-56. During 1951-52 the amount was 8.77 per cent and 11.74 per cent during 1994-95. With the fluctuations of 3.01 per cent during 1952-53. This shows that the plan expenditure for higher education in the state is between the range of 3.01 per cent to 44.86 per cent. The amount spent for special education is with the fluctuations if increasing and decreasing trends with of Rs. 3.44 per cent during 1951-52 to Rs. 3.56 per cent during 1994-95 is dipped to Rs. 1.76 per cent during 1974-75 and increased to Rs. 17.06 per cent during 1986-87. This was because in the year 1984-85 the adult education has given more importance. In the case of general education the trend has been decreasing with of Rs. 41.66 in 1951-52 to Rs. 10.40 per cent in 1994-95 is dipped to Rs. 5.755 during 1983-84.

Plan expenditure for education is increasing. The emphasis is more on primary education. Followed by University/Higher education. The secondary and special education is given usual importance. General education is given low emphasis comparatively.

Table 4.16 indicate the plan period-wise expenditure for education in Karnataka. The percentage of expenditure for different sectors of education when the plan expenditure for a particular plan is taken as 100 per cent also indiacted.

There is an increase in the absolute amount of expenditure given in lakhs at current prices from Ist plan period with of Rs. 1307.28 to the VIII plan of Rs. 60685.40 by and large, however during the 1978-80 there has been a sharp decrease in the expenditure from Rs. 16066.75 in IV plan to Rs. 2275.17 in Janata period followed by Rs. 2694.02 in V plan. This shows

Table 4.16

Plan (Period-wise) Expenditure for Education in Karnataka and Percentage Expenditure for Different Sectors of Educations in Different Plan

(Rs. in Lakhs at Current Prices)

Plan	*Plan Allocation for Edu.*	*Sectorwise Allocations as Percentage to Total Plan Allocations*					
		Primary	*Sec.*	*High./ Univ.*	*Spec.*	*Gen.*	*Total*
1	2	3	4	5	6	7	8
First Plan 51-52 to 55-56	1307.28	42.00	20.00	13.77	3.83	20.40	100.00
Second Plan 56-57 to 60-61	4498.07	59.26	11.44	10.23	4.95	14.12	100.00
Third Plan 61-62 to 65-66	9456.28	55.52	14.85	11.13	4.53	13.97	100.00
Annual Plan 66-67 to 68-69	9847.33	52.98	18.05	10.61	2.36	16.00	100.00
Fourth Plan 66-67 to 68-69	16066.75	48.94	19.26	13.19	3.34	15.27	100.00
Fifth Plan 74-75 to 77-78	2694.02	41.80	10.54	31.93	2.71	13.02	100.00
Janata Period 78-79 to 79-80	2275.17	38.16	15.60	24.96	3.52	17.76	100.00

(*Contd.*)

1	2	3	4	5	6	7	8
Sixth Plan							
85-86 to 89-90	11765.93	34.33	19.28	32.15	7.42	6.82	100.00
Seventh Plan 85-86 to 89-90	17448.95	37.24	18.37	19.36	11.94	13.09	100.00
Late Period 90-91 to 91-92	19208.38	47.53	24.19	13.52	7.94	6.82	100.00
Eighth Plan 92-93 to 94-95	60685.40	52.57	22.27	11.21	3.93	10.02	100.00

Notes:

1. From 1964-65 University Education includes Technical Education.
2. From 1972-73 University Education includes PUC Education.

a lack of consostent trend of increase which indicates a lack of commitment of the governmernt to education.

Similar trend is shown in the expenditure for different sectors of education. While the expenditure for primary education in increased from 42.00 per cent in I plan to 59.26 per cent in the II plan. It went on decreasing there afterwards right up to VII plan. During the VI plan period it was only 34.33 per cent. Later during the VII and VIII plan periods there has been a moderate increase in it with the percentage of Rs, 47.53 per cent and 52.57 per cent. The percentage of expenditure for secondary education is ranged between 11.44 per cent during II plan 24.19 per cent during late period plan. The expenditure has shown decreasing and increasing trends with of 20.00 per cent during I plan and with of 22.27 per cent during VIII plan period.

Higher/university education expenditure has shown with fluctuations with 13.77 per cent in I plan to 11.21 per cent in VIII plan. Dipped to 10.23 per cent in II plan increased 32.15 per cent in VI plan. This shows that a very high extent of disparities exist in the expenditure in different sectors of primary and secondary sectors. The plan periodwise educational expenditure for special education is neither increased or decreased because in plan the amount was 3.83 per cent during VIII plan the amount was of 3.93 per cent. However during VII plan the expenditure was rose to 11.94 per cent. The plan period wise educational expenditure for general education is with fluctuations of decreasing and increasing

The Table 4.17 reveals the non-plan expenditure. As mantioned in plan-allocation and plan expenditure even is non-plan expeniture also the gap between non-plan allocation and non-plan expenditure is found. The non-plan expenditure is lower than the nonplan allocation and it results in chain impact on the development of education. Any budget allocation has to be more or less should be nearer to the true expenditure. A clear balance as desirable between allocation and expenditure. Eithter one of them be neither low or high. Hence, before taking any action one has to give proper thought to budget.

Graph -(8) Plan (period-wise) Expenditure for Educaion and Percentage of Expenditure for Different Sectors of Education in Karnataka

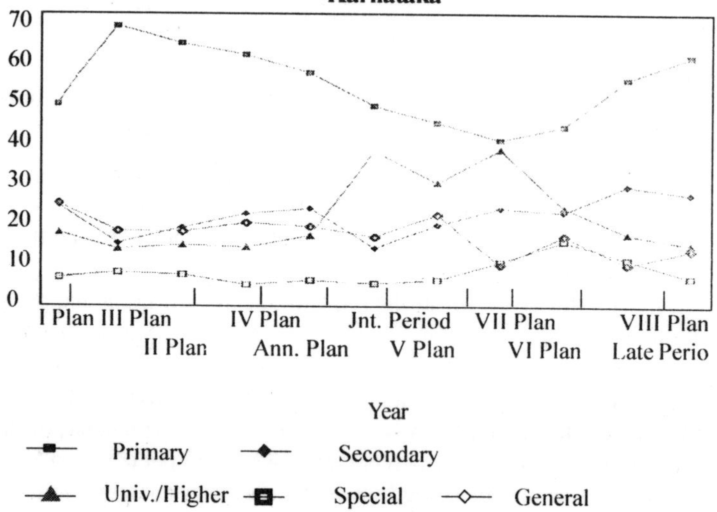

Table 4.17
Non-Plan Expenditure for Educaiton in Karnataka From 1972-73 to 1994-95 and the Expenditure for Different Sectors of Education

(Rs. in Lakhs)

			Sectorwise Allocations as Percentage to Total Plan Allocations				
Sl. No.	*Year*	*Non Plan Allocation for Edu.*	*Primary*	*Sec.*	*High./ Univ.*	*Spec.*	*General.*
1	2	3	4	5	6	7	8
1.	1972-73	5912.95	3335.99	1372.68	883.38	34.66	285.76

(*Contd.*)

2.	1973-74	6357.37	3683.86	1464.58	928.41	30.67	249.80
3.	1974-75	7826.29	4500.18	1758.79	1184.61	49.90	225.79
4.	1975-76	8803.37	4964.30	2033.83	1507.45	41.71	256.05
5.	1976-77	9694.37	5459.01	2117.92	1775.21	45.94	296.27
6.	1977-78	10932.14	6018.88	2411.25	2137.32	49.50	315.17
7.	1978-79	11916.50	6439.40	2686.82	2345.89	57.54	386.29
8.	1979-80	13973.34	7806.19	3017.45	2634.07	87.85	427.77
9.	1980-81	16134.86	9072.05	3389.89	3072.89	91.63	508.25
10.	1981-82	18461.75	10460.97	3962.61	3377.77	100.13	560.25
11.	1982-83	22416.94	12363.76	4729.98	4459.49	149.74	713.95
12.	1983-84	24248.82	13448.47	5282.09	4652.00	86.79	779.44
13.	1984-85	28615.49	15449.63	6324.65	5644.63	134.34	1062.21
14.	1985-86	35842.19	18808.65	9990.04	5731.75	41.96	1259.70
15.	1986-87	41672.28	21917.94	11734.06	6361.34	391.95	1216.99
16.	1987-88	53921.03	27592.12	16652.79	8142.17	67.47	1466.45
17.	1988-89	59420.50	34462.44	16458.83	10301.25	18.20	1479.79
18.	1989-90	66656.61	35040.49	18376.26	11567.85	142.89	1628.08
19.	1990-91	71621.50	37422.27	19693.95	12433.94	39.14	2085.90
20.	1991-92	85518.23	41047.94	25123.28	17180.14	56.11	2108.96
21.	1992-93	95113.57	45868.41	30695.59	16239.33	76.26	2233.98
22.	1993-94	106851.09	52717.59	32743.47	18917.23	87.67	2385.11
23.	1994-95	119751.29	59212.15	35998.80	21840.59	83.01	2616.74

Table 4.18

Compound Growth Rate of Non-Plan Expenditure for Education in Karnataka from 1972-73 to 1994-95

			Sectorwise Allocations as Percentage to Total Plan Allocations				
Sl. No.	*Year*	*Plan Allocation for Edu.*	*Primary*	*Sec.*	*Higher/ Univ.*	*Special*	*General*
1	2	3	4	5	6	7	8
1.	1972-73 to 1981-82	13.37	13.49	12.26	17.03	13.70	9.86
2.	1982-83 to 1991-92	16.81	15.52	20.96	16.09	-13.74	12.51

1	2	3	4	5	6	7	8
3.	1992-93 to 1994-95	12.21	13.62	8.29	15.97	4.33	8.23
4.	1972-73 to 1994-95	15.37	14.44	17.40	15.70	1.99	13.06

The Table 4.18 has also been worked out for non-plan expenditure. Here the state education department successfully utilised the funds. Non-plan allocation showed 15.42 per cent growth rate per annum and the expenditure also in the same, i.e., 15.37 per cent . Not only primary education sector but all other sectors have shown positive growth rate except special education sector eventhough it is positive but is very less, i.e., 1.99 per cent. However non-plan expenditure on special education is greater than allocation which is only 0.05 per cent. Interestingly one can find that under non-plan allocation and non-plan expenditure. The salaries of the employees are included. Consequently the growth rate is positive in these sectors. It can be conclude that other than salaries where there is a real progress, that, can be appreciated. But in real terms true effort has to be made for the real development which is lacking in the state.

The trends observed in table 18 are depicted in graph 9.

Graph -(9) Compound Growth Rate of Non-plan Expenditure for Education in Karnataka.

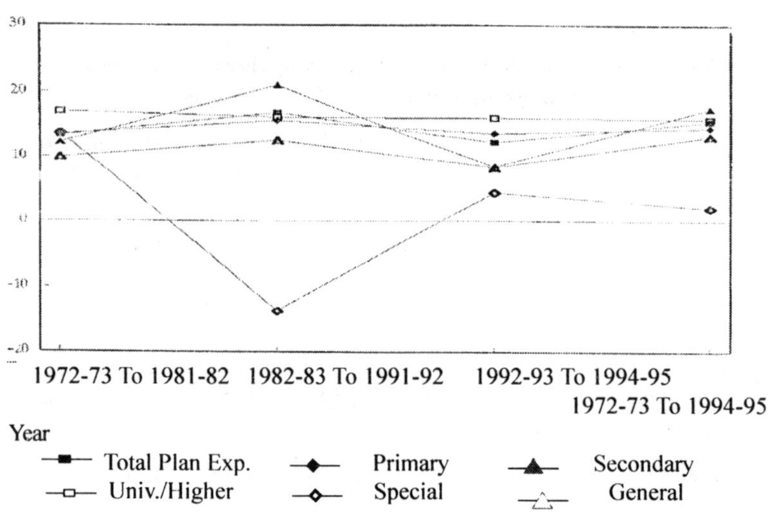

Table 4.19

Non-Plan Expenditure for Education in Karnataka During 1972-73 to 1994-95 and the Percentage of Non-Plan Expenditure for Different Sectors of Education

(Rs. in Lakhs at Current Prices)

Sl. No.	Year	Non-Plan Allocation for Edu.	Sectorwise Allocations as Percentage to Total Non-plan Allocations					
			Primary	Sec.	High. Univ.	Spe-cial	Gen-eral	Total
1	2	3	4	5	6	7	8	9
1.	1972-73	5912.95 (100)	56.42	23.21	14.95	0.59	4.85	100.00
2.	1973-74	6357.57 (100)	57.95	23.03	12.62	0.48	3.92	100.00
3.	1974-75	7826.29 (100)	57.50	22.47	16.50	0.64	2.89	100.00
4.	1975-76	8803.37 (100)	56.39	23.10	17.12	0.47	2.92	100.00
5.	1976-77	9694.37 (100)	56.31	21.85	18.32	0.47	3.05	100.006
6.	1977-78	10932.14 (100)	55.06	22.06	19.55	0.45	2.88	100.00
7.	1978-79	11916.50 (100)	54.04	22.56	19.68	0.48	3.24	100.00
8.	1979-80	13973.34 (100)	55.86	21.59	18.85	0.63	3.06	100.00
9.	1980-81	16134.86 (100)	56.23	21.00	19.05	0.57	3.15	100.00
10.	1981-82	18461.75 (100)	56.66	21.46	18.30	0.54	3.04	100.00
11.	1982-83	22416.90 (100)	55.15	21.10	19.89	0.67	3.19	100.00
12.	1983-84	24248.82 (100)	55.46	21.78	19.18	0.36	3.21	100.00
13.	1984-85	28615.49 (100)	53.99	22.16	19.73	0.47	3.71	100.00
14.	1985-86	35842.19 (100)	52.49	27.87	15.99	0.13	3.52	100.00
15.	1986-87	41622.28 (100)	52.66	28.19	15.28	0.94	2.92	100.00
16.	1987-88	53921.03 (100)	51.17	30.88	15.10	0.13	2.72	100.00
17.	1988-89	19420.1 (100)	52.44	27.7	17.34	0.03	2.49	100.00
18.	1989-90	66656.61 (100)	52.58	27.57	16.48	0.89	2.48	100.00
19.	1990-91	71621.50 (100)	52.25	27.42	17.38	0.06	2.91	100.00

1	2	3	4	5	6	7	8	9
20.	1991-92	85518.23 (100)	47.99	29.38	20.08	0.08	2.47	100.00
21.	1992-93	95113.57 (100)	48.22	32.27	17.07	0.08	2.36	100.00
22.	1993-94	106851.9(100)	49.35	30.64	17.76	0.08	2.23	100.00
23.	1994-95	119751.2 (100)	49.45	30.06	18.24	0.07	2.18	100.00

Notes:

1. From 1972-73 University Education includes PUC Education.
2. From 1972-73 General Education includes Sports, Youth Welfare, Art & Cultural Education.
3. From 1984-85 Higher Education includes PUC and Language Development Education.
4. From 1984-85 Special Education includes Adults Education.

It is evident from the Table 4.11 and 19, that there is not so much variation between the non-plan allocation and the non-plan expenditure. The percentage of expenditure for different sectors of education have been more or less stable with minor alternations during the period. The total non-plan expenditure for education indiactes a trend of increase from Rs. 5912.95 in 1972-73 to 119751.29 during 1994-95 which is steadily increasing.

The percentage of non-plan expenditure for primary education was maximum in 1981-82, i.e., 56.66 per cent. It was above 50 per cent for all the years from 1972-73 to 1990-91 but declined below 50 per cent after 1990-91. It was 49.45 per cent in 1994-95. The trend shows that the sectorwise percentage of non-plan expenditure on primary sector has slight a decreasing trend after 1990s. Similarly the percentage trends in secondary education indicate steadily increasing with of 23.21 per cent in 1972-73 to Rs. 30.06 per cent during 1994-95. From 1985-86 onwards there have been major fluctuations in the percentage of expenditure for higher/university education with Rs. 14.95 per cent during 1972-73 to 19.735 during 1984-85. This was a boon period for higher education and in 1994-95 the percentage was 18.24 per cent. In case of special education it is observed a descreasing and increasing trend with 0.59 per cent in 1972-73 to Rs. 0.07 per cent in 1994-95. Fallen to Rs. 0.3 per cent during 1988-89 and increased Rs. 0.94 per cent during 1986-87. The general education has decreasing trend with 4.85 per cent during 1972-73 to 2.18 per cent during 1994-95.

Non-plan expenditure is increasing as the emphasis is more on primary sector. But is decreasing in post 90s increasing trend in secondary and higher/university education. Less emphasis is observed on both special and general education during the same period.

Table 4.20

Non-Plan Expenditure (Plan Period-wise) for Education in Karnataka and Percentage of Expenditure for Different Sectors of Education in Different Plans

(Rs. in Lakhs at Current Prices)

Plan	*Non-Plan Allocation for Edu.*	*Sectorwise Allocations as Percentage to Total Non-Plan Expenditure*					
		Primary	*Sec.*	*High./ Univ.*	*Spec.*	*Gen.*	*Total*
1	2	3	4	5	6	7	8
Fourth Plan 72-73 to 73-74	12270.33	54.58	23.89	17.97	0.16	2.99	100.00
Fifth Plan 74-75 to 77-78	37256.17	56.21	22.35	18.01	0.50	2.93	100.00
Janata Period 78-79 to 79-80	25889.84	55.03	22.03	19.24	0.56	3.14	100.00
Sixth Plan 80-81 to 84-95	109877.86	55.33	21.56	19.30	0.51	3.30	100.00
Seventh Plan 85-86 to 89-90	257619.56	52.25	28.45	16.34	0.22	2.74	100.00
Late Period 90-91 to 91-92	157139.73	49.94	28.49	18.85	0.06	2.66	100.00

Eighth Plan							
92-93 to 96-97	321715.95	49.05	30.91	17.72	0.07	2.25	100.00

Notes: 1. From 1972-73 University Education includes PUC Education.

2. From 1972-73 General Education includes Sports, youth welfare, Art and Cultural Education.

3. From 1984-85 Higher Education includes PUC and Language Development Education.

4. From 1984-85 Special Education includes Adults Education.

The Table 4.20 reveals the plan period-wise non-plan expenditure for education with fluctuation of decreasing and increasing. It is evident that from one plan to another there is a greater fluctuation of sudden increase and decrese in another plan. During IV plan the non-plan expenditure is Rs. 12270.33 which increased to 321715.95 during VIII plan.

The percentage of non-plan expenditure for primary education has decreased from Rs. 54.98 per cent during IV plan to 49.05 per cent during VIII plan. Except in V plan, it raised to Rs. 56.21 per cent. The non-plan expenditure for secondary education as decreased steadily from 23.89 per cent during IV plan 21.56 per cent during VI plan. Later on it increder Rs. 28.45 per cent during VII plan to Rs. 30.91 per cent during VIII plan. Followed by university/higher education which is between 17.97 per cent during IV plan to 17.72 during VIII plan. It has fallen to 16.34 per cent in VII plan and raised to 19.30 per cent during VI plan. The non plan expenditure for special education has increasing trend of Rs. 0.16 per cent during Iv plan to 0.51 per cent during VI plan later on it was decrese to 0.06 per cent and 0.07 per cent during late period and VIII plan periods respectively. The general education has increased and decreased priority from 2.99 per cent during IV plan to 2.25 per cent in VIII plan except 1978-79 and VI plan period.

Plan period-wise non-plan expenditure for education is increasing. Primary education is given more priority intially but it is slightly declining after 90s. Whereas owed by higher/university education. Priority has been steadily decreasing to special and general education. The trends observed in Table 20are depicted in Graph 10.

Graph -(10) Non-Plan Expenditure (plan period-wise) for Education and Percentage of Expenditure for Different Sectors of Education in Karnataka

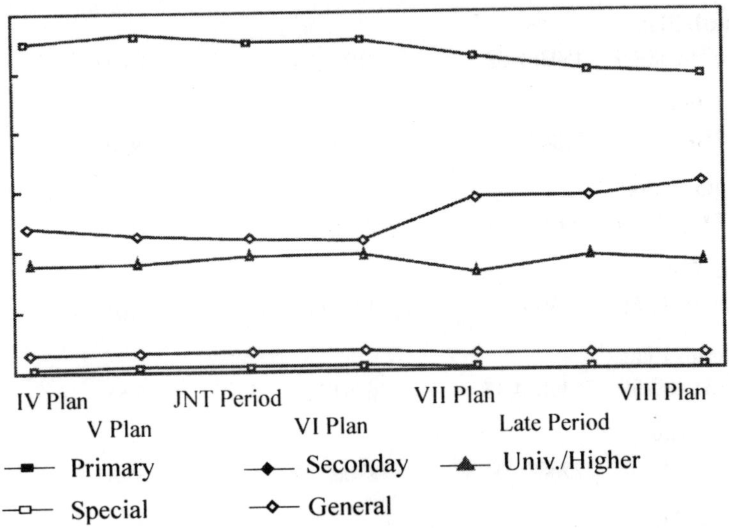

Table 4.21

Plan (Period-wise) Total Allocations for All Sectors and Plan Non-Plan Allocations for Education in the State and Percentage of Total Allocations for Education to Total Allocations for all Sectors in the State

(Rs. in Lakhs at Current Price)

Plan	*Total Allocation for All Sectors*	*Allocation for Education*	*%age of Educational Allocation in Total Allocations*
1	2	3	4
First Plan 51-52 to 55-56	79421.18	1821.06	2.29
Second Plan 56-57 to 60-61	350985.89	5366.45	1.53
Third Plan 61-62 to 65-66	345605.68	9916.07	2.87

1	2	3	4
Annual Plan 69-70 to 73-74	248887.93	9927.60	3.99
Fourth Plan 66-67 to 68-69	450365.02	71923.74	15.97
Fifth Plan 74-75 to 77-78	518437.44	41507.15	8.01
Janata Period 78-79 to 79-80	366170.56	58489.00	15.97
Sixth Plan 80-81 to 84-85	1673939.15	117311.00	7.01
Seventh Plan 85-86 to 89-90	3549824.37	267913.11	7.55
Late Period 90-91 to 91-92	2296885.03	187062.17	8.14
Eighth Plan 92-93 to 96-97	10030761.60	805655.92	8.03

Table 4.21shows the details of total allocations for all sectors and allocations for education as percentage of total allocations for all sectors of the economy. The total allocation for all sectors was of Rs. 79421.18 during I plan and it was of Rs. 10030761.60 during VIII plan. The trend indicates fluctuations decreasing in III plan and annual plan comparatively from II plan. Further the total allocations for all sectors in increasing except only janata period it is decreased to Rs. 36617056. However, overall observation on total allocation for all sectors are with the fluctutions of decreasing and increasing trend. With the comperision to total allocation for all sectors the allocation for education during various plan is not having steadily increasing trend. It was Rs. 1821.06 during I plan and 805655.92 during VIII plan period. But it was Rs. 71923.74 during IV plan. Comaritvely from IV whereas an increasing tendency in the total allocations.

The percentage of education allocation in total allocation is ranged between 1.53 per cent during II plan to 15.97 per cent during IV Janata period plan. While, during the I plan, the percentage of allocations was 2.29 per cent during III plan it was 2.87 per cent it attracted the high percentage only during IV and Janata period as mentioned above. The percentage of allocations for the I plan dropped down to 8.01 per cent and in the eight plan . This was at the 8.03 per cent. There is no normal trend observed in the percentage of allocations to education to the total allocation for all sector of the economy since the percentage have neither gone on increasing nor decreasing over the plan period. This shows the arbitrary nature of allocation amde for education.

Total allocations for all sectors economy are increasing, including for education sector. The emphasis on allocation is not satisfactory as the percentage has severe ups and downs trends.

The trends observed in Table 21 are depicted in graph 11.

Graph -(11) Plan (period-wise) Total Allocations for All Sectors and Percentage of Total Allocations for Education to Total Allcations for All Sectors in Karnataka

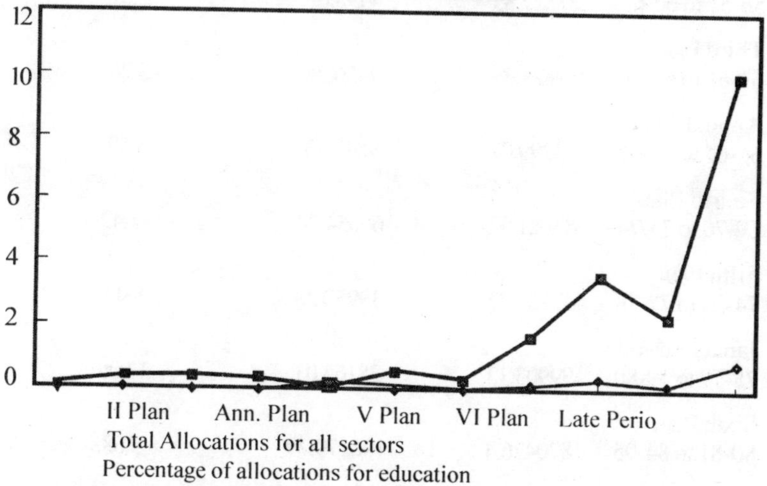

Table 4.22 indicates the plan period wise total expenditure for education as percentage of the total expenditure for all the sectors of economy. The total expenditure for all the sectors of economy is Rs. 65759.20 during first plan and with of Rs. 7727759.19 during VIII plan. From I to IV plan the trend is increasing in total expenditures for all sectors of ecomony, while during Janata period it has decreased to Rs. 199903.13 followed by Rs. 447721.27 during V plan. During this period there were internal disturbances, and emergency was also imposed. After emergency was lifted, the elections were declared to the parliament and subsequently new government came to power. The new government dropped the five year plans and tried to implement yearly plans. Because of the reason the

Table 4.22

Plan (Period Wise) Total Expenditure for all Sectors and Plan and Non-plan Expenditures for Education in the State and Percentage of Total Expenditures for all Sectors in the State

(Rs. in Lakhs at Current Price)

Plan	*Total Expenditure for All Sectors*	*Expenditure for Education*	*%age of Educational Expenditure in Total Expenditures*
1	2	3	4
First Plan 51-52 to 55-56	65759.2	1307.28	1.99
Second Plan 56-57 to 60-61	223527.83	4498.07	2.01
Third Plan 61-62 to 65-66	289821.76	9456.28	3.26
Annual Plan 66-67 to 68-69	274299.07	9847.33	3.59
Fourth Plan 69-70 to 73-74	583681.97	66654.24	11.42
Fifth Plan 74-75 to 77-78	447721.27	39950.20	8.92
Janata Period 78-79 to 79-80	199903.13	28165.01	14.09
Sixth Plan 80-81 to 84-95	1870476.4	106179.79	5.68
Seventh Plan 85-86 to 89-90	3871267.93	274911.56	7.00
Late Period 90-91 to 91-92	1295145.90	176348.11	13.62
Eighth Plan 92-93 to 94-95	7727758.19	382401.35	4.94

total expenditure for all sectors of economy has decreased comparatively to other plans.

The expenditure for education during various plans is with

fluctuations of decreased and increased tendency. During I plan Rs. 1307.28 it was increased up to IV plan with of Rs. 66654.24. During V plan and Janata period plan, it was dropped down to Rs. 39950.20 and 28165.01 respectively during VI and VII plan period the increasing trend is found. In later plan period it is Rs. 176348.11 which is high during 1992-93 to 1994-95 period with of Rs. 382401.35.

The percentage of educational expenditue to total expenditure has fluctuations of increase and decrease while, the IV plan (11.09%) and the Janata plan period (14.09%) and the later period (13.62%) had higher percentages. The other plan periods from V plan period onwards had moderate percentages and I, II, III annual and VIII plans with of 1.99%, 2.01%, 3.26%, 3.59% and 4.94% respectively had lower percentage.

Here also there is no any consistent trend that is evident as there are fluctuations in the percentage share of education in total expenditure. Total expenditure for all sectors of economy is also fluctuating during this period.

Thus, it is observed that expenditures for education are increasing, or decreasing along with the fluctuations in the total expenditures for all sectors of economy. The percentage of educational expenditure to total expenditure is also indicating a increasing and decreasing trend.

The trends observed in Table 22 is depcted in the Graph 12.

Graph-(12) Plan (Period-wise) total Expenditure for all Sectors and Percentage of total Expenditure for Education to total Expenditure for all Sectors in Karnataka

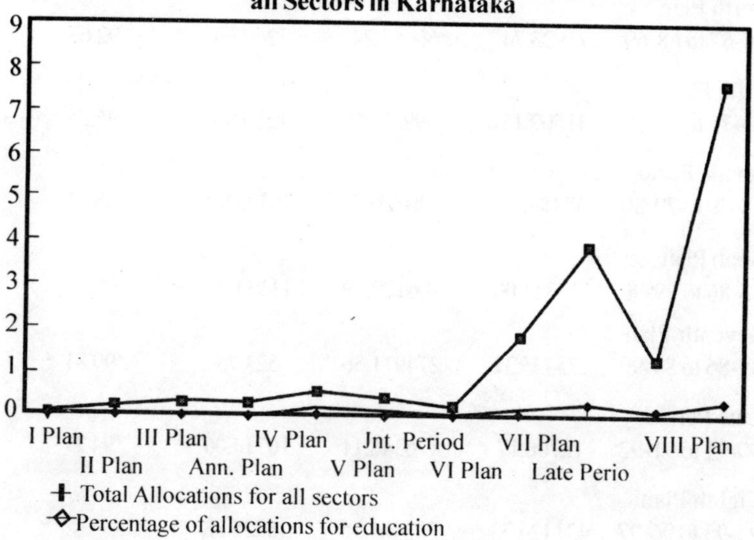

Table 4.23

Plan (Period-wise) (I) Total Allocations and Total Expenditure for Education (II) Difference between the Total Allocations and the Total Expenditure for Education and (III) Percentage of Total Educational Expenditure to Total Allocations for Education in Karnataka

(Rs. in Lakhs at Current Prices)

Plan	*Total Allocations for Education*	*Total Expenditure for Education*	*Total Allocations Minus Total Expenditures*	*%age Expenditures with Allocations*
1	2	3	4	5
First Plan 51-52 to 55-56	1821.06	1307.28	573.78	71.79
Second Plan 56-57 to 60-61	5366.45	4498.07	868.38	83.82
Third Plan 61-62 to 65-66	9916.07	9456.28	459.79	95.36
Annual Plan 66-67 to 68-69	9927.60	9847.33	80.27	99.19
Forth Plan 66-67 to 68-69	71923.74	66654.24	5269.50	92.67
Fifth Plan 74-75 to 77-78	41507.15	39950.20	1556.95	96.25
Janata Period 78-79 to 79-80	58489.00	28165.01	30323.99	48.15
Sixth Plan 85-86 to 89-90	117311.00	106179.79	11131.21	90.51
Seventh Plan 85-86 to 89-90	275435.31	274911.56	523.75	99.81
Late Period 90-91 to 91-92	18706.17	176348.11	10714.06	94.27
Eighth Plan 92-93 to 96-97	431126.73	382401.35	48725.38	

Table 4.23 shows the total allocations for education and total expenditure for education in Karnataka during the plan periods. The total allocations for reduction is increased from First plan with of Rs. 1821.06 to 71923.74 during IV plan. During V plan it is dropped down to Rs. 41507.15 lateron it is increased from 1979 to VIII plan the total allocation for education is Rs. 431126.73 in between during the late period it was decreased with of Rs. 187062.17 it is comparatively total expenditure for education is having a trend of increase or decrease with the increase or decrease of total allocation for education. The V plan with of Rs. 39950.20, during Janata period plan Rs. 28165.01 and late period Rs. 176348.11, whereas a trend increase of total allocations for education leads to the expenditures for education also. Through during first plan total expenditures for education is Rs. 1307.26 and during VIII plan the total expenditures for education is Rs. 38240.35.

The total educational expenditure as a percentage to total allocations ranged from 48 per cent in the Janata plan period to 99.81 per cent in VII plans. During the I plan, II and the V plan periods, the total expenditures or percentage to total allocations has been respectively 71.74 per cent, 83.82 per cent and 89.00 per cent. Total educational expenditure has kept the highest confirmity with the total educational allocations during the VII plan (99.81 %). Annual plans (99.19 %), V plan (96.25 %), III plan (95.36 %), VI plan (90.51 %) and the late period (94.27 %).

It is often found that as plans are not implemented effectively, there is always a gap between the allocations and the actual expenditures that are made. Therefore it is not possible to attain the targets fixed. Hence it is essential to observe the gaps in allocations and expenditures to assess the realisation of goals in the field of education. Table XIII indicates these gaps in allocations and expenditures. It is observed that there is no 100% utilisation of total allocations. The percentage of utilisation fluctuates across the years. It is as high as 99.81% during seventh plan and as low as 48.51% during Janata period. The overall utilisation is above 90%. This indicates that except during first two plans and Janata period. The utilisation percentage is very high, i.e., 90% and above. This means during these years the resources allocated to education are utilised efficiently.

Table 4.24

Plan Expenditure for Education in Karnataka from 1960-61to 1994-95 at Current and Constant Prices (Rs. In Lakhs with Base Year 1960-61)

(Rs. in Lakhs with Base Year 1980-81)

Sl No.	*Year*	*Plan Educ. Expen. in Current Prices*	*Plan Educ. Expen. in Constant Prices*	*Sl. No.*	*Year*	*Plan Educ. Expen. in Current Prices*	*Plan Educ. Expen. in Constant Prices*
1	2	3	4	5	6	7	8
1.	1960-61	1247.27	1247.27	19.	1978-79	1478.83	329.06
2.	1961-62	1440.23	1334.29	21.	1980-81	1047.36	1047.36
3.	1962-63	1662.47	1487.40	20.	1979-80	796.34	156.02
4.	1963-64	1826.39	1484.02	22.	1981-82	1330.49	469.90
5.	1964-65	2066.91	1450.06	23.	1982-83	2067.09	673.25
6.	1965-66	2460.27	1620.94	24.	1983-84	3016.17	859.85
7.	1966-67	2838.21	1581.70	25.	1984-85	4304.83	1138.93
8.	1967-68	3152.93	1638.99	26.	1985-86	2214.64	50.93
9.	1968-69	3856.19	1923.38	27.	1986-87	2129.47	481.18
10.	1969-70	4257.53	2015.68	28.	1987-88	3311.35	677.54
11.	1970-71	5379.30	2366.76	29.	1988-89	4517.23	832.67
12.	1971-72	5420.27	2311.51	30.	1989-90	5276.26	895.04
13.	1972-73	446.10	224.61	31.	1990-91	8587.10	1303.37
14.	1973-74	563.56	171.37	32.	1991-92	10620.48	1365.50
15.	1974-75	386.81	99.21	33.	1992-93	14662.24	1721.48
16.	1975-76	496.75	130.93	34.	1993-94	20961.15	2242.74
17.	1976-77	789.26	208.90	35.	1994-95	25062.01	2397.50
18.	1977-78	1021.20	235.93				
Annual average Rate of growth of increase		– 36.15	– 87.48			2292.87	128.91

Table 4.24 gives the details on plan expenditure for education in terms of current and constant prices from 1960-61 to 1979-80 and 1980-81 to 1994-95. The plan educational expenditure in current prices is ranged between Rs. 386.81 during 1974-75 to Rs. 5420.27 during 1971-72. The current educational expenditure is increasing from 1247.27 in 1960-61 to 1971-72 that is the right amount spent on education in current prices. Later on from 1972-73, 1973-74, 1975-76, 1976-77 and 1979-80 has decreased to low level, i.e., 446.10, 563.56, 496.75, 789.26 and 796.79. In terms of constant prices it has increased in 1971-72, further it has decreased later on, where the expenditure at the constant prices is converted to constant prices with 1960-61 as the base year. For education during 1979-80 for a current expenditure of Rs. 796.34 the expenditure at the constant prices is only 156.02 the total expenditure for education at current prices has grown at annual average rate of growth of increase of 36.15 where as it has grown in terms of constant prices at annual average rate of growth of increase of 87.48. From 1980-81 onwards plan educational expenditure is between 1047.36 in 1980-81 to Rs. 25062.01 during 1994-95. The current expenditure is increasing the stagnation period was that of Rs. 2214.64 and 2129.47 during 1985-86 and 1986-87 respectively. In terms of constant prices it has been decreasing up to 1989-90. Though it was increased to Rs. 1138.93 in the year 1984-85. The range of plan educational expenditure at constant prices Rs. 469.90 during 1981-82 to 2397.50 during 1994-95 with both decreasing and increasing trends when the expenditure at the current prices is converted into constant prices with 1980-81 for the base year. For education during 1994-95 for a current expenditure of Rs. 25062.01, the expenditure at the constant prices is only Rs. 2397.50.

This shows that there is no increase in the old expenditure for education over the period. Whatever increase had been there it had been magnified due to the increase in the prices. The total expenditure for education at current prices has grown at annual average rate of growth of increase of 2292.87 whereas it has growth in terms of constant prices only at annual average rate of growth of increase rate of Rs. 128.91, during the decade 1960-72 the expenditure both at current and constant prices is increasing but after that till 80's it is very low i.e. below 1.5 crores at current prices and below 250 at constant prices. Thus during this period both in terms of current and constant price the expenditure is very low. During the next fifteen years 1980-81 to 1994-95. The expenditure at current as well as constant prices is fluctuating. Still the average rate of increase is 2292.87 at current price but it is very low, i.e., 128.91 at constant price. Thus the current price figures may give a substantial increase in expenditure at least in some years but it is very low when estimated in terms of constant price. (1960-61 base) in current prices, plan educational expenditure has not showed an increasing trend. Constant prices with 1960-61 base is also not showing an increasing trend. 1980-81 prices, in current on plan educational expenditure is increasing with 1980-81 base prices the plan educational expenditure in constant prices is increasing.

Table 4.25
Non-Plan Expenditure for Education in Karnataka from 1972-73 to 1994-95 for Current and Constant Prices

(Rs. in lakhs with base year 1960-61) (Rs. in Lakhs with base year 1980-81)

Sl No.	*Year*	*Plan Educ. Expen. in Current Prices*	*Plan Educ. Expen. in Constant Prices*	*Sl. No.*	*Year*	*Plan Educ. Expen. in Current Prices*	*Plan Educ. Expen. in Constant Prices*
1	2	3	4	5	6	7	8
1.	1972-73	5912.95	2977.17	12.	1983-84	24248.82	6912.83
2.	1973-74	6357.37	1933.15	13.	1984-85	28516.49	7570.84
3.	1974-75	7826.27	2007.31	14.	1985-86	35842.19	8916.41
4.	1975-76	8803.37	2320.4	15.	1986-87	41779.23	9440.57
5.	1976-77	9694.37	2565.87	16.	1987-88	53921.03	11032.89
6.	1977-78	10932.14	2525.68	17.	1988-89	59420.5	10953.09
7.	1978-79	11926.5	2651.59	18.	1989-90	66656.61	11307.31
8	1979-80	13973.34	2737.64	19.	1990-91	71621.5	10869.86
9.	1980-81	16134.86	16134.56	20.	1991-92	85518.23	10995.31
10.	1981-82	18461.75	7301.22	21.	1992-93	95113.57	11167.23
11.	1982-83	22416.94	7301.22	22.	1993-94	106851.09	11432.57
				23.	1994-95	119751.29	11455.73
Annual Average Rate of Growth of Increase		136.32	– 8.04			642.19	– 2.82

Table 4.25 gives the details of growth of non-plan expenditure at current and constant prices, with base years 1960-61 to 1980-81. The

former period, IV and Vth plan period, i.e., 1972-73 to 1979-80. Non-plan educational expenditure at current prices has grown from Rs. 5912.95 to Rs. 13973.34. The non-plan expenditure during the same period has grown at constant prices from Rs. 2977.17 to 2737.64 the annual average rate of growth of increase at current prices is of 136.32 whereas its growth at constant prices is 8.04. And for the later period, for the period 1980-81 to 1994-95. The non-plan educational expenditures at current prices has grown from Rs. 16134.86 to 119751.29 respectively. The non-plan expenditure during the same period has given at constant prices from Rs. 16134.56 to Rs. 11455.73. With fluctuations of decreased and increased the annual average rate of growth of increase in non-plan educational expenditure at current prices is 642.19, whereas its growth at constant prices is only 2.82 which is very cheaper.

It is thus observed that while expenditure at current prices indicates a positive growth rate for both periods 1972-73 to 1979-80 and 1980-81to 1994-95 the average rate of increase is 136.32 in the first period and 642.19 for the latter period. But the picture is reverse when the estimates are made at constant prices. It is thus clear that the real rate of increase in expenditure is negative. The growing expenditure effect is nullified by the price rise in the economy. But when compared with plan expenditure, there is stability in non-plan expenditure as indicated by low negative rates of average increase in expenditures, i.e., – 8.04 and – 2.82 respectively.

Table 4.26

Non-Plan Expenditure for Education in Karnataka from 1972-73 to 1994-95 for Current and Constant Prices

(Rs.in Lakhs with base year 1960-61) (Rs. in Lakhs with base year 1980-81)

Sl No.	*Year*	*Total Educ. Expen. in Current Prices*	*Total Educ. Expen. in Constant Prices*	*Sl. No.*	*Year*	*Total Educ. Expen. in Current Prices*	*Total Educ. Expen. in Constant Prices*
1.	1960-61	1247.27	1247.27	1.	1980-81	17182.21	
	17182.21						
2.	1961-62	1440.23	1334.29	2.	1981-82	19792.24	
	6990.27						
3.	1962-63	1662.47	1487.40	3.	1982-83	24484.03	
	7374.47						
4.	1963-64	1826.39	1484.02	4.	1983-84	27264.98	
	772.67						

Sl No.	Year	Total Educ. Expen. in Current Prices	Total Educ. Expen. in Constant Prices	Sl. No.	Year	Total Educ. Expen. in Current Prices	Total Educ. Expen. in Constant Prices
5.	1964-65	2066.91	1450.06	5.	1984-85	39320.32	8707.77
6.	1965-66	2460.27	1620.94	6.	1985-86	38056.83	9467.34
7.	1966-67	2838.21	1581.70	7.	1986-87	43751.75	3886.56
8.	1967-68	3152.93	1638.99	8.	1987-88	57232.38	11710.43
9.	1968-69	3856.19	1923.38	9.	1988-89	63937.73	11785.76
10.	1969-70	4257.53	2015.68	10.	1989-90	71932.87	12202.35
11.	1970-71	5379.30	2366.76	11.	1990-91	80209.40	12173.23
12.	1971-72	5420.27	2311.51	12.	1991-92	96138.71	12360.81
13.	1972-73	6359.05	3201.78	13.	1992-93	109775.81	12888.72
14.	1973-74	6920.93	2104.52	14.	1993-94	127812.24	13675.32
15.	1974-75	8213.10	2106.52	15.	1994-95	144813.30	13853.22
16.	1975-76	9300.12	2451.33				
17.	1976-77	10483.63	2774.77				
18.	1977-78	11953.35	2761.61				
19.	1978-79	13395.32	2980.64				
20.	1979-80	14769.69	2893.63				
Annual average rate of growth of increase		1084.16	131.99			742.81	-19.37

The table 4.26 contains the details on the growth of total expenditure both plan and non-plan at current and constant prices with base years (1960-61 to 1980-81), with base year 1960-61. The total educational expenditure at current prices has rose from 1247.27 during 1960-61 to Rs. 14769.69 during 1979-80. At constant prices which was 1247.27 during 1960-61 has increased to Rs. 3201.78 during 1972-73. Later on with increasing trend with of Rs. 2893.63 during 1979-80. The total educational expenditure at current prices has grown at annual avberage rate of growth of increase Rs. 1084.16 value and it has growth in terms of constant prices only at annual average rate of growth of increase of Rs. 131.99.

With 1980-81 base year, The constant prices of total educational expenditure range between Rs. 772.67 during 1983-84 to 13853.22 during 1994-95. During 1980-81 the amount was Rs. 17182.21. later on increasing trend is showed except 1986-87 with Rs. 3386.56 followed by 1983-84. Interms of current prices it rose from Rs. 17182.21 during 1980-81 to Rs. 144813.30 during 1994-95. The total educational expenditure at current prices has annual average rate of growth of increase of 742.81 and it has grown interms of constant prices only at annual avreage rate of growth of increase of Rs. 19.37. Apparently it appears that the percentagw increase at current prices is for more than percentage of increase at constant prices.

The analysis of plan and non-plan expenditure together gives a better picture about the resources transfer to educational sector. This indicates stabilty to a large extent or the I period (1960-61 to 1979-80). The avrage rate of increase is positive both at current and constant prices i.e. 1084.16 and 131.99. Much above those given by plan expenditure on education. Even for the latter period, it holds good. However it is observed that though expenditure at current prices indicates a positive increase the position is reverse when esimated at constant prices.

The trend find in Table 4.30 are depicted in Graph 13.

Graph -(13) Total expenditure for education at current and constant prices with base years (1960-61) and (1980-81).

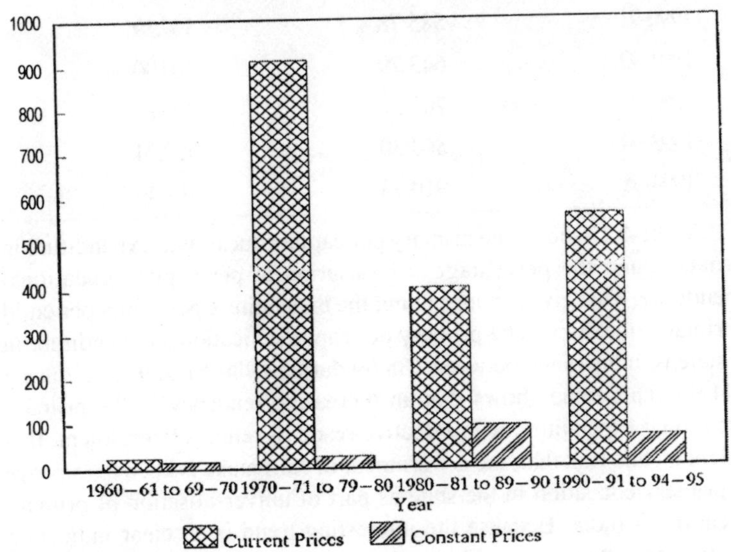

Table 4.27
Primary Per Capita Educational Expenditure in Karnataka and Index Number of Primary per Capita Educational Expenditure

(1980-81 to 1994-95)

Sl. No.	*Year*	*Primary per capita Enrolment Educational Expenditure*	*% of Variation in Primary per capita Educational Expenditure*
1.	1980-81	188.00	100.00
2.	1981-82	209.56	111.47
3.	1982-83	247.88	118.29
4.	1983-84	448.10	180.77
5.	1984-85	306.10	68.31
6.	1985-86	347.72	113.60
7.	1986-87	383.18	110.19
8.	1987-88	449.88	117.41
9.	1988-89	493.91	109.79
10.	1989-90	545.97	110.54
11.	1990-91	585.78	107.29
12.	1991-92	643.79	109.90
13.	1992-93	703.38	109.26
14.	1993-94	863.30	122.74
15.	1994-95	910.73	105.49

Table 4.27 shows the primary per capita educational expenditure in Karnataka and the percentage of variation in per capita educational expenditure. This gives an idea about the expenditure per capita per child in primary education. The primary per capita educational expenditure in the state is in the range between 188.00 during 1980-81 to 910.73 during 1994-95. This trend shows that an increasing tendency in the primary educational expenditure with effective result of retuns of enrolment. It is evident on this task that, the government of Karnataka is keen to improve the primary education in the state as part of universalisation of primary education in India. Because the interesting trend is an clear indication that, the expenditures on primary education is continuously increasing by

the government. It also indicates the increasing availability of basic primary education to a large section of child population in the age group of 5 to 11.

The percentage of variation in per capita educational expenditure over the previous year in each time period indicates wide differences in it. It is as high as 180.77 between 1983-84 and 1984-85 and as low as 68.31 during the succeeding year. The normal range is between 100 to 125 per cent. The positive variation in all the years except 1984-85 indicates the growing per capita expenditure on primary education. Primary per capita educational, expenditure is increasing consistently, Percentage of variation in per capita educational expenditure is also increasing.

The trend observed in Table 27 are depicted in Graph 14.

Graph -(14) Primary Per Capita Educational Expenditure and Index Number of Primary Per Capita Educational Expenditure

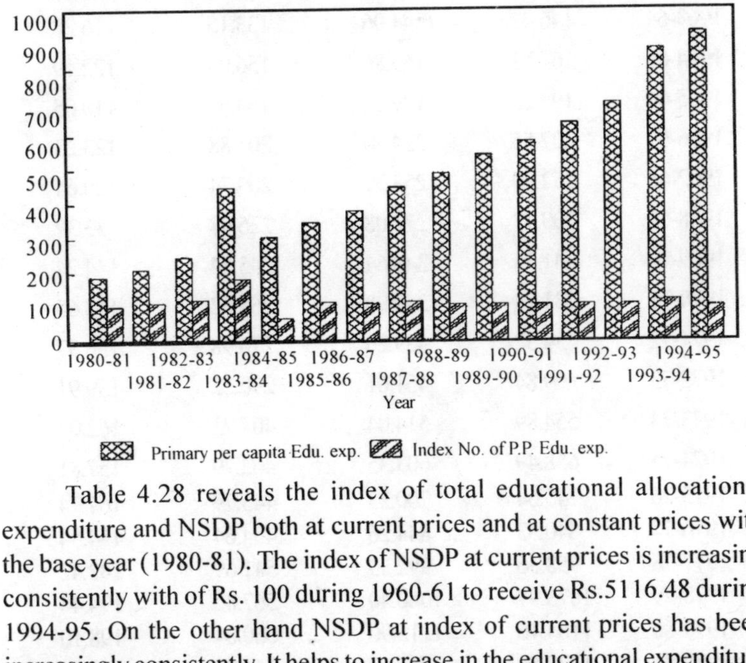

Table 4.28 reveals the index of total educational allocations, expenditure and NSDP both at current prices and at constant prices with the base year (1980-81). The index of NSDP at current prices is increasing consistently with of Rs. 100 during 1960-61 to receive Rs.5116.48 during 1994-95. On the other hand NSDP at index of current prices has been increasingly consistently. It helps to increase in the educational expenditure in the state. Simiiarly the index of NSDP at constant prices is increased with fluctuations. Though the index of NSDP at constant prices reached from Rs. 100 in 1960-61 to 399.41 in 1994-95. However their fluctuations of decrease and increase in this trend. In any state this trend. In any state this would not be happend because NSDP at constant prices will be the

Table 4.28
Index of Total Educational Allocations, Expenditure and NSDP at Current and Constant Prices

Sl. No.	*Year*	*Indexof total Educational expenditure*	*Index of total Educational Allocations*	*Index of NSDP at Current Prices*	*Index of NSDP at Constant Prices*
1	2	3	4	5	6
1.	1960-61	100.00	100.00	100.00	100.00
2.	1961-62	115.47	119.20	111.88	106.11
3.	1962-63	133.29	134.34	115.55	110.11
4.	1963-64	146.43	141.96	133.15	116.28
5.	1964-65	165.71	165.86	156.08	122.19
6.	1965-66	197.25	189.12	164.57	110.05
7.	1966-67	227.55	224.90	201.88	123.23
8.	1967-68	252.79	253.39	209.74	120.64
9.	1968-69	309.17	273.08	226.98	133.37
10.	1969-70	341.35	348.64	245.44	144.24
11.	1970-71	431.24	369.98	268.52	148.65
12.	1971-72	434.57	429.20	276.98	150.97
13.	1972-73	509.84	451.61	290.22	139.91
14.	1973-74	554.89	514.04	407.73	162.03
15.	1974-75	658.49	603.35	462.79	157.81
16.	1975-76	745.64	700.23	445.79	167.74
17.	1976-77	840.53	844.26	454.64	154.54
18.	1977-78	958.36	992.23	541.69	183.42
19.	1978-79	1073.97	1080.40	567.82	194.44
20.	1979-80	1184.16	1115.90	660.84	198.10
21.	1980-81	1377.58	1215.19	744.07	187.66
22.	1981-82	1586.84	1425.37	855.41	200.09
23.	1982-83	1963.01	1811.81	950.46	204.94
24.	1983-84	2185.97	2013.74	1147.55	219.52
25.	1984-85	2639.39	2412.98	1291.38	235.88
26.	1985-86	3051.21	2799.89	1360.78	226.15

Contd.

1	2	3	4	5	6
27.	1986-87	3507.80	3324.05	1562.49	247.37
28.	1987-88	4588.61	4058.41	1789.11	264.76
29.	1988-89	5126.21	4677.51	2086.95	287.61
30.	1989-90	5767.22	5986.39	2370.12	303.82
31.	1990-91	6430.80	6649.65	2740.98	306.34
32.	1991-92	7707.93	7508.11	3553.63	345.05
33.	1992-93	8801.29	9221.48	3889.18	353.35
34.	1993-94	10247.36	10970.66	4463.06	381.17
35.	1994-95	11610.42	12437.58	5116.48	399.41

real income of the state. If this inflation is created it will be very difficult to implement the plan objective. In order to spend the amount of education, the index of total educational expenditure is increased. Index of NSDP at current prices increased consistently. But the index of NSDP at constant prices is with fluctuations of decreasing and increasing trend exists in the State.

The index of total educational allocation is increased consistently from Rs. 100 during 1960-61 to 12437.58 during 1994-95. The index of total educational allocation is to compare the relative prices in two different places. It is thus always measured a relative to a base level of 1980-81. In the state of karnataka the trend is in the index of total educational allocation has been increasing consistently. This shows that the commitment of the government in the development of education in the state. State has considered that education is one of the most important factors. Therefore it has given more emphasis on the expenditure for education.

The index of total educational expenditure is increased consistently from Rs. 100 during 1960-61 to Rs. 11610.42 during 1994-95. The index of total educational expenditure is to compare the relatives prices in two different places. It is thus always measured a relative to a base level of 1980-81. In the state of Karnataka the trend is in the index of total educational expenditure has been increasing consistently. This shows that the commitment of the government in the development of education in the state. It has considered that education is one of the most important factor, therefore they have given more emphasis on the expenditure for education.

The index of total educational expenditure when compared with total educational allocations indicates a value that is comparatively lesser than the other one. This implies that the gap exists between the allocations and actual expenditures. However the size of the gap is very small (except in few years). This means the expenditures are closer to allocations and hence there is a proper utilisation of funds.

To estimates the buoancy of educational expenditure and allocations with that of state SDP at current and constant prices, it is observed that the index of education either in terms of allocations of actual expenditures is increasing rapidly when compared with the index of SDP either at current or constant prices. This indicates comparatively growth in both allocations and expenditure to education sector than the actual growth in SDP both at current and constant prices.

Percentage variation in expenditure on education is higher than the variation in NSDP, which indicates that the expenditure on education education is subject to more fluctuations, that in NSDP which may due to varying importance attached to education in these periods.

Table 4.29

Percentage of Change in Variable

Sl. No.	Year	Expenditure on Education	NSDP at Current Prices	NSDP at Constant Prices
1.	1960-61 to 1969-70	24.14	14.55	4.43
2.	1970-71 to 1979-80	17.46	14.61	3.33
3.	1980-81to 1989-90	31.86	21.85	6.19
4.	1990-91 to 1994-95	16.11	17.33	6.80

Table 4.30

Elasticity of Expenditure at Current and Constant Prices

Sl. No.	Year	Elasticity at Current Prices	Elasticity at Constant Prices
1.	1960-61 to 1969-70	1.66	5.45
2.	1970-71 to 1979-80	1.19	5.24
3.	1980-81to 1989-90	1.46	5.15
4.	1990-91 to 1994-95	0.93	2.65

The elasticity is greater than one, which indicates that expenditure on education is more sensitive to changes in NSDP.

The obtained 'r' value 0.9971 is > than the tabled value (0.428) and significance. On the basis of this, it may be concluded that there is

Table 4. 31
Coefficient Correlation between GSDP and Allocations for Education at Current Prices

Varriable	*Cases*	*Mean*	*Std. Dev*
GSDP	35	959774.6571	1140579.7418
ALLO	35	32301.1083	43434.8519

Variable	*Cases*		*cross-prod dev.*	*Varience - Cover*
GSDP	ALLO	35	1679452451175.8	4939566038.700

---Correlation Coefficient---

	GSDP		ALLO	
		1,0000		.9971**
	(.35)		(.35)	
	p = .		p = .000	
ALLO		.9971**	1,0000	
	(.35)		(.35)	
	p = .000		p = .	

(Coefficient/(Cases) / 2-tailed significance)
**Sugnificance at.001 level.

significant ralation between GSDP and allocations on education at current prices. The expenditure on education is increasing with increase in GSDP which clearly observed through high value (positive) correlation between the two.

Table 4.32
Coefficient Correlation between GSDP and Allocations for Education at Constant Prices

Varriable	*Cases*	*Mean*	*Std. Dev*
GSDP	35	658803.2571	286622.2479
ALLO	35	32301.1083	43434.8519

Variable	*Cases*		*cross-prod dev.*	*Varience - Cover*
GSDP	ALLO	35	404383797259.47	118993641095.867

---Correlation Coefficient---

	GSDP	ALLO
	1,0000	.9554**
	(.35)	(.35)
	p = .	p = .000
ALLO	.9554**	1,0000
	(.35)	(.35)
	p = .000	p = .

(Coefficient/(Cases)/2-tailed significance)

** Significance at .001 level.

The obtained 'r' value 0.9554 is > than the tabled value (0.428) and significance at 0.01 level of significance at 0.01 level of significance. On the basis of this, it may be concluded that there is significant relation between GSDP and allocations on education at constant prices. The expenditure on education is increasing with increase in GSDP which is clearly observed through high value (positive) correlation between the two.

Table 4.33

Coefficient Correlation between GSDP and Expenditure on Education at Current Prices

Variable	*Cases*	*Mean*	*Std. Dev*
GSDP	35	958926.0857	1141174.9502
EXP	35	30637.3531	39189.2647

Variable	*Cases*	*Cross-Prod Dev.*	*Variance - Covar*
GSDP	ALLO 35	404383797259.47	118993641095.867

---Correlation Coefficients---

	GSDP	EXP
GSDP	1,0000	.9981**
	(.35)	(.35)
	p = .	p = .000
EXP	.9981**	1,0000
	(.35)	(.35)
	p = .000	p = .

(Coefficient/(Cases)/2-tailed significance)

** Significance at .001 level.

The obtained 'r' value 0.9981 is > than the tabled value (0.428) and significance. On the basis of this, it may be concluded that there is significant relation between GSDP and expenditure on education at current prices. The expenditure on education is increasing with increase in GSDP which clearly observed through high value (positive) correlation between the two.

The obtained 'r' value 0.9672 is > than the tabled value (0.428) and significance at 0.01 level of significance. On the basis of this, it may be concluded that there is significant relation between GSDP and expenditure on education at constant prices. The expenditure on education is increasing with increase in GSDP which clearly observed through high value (positive) correlation between the two.

Table 4.34

Coefficient Correlation between GSDP and Expenditure for Education at Constant Prices

Variable		*Cases*	*Mean*	*Std. Dev.*
GSDP		35	658803.2751	286622.2479
EXP		35	30637.3531	39189.2647
Variable		*Cases*	*Cross-Prod dev.*	*Variance - Covar*
GSDP	EXP	35	369361941415.61	10863586512.224

---Correlation Coefficients---

	GSDP	Exp
GSDP	1,0000	.9672**
	(35)	(35)
	P=.	P= .

(Coefficient/(Cases) / 2-tailed significance)

**Sugnificance at 0.001 level.

Table 4.35

Coefficient Correlation between NSDP and Allocations for Education at Current Prices

Variable	*Cases*	*Mean*	*Std. Dev.*
NSDP	35	857421.0286	1003716.6184
ALLO	35	32301.1083	43434.8519

Variable		*Cases*	*Cross-Prod Dev.*	*Variance - Covar*
NSDP	ALLO	35	1477753276633.7	4346331665.696

---Correlation Coefficients---

	NSDP	ALLO
NSDP	1,0000	.9970**
	(35)	(35)
	P=.000	P= .
ALLO	.9970**	1,0000
	(35)	(35)
	P = .000	P =.

(Coefficient/(Cases) / 2-tailed significance)
**Sugnificance at.001 level.

The obtained 'r' value 0.9970 is > than the tabled value (0.428) and significance at 0.01 level of significance. On the basis of this, it may be concluded that there is significant relation between NSDP and allocations on education at current prices. The expenditure on education is increasing with increase in NSDP which clearly observed through high value (positive) correlation between the two.

Table 4.36

Coefficient Correlation between GSDP and Allocations for Education at Constant Prices

Variable	*Cases*	*Mean*	*Std. Dev.*
NSDP	35	596067.942	249597.8434
ALLO	35	32301.1083	43434.8519

Variable		*Cases*	*Cross-Prod Dev.*	*Variance - Cover*
NSDP	ALLO	35	352398140084.43	10364651178.954

---Correlation Coefficients---

	GSDP	ALLO
NSDP	1,0000	.9560**
	(35)	(35)
	P =.	P = .000
ALLO	.9560**	1,0000

(35)	(35)
P=.000	P=.

(Coefficient/(Cases) / 2-tailed significance)
**Significance at .001 level.

The obtained 'r' value 0.9556 is > than the tabled value (0.428) and significant at 0.01 level of significance. On the basis of this, it may be concluded that there is significant relation between NSDP and allocations on education at current prices. The expenditure on education is increasing with increase in NSDP which is clearly observed through high value (positive) correlation between the two.

Table 4.37

Coefficient Correlation between NSDP and Expenditure for Education at Current Prices

Variable	*Cases*	*Mean*	*Std. Dev*
NSDP	35	857421.0286	1003716.6184
EXP	35	30637.3531	39189.2647

Variable		*Cases*	*Cross-Prod Dev.*	*Variance - Covar*
GSDP	ALLO	35	352398140084.43	10364651178.54

---Correlation Coefficients---

	NSDP	EXP
NSDP	1,0000	.9980**
	(35)	(35)
	P=.	P=.000
EXP	.9980**	1,0000
	(35)	(35)
	P=.000	P=.

(Coefficient/(Cases) / 2-tailed significance)
**Significance at .001 level.

The obtained 'r' value 0.9980 is > than the tabled value (0.428) and significant at 0.01 level of significance. On the basis of this, it may be concluded that there is significant relation between NSDP and allocations on education at current prices. The expenditure on education is increasing with increase in NSDP which clearly observed through high value (positive) correlation between the two.

Table 4.38

Coefficient Correlation Between GSDP and Expenditure for Education at Constant Prices

Varriable	*Cases*	*Mean*	*Std. Dev.*
NSDP	35	596067.94	249597.84
EXP	35	30637.35	39189.26

Variable	*Cases*	*Cross-Prod Dev.*	*Variance - Covar*
GSDP	EXP 35	321788235216.02	9464359859.29

---Correlation Coefficient---

	NSDP	EXP
NSDP	1,0000 (35) P=.	.9676** (35) P=.000
ALLO	.9676** (35) P=.000	1,0000 P=.

(Coefficient/(Cases) / 2-tailed significance)
**Significance at .001 level.

The obtained 'r' value 0.676 is > than the tabled value (0.428) and significant at.001 level of significance. On the basis of this, it may be concluded that there is significant relation between NSDP and allocations on education at current prices. The expenditure on education is increasing with increase in NSDP which is clearly observed through high value (positive) correlation between the two.

5

Expenditure on Education in Southern States

In the last chapter the analysis of expenditure and allocation for education in the state of Karnataka has been done. In this chapter an attempt has made to analyse the expenditure for education in southern states like Andhra Pradesh, Kerala,Tamil Nnadu, Maharashtra and in Union Territory such as Pondichery. The comparative analysis would help for further plans, particularly on expenditure for education . With the proper plans of educational expenditure one can achieve the over all development of the country.

Table 5.1

Expenditure for Education as Percentage to Total State Budget and State Domestic Product SDP in the State of Andhra Pradesh

(Rs. in Lakhs)

Sl No.	*Year*	*Exp. of Education*	*Total State Budget*	*SDP*	*% of Edu. Expenditure to State Budget*	*% of Exp. Budget to SDP*
1	2	3	4	5	6	7
1.	1951-52	409.30	2787.44	-	14.68	-
2.	1952-53	424.35	2532.80	-	!6.75	-
3.	1953-54	709.43	3926.68	-	18.07	-
4.	1954-55	945.65	5336.19	-	17.72	-
5.	1955-56	1050.43	5795.88	-	18.12	-

1	2	3	4	5	6	7
6.	1956-57	1025.27	2450.41	-	41.84	-
7.	1957-58	1036.92	5510.92	-	18.82	-
8.	1958-59	1256.47	6341.97	-	19.81	-
9.	1959-60	1530.16	7462.81	-	20.50	-
10.	1960-61	1738.00	8498.39	98320.00	20.45	1.77
11.	1961-62	2122.93	9063.87	107960.00	23.42	1.97
12.	1962-63	2196.96	10833.59	111760.00	20.28	1.97
13.	1963-64	2311.25	12571.18	131900.00	18.39	1.75
14.	1964-65	2582.98	13842.93	150980.00	18.68	1.71
15.	1965-66	2758.23	15956.58	152080.00	17.29	1.81
16.	1966-67	3288.20	18467.85	178250.00	17.80	1.84
17.	1967-68	3760.79	18980.51	202470.00	19.81	1.86
18.	1968-69	4636.00	23009.00	204260.00	20.15	2.27
19.	1969-70	5173.00	27668.00	219640.00	18.70	2.36
20.	1970-71	6205.00	29667.00	252280.00	20.92	2.46
21.	1971-72	6616.00	32487.00	275800.00	20.37	2.40
22.	1972-73	6753.00	35275.00	294790.00	19.14	2.29
23.	1973-74	8743.00	41633.00	392600.00	21.00	2.23
24.	1974-75	9296.00	43009.00	472220.00	21.61	1.97
25.	1975-76	11609.00	50504.00	421800.00	22.99	2.75
26.	1976-77	13224.00	61794.00	427560.00	21.40	3.09
27.	1977-78	14845.00	74226.00	499400.00	20.00	2.97
28.	1978-79	16335.00	82722.00	551110.00	19.75	2.96
29.	1979-80	18692.00	101493.00	612760.00	18.42	3.05
30.	1980-81	22645.00	116113.00	732400.00	19.50	3.09
31.	1981-82	27250.00	138629.00	897430.00	19.66	3.04
32.	1982-83	34018.00	150650.00	970170.00	22.58	3.51
33.	1983-84	42461.00	204193.00	1151610.00	20.79	3.69
34.	1984-85	46666.00	246282.00	1196190.00	18.95	3.90
35.	1985-86	52986.00	278051.00	1341150.00	19.06	3.95
36.	1986-87	56162.00	324450.00	1424190.00	17.31	3.94
37.	1987-88	67518.00	344098.00	1737490.00	19.62	3.89
38.	1988-89	75415.00	424572.00	2208890.00	17.76	3.41
39.	1989-90	99814.00	471512.00	2499140.00	21.17	3.99
40.	1990-91	98842.00	550478.00	3016780.00	17.96	3.28
41.	1991-92	112346.00	645156.09	—	17.41	—
42.	1992-93	135531.00	714754.71	3970410.00	18.96	3.41
43.	1993-94	166115.00	792466.26	—	20.96	—

Table 5.1 reverses the expenditure for education as percentage to total state budget and state domestic product (SDP) in the neighbouring state of Andhra Pradesh. The expenditure for reduction is consistently increasing from Rs. 409.30 lakhs in 1951-52. In the state of Andhra Pradesh the educational expenditure has been given an importance in order to eradicate the low literacy rate in the state and also to implement the central government, programme of universalization of primary education in the country. There is a short stagnation during 1961-62 and 1962-63 with the Rs. 2122.93 and 2196.96 respectively. The expenditure for education has increased to a high amount during the year 1979-80, 1981-82, 1982-83 and 1985-86 with the amount Rs. 18682.00, 27250.00, 34018.00 and 52986.00 respectively. The total educational expenditure in the state of Andhra Pradesh is higher than Karnataka. In Andhra Pradesh during the 1951-52 total education and expenditure was Rs. 407.30 whereas in the state of Karnataka in the same year was Rs. 285.03 and in the year 1993-94 Andhra Pradesh has spent Rs. 166115.00 whereas Karnataka has spent Rs. 127812.24. This trend clearly shows that the government of Andhra Pradesh is spending more on education than Karnataka state.

In Andhra Pradesh the total state budget is ranged between Rs. 2450.41 during 1956-57 to Rs. 792466.26 during 1993-94 total state budget is increasing with of Rs.2787.44 during 1951-52, except during the 1952-53 with the amount Rs. 2532.80 followed by 1956-57 in the next year total state budget has been increasing steadily. However, the size of the state budget is smaller than in Karnataka.

The percentage of educational expenditure to state budget is in the range between 14.86 per cent during 1951-52 to 20.96 per cent during 1993-94. However the percentage of educational expenditure to state budget is increasing and decreasing with fluctuations. Compared to this the percentage of educational expenditure to all sectors in the state of Karnataka is lesser than the state of Andhra Pradesh, during the year 1951-52 in Karnataka the percentage was (1.79 per cent) whereas in Andhra Pradesh the percentage was (14.86 per cent) during the year 1994-95 the percentage was (4.98 per cent) in Karnataka, whereas (20.96 per cent) in the Andhra Pradesh.

Thus in Karnataka, the absolute expenditure on education is increasing consistently giving an impression that the state is anxious to raise the level of literacy and build a high manpower stock yet, when compared to the neighbouring state of Andhra Pradesh. The expenditure in absolate amount as well as in terms of percentage is very low while in Karnataka the share of education in total allocations never exceeded over 10 per cent. The picture in Andhra Pradesh indicates that the expenditure is above 15 per cent in all the years. It is as the average in the range of 18 to 20 per cent. Further the size of Andhra Pradesh budget is comparatively smaller than that of Karnataka. This indicates that the efforts for formulation of human capital in Karnataka are lesser than those compared with other states. As indicated by the comparison done here with the neighbouring state of Andhra Pradesh.

Table 5.2
Expenditure for Education as Percentage to Total State Budget and State Domestic Product SDP in the State of Kerala

(Rs. in Lakhs)

Sl No.	*Year*	*Exp. of Education to State*	*Total State Budget SDP*	*SDP*	*% of Edu. Expenditure*	*% of Exp. Budget to*
1	2	3	4	5	6	7
1.	1951-52	247.57	1362.86	-	18.17	-
2.	1952-53	291.26	1598.38	-	18.22	-
3.	1953-54	304.18	1455.79	-	20.89	-
4.	1954-55	329.70	1268.38	-	25.99	-
5.	1955-56	476.64	1966.22	-	24.24	-
6.	1956-57	672.83	2192.76	-	30.68	-
7.	1957-58	1007.32	2976.14	-	33.85	-
8.	1958-59	1316.96	3562.19	-	36.97	-
9.	1959-60	1475.22	4092.79	-	36.04	-
10.	1960-61	1616.80	4600.85	43220.00	35.14	3.74
11.	1961-62	1854.85	5361.22	46720.00	34.60	3.97
12.	1962-63	1914.14	6633.82	48750.00	28.85	3.93
13.	1963-64	2109.47	7091.95	51860.00	29.74	4.07
14.	1964-65	2307.49	7486.25	61110.00	30.82	3.78
15.	1965-66	2837.43	8182.58	71070.00	34.68	3.99
16.	1966-67	3470.24	9853.89	76500.00	35.22	4.54
17.	1967-68	4143.12	12386.58	91940.00	33.45	4.51
18.	1968-69	4664.00	13558.00	99400.00	34.40	4.69
19.	1969-70	5500.00	15109.00	111100.00	36.40	4.95
20.	1970-71	6009.00	16380.00	125460.00	36.68	4.79
21.	1971-72	6535.00	18651.00	127610.00	35.04	5.12
22.	1972-73	7046.00	20435.00	145720.00	34.48	4.84
23.	1973-74	8234.00	23732.00	182300.00	34.70	4.52
24.	1974-75	10318.00	28766.00	208550.00	35.87	4.95

Contd.

1	2	3	4	5	6	7
25.	1975-76	12897.00	45504.00	222820.00	28.34	5.79
26.	1976-77	14103.00	38959.00	239840.00	36.20	5.88
27.	1977-78	14527.00	41589.00	252050.00	34.93	5.76
28.	1978-79	14527.00	41589.00	275350.00	34.93	5.28
29.	1979-80	18460.00	99162.00	315560.00	18.62	5.85
30.	1980-81	21099.00	66761.00	382270.00	31.60	5.52
31.	1981-82	24006.00	78339.00	471150.00	30.64	5.63
32.	1983-84	30709.00	99244.00	552330.00	30.94	5.56
33.	1984-85	34595.00	13866.00	614150.00	30.38	5.63
34.	1985-86	41103.00	144533.00	650340.00	28.44	6.32
35.	1986-87	47682.00	165477.00	735440.00	28.81	6.48
36.	1987-88	50012.00	178068.00	825760.00	28.09	6.06
37.	1988-89	56875.00	206100.00	918170.00	27.60	6.19
38.	1989-90	62379.00	229809.00	1066460.00	27.14	5.85
39.	1990-91	76134.00	282495.00	1206180.00	26.95	6.31
40.	1991-92	82132.00	321645.75	—	25.53	—
41.	1992-93	95892.00	385125.03	—	24.90	—
42.	1993-94	113069.00	430675.48	1694460.00	26.25	6.67

Table 5.2 reveals that the expenditure for education as persentage to total state budget and state of Kerala

The expenditure for education in Kerala was in the range of Rs. 247.57 lakhs during 1951-52 to Rs. 113069.00 lakhs during 1993-94. The educational expenditure is consistently increasing. Since Kerala has achieved the highest literacy rate in India, the Government of India had declared it as 100 per cent literacy state. But, this has to be compared carefully. In Kerala from 1951-52 to 1954-55 the educational expenditure was less than Karnataka during 1951-52 it has spent 247.57, in 1952-53 Rs. 291.26, in 1953-54 Rs. 304.18 and in 1954-55 Rs. 329.70 during the respective years in Karnataka the amount spent was Rs. 285.03, Rs. 316.88, Rs. 323.44 and Rs. 342.65 from 1955-56 to 1985-86. Kerala has increased the educational expenditure but Karnataka has spent Rs. 43751.75 whereas Kerala has spent Rs. 47682.00 and in the year 1993-94 Karnataka has spent Rs. 127812.24 but Kerala has spent only Rs. 113069.00 with this comparative expenditure Kerala has surprisingly achieved 100 per cent of literacy. Where as Karnataka has failed. This trend makes us to review the commitment among the administrators and policy makers.

Total state budget is consistently increasing from Rs. 1362.00 during 1951-52 to Rs. 430675.48 during 1993-94. The trend shows that an increasing tendency in expenditure in all the sector of economy. SDP of the state is consistently increasing from Rs. 43220.00 in 1960-61 to Rs. 1694460.00 in 1993-94. Because of the increase in the SDP made there is increase in the educational expenditure in the state.

The percentage of educational expenditure to state budget is ranging between 18.17 the lowest during 1951-52 to 36.97 per cent the highest during 1958-59. However in Kerala this trend is with the fluctuations of decreasing and increasing with of 26.25 per cent during 1993-94. The percentage of educational expenditure the state budget in Kerala is ranged between 18.17 per cent to 36.97 per cent whereas in Karnataka the range is between 0.12 per cent to 10.74 per cent.

In Kerala the educational expenditure is increasing total state budget is also increasing with an increased SDP. Percentage of educational allocations to state budget steadily increasing percentage of expenditure, budget to SDP is increasingly steadily. Comparatively in recent years Kerala is spending less amount for education whereas Karnataka has started spending of more amount. For some years Karnataka had shown negligency in the educational expenditure. Though Karnataka is spending more in education than Kerala. The percentage of educational expenditure to state budget in Karnataka is very less when compared to Kerala.

Thus the high literacy rate of Kerala is an intone of substantial part of state budget devoted to development of educational facilities.

Table 5.3

Expenditure for Education as Percentage to Total State Budget and State Domestic Product SDP in the State of Maharashtra

(Rs. in Lakhs)

Sl No.	*Year*	*Exp. of Education*	*Total State Budget*	*SDP*	*% of Edu. Expenditure to State Budget*	*% of Exp. Budget to SDP*
1	2	3	4	5	6	7
1.	1951-52	1210.42	6257.75	-	19.34	-
2.	1952-53	1308.86	6844.27	-	19.12	-

1	2	3	4	5	6	7
3.	1953-54	1281.96	7111.84	-	18.02	-
4.	1954-55	1411.34	7102.91	-	19.87	-
5.	1955-56	1587.47	7817.35	-	20.31	-
6.	1956-57	1998.96	9236.17	-	21.64	-
7.	1957-58	2360.85	11508.45	-	20.51	-
8.	1958-59	2475.67	12827.44	-	19.30	-
9.	1959-60	2787.39	14921.44	-	18.68	-
10.	1960-61	2321.56	11926.52	159740.00	19.47	1.45
11.	1961-62	2449.36	12626.69	164730.00	19.40	1.49
12.	1962-63	2241.16	14637.88	181240.00	15.31	1.24
13.	1963-64	3045.30	16858.17	203690.00	18.06	1.50
14.	1964-65	3511.42	20351.91	226630.00	17.25	1.55
15.	1965-66	4060.60	24112.14	235450.00	16.84	1.72
16.	1966-67	4241.39	28383.65	275900.00	14.94	1.54
17.	1967-68	5688.36	31117.52	313090.00	18.25	1.85
18.	1968-69	7319.00	36614.00	332310.00	19.99	2.20
19.	1969-70	8776.00	39710.00	365640.00	22.10	2.40
20.	1970-71	9811.00	46002.00	387550.00	21.33	2.53
21.	1971-72	10212.00	53988.00	409440.00	18.92	2.49
22.	1972-73	11627.00	65065.00	434220.00	17.87	2.68
23.	1973-74	14323.00	81381.00	575790.00	17.60	2.49
24.	1974-75	16217.00	73915.00	735930.00	21.94	2.20
25.	1975-76	19339.00	91657.00	767660.00	21.10	2.52
26.	1976-77	20763.00	102787.00	857360.00	20.20	2.42
27.	1977-78	22878.00	112674.00	961640.00	20.30	2.38
28.	1978-79	28174.00	140720.00	1064540.00	20.02	2.65
29.	1979-80	32213.00	159892.00	1214190.00	20.15	2.65
30.	1980-81	38609.00	191704.00	1511340.00	20.14	2.55
31.	1981-82	42297.00	223803.00	1696580.00	18.90	2.49
32.	1982-83	49712.00	262808.00	1827740.00	18.92	2.72
33.	1983-84	57370.00	318121.00	2115170.00	18.03	2.71
34.	1984-85	68969.00	387984.00	2283270.00	17.78	3.02
35.	1985-86	79884.00	449080.00	2646390.00	17.79	3.02

1	2	3	4	5	6	7
36.	1986-87	95001.00	550445.00	2812010.00	17.26	3.38
37.	1987-88	104873.00	550445.00	3328250.00	19.05	3.15
38.	1988-89	122468.00	654065.00	4012370.00	18.72	3.05
39.	1989-90	153535.00	784828.00	4863940.00	19.56	3.16
40.	1990-91	170615.00	875367.00	5685630.00	19.49	3.00
41.	1991-92	205464.00	1004871.80	-	20.45	-
42.	1992-93	230512.00	1148641.41	7548130.00	20.07	3.05
43.	1993-94	223046.00	1250064.09	-	17.84	-

Table 5.3 shows that the expenditure of education as percentage to total state budget and state domestic product (SDP) in the state of Maharashtra. The expenditure for education is consistently increasing from rate Rs. 1210.42 during 1951-52 to Rs. 223046.00 during 1993-94. The highest amount spent in the year 1992-93 with Rs. 230512.00. This trend shows that in the state of Maharashtra, the educational expenditure has been given more importance in order to provide education for all sections of the state. Comparatively the total educational allocations in Maharashtra is highest than the state of Karnataka. In Maharashtra the total state budget is increasing consistently from Rs. 6257.75 during 1951-52 to Rs. 1250064.09 during 1993-94. The SDP is consistently incresing from Rs. 159740.00 during 1960-61 to Rs. 7548130.00 during 1992-93. In Maharashtra during 1951-52 the expenditure was Rs. 1210.42 whereas in Karnataka Rs. 285.03 and in Karnataka during 1993-94 Rs. 127812.24 whereas in Maharashtra Rs. 223046.00 whereas in Karnataka in was Rs. 223046.00.

The percentage of educational expenditure to state budget is ranged between 14.94 per cent during 1966-67 to 21.94 during 1974-75. However, this trend has not showed any consistent increase. During 1951-52 it was 19.34 per cent and during 1993-94 it was 17.84 per cent. In between there are many fluctuations of increase or decrease.

The percentage of educational expenditure in Karnataka is ranged between 0.12 per cent to 10.74 per cent whereas in Maharashtra it was 14.94 per cent to 21.94 per cent.

Educational expenditure is increasing as total state budget is also increasing. Subsequently there has been increase in S.D.P. The percentage of educational expenditure to state budget is not more, educational expenditure in Maharashtra is more than Karnataka expenditure for all sectors in Maharashtra is lesser than Karnataka. The percentage of educational expenditure to state budget is more in Maharashtra than Karnataka.

Table 5.4

EXPENDITURE FOR EDUCATION AS PERCENTAGE TO TOTAL STATE BUDGET AND STATE DOMESTIC PRODUCT SDP IN THE STATE OF TAMIL NADU

(Rs. in Lakhs)

Sl No.	*Year*	*Exp. of Education*	*Total State Budget*	*SDP*	*% of Edu. Expenditure to State Budget*	*% of Exp. Budget to SDP*
1	2	3	4	5	6	7
1.	1951-52	1101.10	6434.96	-	17.11	-
2.	1952-53	1196.02	6840.71	-	17.48	-
3.	1953-54	1053.06	5963.83	-	17.66	-
4.	1954-55	919.13	4724.52	-	19.45	-
5.	1955-56	1093.29	5455.81	-	20.04	-
6.	1956-57	1026.98	5686.67	-	18.06	-
7.	1957-58	1115.63	5915.02	-	18.86	-
8.	1958-59	1221.99	6835.37	-	17.88	-
9.	1959-60	1514.70	8057.71	-	18.80	-
10.	1960-61	1838.74	9109.43	111180.00	20.19	1.65
11.	1961-62	2346.48	10179.11	113980.00	23.05	2.06
12.	1962-63	2576.00	12180.83	116750.00	21.15	2.21
13.	1963-64	2741.45	13499.74	125060.00	20.31	2.19
14.	1964-65	3173.86	15129.80	140350.00	20.98	2.26
15.	1965-66	3785.13	18066.35	149420.00	20.95	2.53
16.	1966-67	4385.63	20142.70	175080.00	21.77	2.50
17.	1967-68	5355.50	26094.00	192630.00	20.04	2.99
19.	1969-70	6574.00	30577.00	214840.00	21.50	3.06
20.	1970-71	7254.00	32148.00	237110.00	22.56	3.06
21.	1971-72	8680.00	39384.00	269620.00	22.04	3.22
22.	1972-73	9636.00	43924.00	283900.00	21.94	3.39

Contd.

1	2	3	4	5	6	7
23.	1973-74	9779.00	46567.00	343230.00	21.00	2.85
24.	1974-75	11340.00	52836.00	363870.00	21.46	3.12
25.	1975-76	12121.00	56336.00	372740.00	21.52	3.25
26.	1976-77	14159.00	62929.00	430390.00	22.50	3.29
27.	1977-78	16061.00	70612.00	470990.00	22.75	3.41
28.	1978-79	18293.00	75351.00	502300.00	24.28	3.64
29.	1979-80	19753.00	84955.00	609520.00	23.25	3.24
30.	1980-81	23507.00	115225.00	721820.00	20.40	3.26
31.	1981-82	26425.00	135989.00	867670.00	19.43	3.05
32.	1982-83	33834.00	157608.00	882090.00	21.47	3.84
33.	1983-84	37104.00	191080.00	1022220.00	19.42	3.63
34.	1984-85	43456.00	221033.00	1202780.00	19.66	3.61
35.	1985-86	52562.00	244975.00	1368230.00	21.46	3.84
36.	1986-87	53040.00	277570.00	1530500.00	19.11	3.47
37.	1987-88	67731.00	337481.00	1816620.00	20.07	3.73
38.	1988-89	76866.00	376304.00	1963160.00	20.43	3.92
39.	1989-90	104296.00	473079.00	2297470.00	22.05	4.54
40.	1990-91	126191.00	564129.00	2591570.00	22.37	4.87
41.	1991-92	143094.00	867952.00	-	16.49	-
42.	1992-93	154619.00	766981.62	3522450.00	20.16	4.39
43.	1993-94	177087.00	830087.45	-	21.33	-

Table 5.4 reveals the expenditure for education as percentage to total state budget and state domestic product (SDP) in the state of Tamil Nadu. The expenditure of education in the state of Tamil Nadu has increased consistently from 1956-57 onwards. From 1951-52 the amount was Rs. 1101.10 during 1953-54, 1954-55 and 1956-57 the amount decreased with the increase in one year. The amount was Rs. 1053.06, Rs. 919.13 and Rs. 1026.98 respectively. However, the educational expenditure was increased to Rs. 177087.00 during 1993-94. This trend shows that Tamil Nadu has given more emphasis on education comparatively.

Because the literacy rate was meadiatory in the state. The government thought to increase the literacy rate in the state by spending more education comparatively to Karnataka. During 1951-52 and 1992-93 Karnataka's amount was Rs. 285.03 and Rs. 127812.24 where as in Tamil Nadu Rs. 1101.10 and Rs. 177087.00 respectively.

The total state budget is consistently increasing from Rs. 6434.96 during 1951-52 to Rs. 830087.48 during 1993-94. The SDP in the state is consistently increasing from Rs. 111180.00 during 1960-61 to Rs. 3522445.00 during 1992-93. This trend showed that the government is trying to increase the people's standard of living, and state domestic product by giving education, awareness, and various kinds of knowledge through spending more on educational sectors in the state since 1951-52.

The percentage of educational expenditure to state budget is ranged between 17.11 per cent in 1951-52 to 24.28 per cent in 1977-78. However this percentage is fluctuating in 1993-94 it reduced to 21.33 per cent. The range of percentage of educational expenditure to state budget in Tamil Nadu is between 17.11 per cent and 24.28 per cent whereas in Karnataka 0.12 per cent to 10.74 per cent. The percentage of expenditure, budget to SDP as a ranged between 1.65 per cent to 4.87 per cent from 1960-61 to 1990-91.

Educational expenditure is increasing as total state budget is increasing. SDP is increasing consistently. The percentage of educational expenditure to state budget steadily increased but with fluctuations. The educational expenditure in Tamil Nadu is higher than the educational expenditure in Karnataka. The percentage of educational expenditure the state budget in Tamil Nadu is also higher than in Karnataka.

Table 5.5

Percentage Expenditure on Each Subsector of Education to Total Expenditure on Education : Andhra Pradesh

Sl No.	*Year*	*Elementry Edu.*	*Secondary Edu.*	*Adult Edu.*	*Technical Edu.*	*Univ./ Higher Edu.*	*Others*	*Total*
1	2	3	4	5	6	7	8	9
1.	1951-52	44.87	24.20	8.90	-	13.70	8.33	100.00
2.	1952-53	46.97	25.26	7.03	-	12.23	8.52	100.00
3.	1953-54	54.39	20.30	6.15	-	9.58	9.59	100.00
4.	1954-55	55.91	17.12	5.13	-	9.67	12.16	100.00
5.	1955-56	49.43	16.13	3.99	-	9.44	21.00	100.00
6.	1956-57	55.76	17.99	5.12	-	10.28	10.84	100.00
7.	1957-58	55.17	19.69	6.06	-	13.62	5.46	100.00
8.	1958-59	50.79	19.62	9.67	-	14.56	5.36	100.00

Contd.

1	2	3	4	5	6	7	8	9
9.	1959-60	51.94	21.39	9.62	-	12.04	5.00	100.00
10.	1960-61	49.18	25.22	11.28	-	9.56	4.76	100.00
11.	1961-62	42.70	26.10	9.14	-	18.58	3.49	100.00
12.	1962-63	43.63	27.05	10.00	-	14.96	4.35	100.00
13.	1963-64	40.79	33.90	10.68	-	10.15	4.48	100.00
14.	1964-65	40.87	34.70	5.42	4.57	9.22	5.52	100.00
15.	1965-66	42.09	30.12	5.90	4.56	10.12	7.21	100.00
16.	1966-67	43.14	31.68	5.06	4.33	9.50	6.30	100.00
17.	1967-68	41.53	33.23	3.93	4.31	11.53	5.47	100.00
18.	1968-69	42.76	34.20	2.87	3.80	10.99	5.38	100.00
19.	1969-70	41.93	33.68	2.70	3.52	13.01	5.17	100.00
20.	1970-71	43.21	33.09	2.41	3.38	13.25	4.66	100.00
21.	1971-72	43.60	33.77	2.08	3.38	14.19	4.97	100.00
22.	1972-73	43.98	34.38	0.83	3.19	15.89	1.73	100.00
23.	1973-74	44.54	32.00	1.12	2.90	17.17	2.27	100.00
24.	1974-75	42.72	32.15	0.76	3.22	18.72	2.44	100.00
25.	1975-76	44.58	31.67	0.56	3.08	17.67	2.43	100.00
26.	1976-77	44.79	30.28	0.50	2.96	19.21	2.27	100.00
27.	1977-78	44.95	30.48	0.05	3.03	18.99	2.50	100.00
28.	1978-79	44.18	29.51	0.04	3.04	20.41	2.82	100.00
29.	1979-80	43.66	29.54	0.41	3.24	20.67	2.47	100.00
30.	1980-81	44.77	29.49	0.44	3.08	19.59	2.62	100.00
31.	1981-82	44.14	29.33	0.45	2.91	20.33	2.83	100.00
32.	1982-83	47.48	27.94	0.46	2.48	19.54	2.10	100.00
33.	1983-84	49.12	26.58	0.42	2.74	18.70	2.43	100.00
34.	1984-85	47.00	28.12	0.18	2.34	19.96	2.40	100.00
35.	1985-86	45.88	28.57	0.66	3.01	19.65	2.22	100.00
36.	1986-87	45.91	27.83	0.63	3.04	20.56	2.03	100.00
37.	1987-88	47.78	28.57	0.68	2.70	19.26	1.01	100.00
38.	1988-89	44.67	30.12	0.77	2.91	20.52	1.02	100.00
39.	1989-90	44.39	27.52	0.69	3.21	23.16	1.01	100.00
40.	1990-91	44.98	28.20	0.66	2.84	21.32	1.00	100.00
41.	1991-92	44.50	29.40	0.61	2.76	21.72	1.01	100.00
42.	1992-93	44.68	28.53	0.91	2.82	22.08	0.97	100.00
43.	1993-94	39.26	24.89	0.76	2.71	18.79	3.60	100.00

Table 5.5 shows the percentage of expenditure on each sub-sector on education to total expenditure on education in Andhra Pradesh. The percentage of expenditure on elementry education is ranged between 39.26

per cent during 1993-94 to 55.91 per cent during 1954-55 during the year 1951-52 it was 44.88 per cent in 1960-61 the trend showed an increasing attitude. Later on the percentage of expenditure on elementry education is with fluctuation of decreasing or increasing. The lack of consistey of the increasing trend of expenditure on elementry education shows that the policy of Government has shifted to another sectors of education, i.e., adult, technical and university/higher education. In order to utilise the use of manpower which is available in the state. Elementary education followed by secondary education is ranged between 16.13 per cent to 34.70 per cent during the period 1955-56 to 1964-65 respectively. However the trend did not show any consistent on the expenditure on secondary education. Further it is observed that the government of Andhra Pradesh has been trying to improve elementary as well as secondary education sectors in the state by spending more on these sectors of education. The adult education was given more importance in the beginning of the plans and later shifted the focus on this sectors. In the 1951-52 it was 8.90 per cent it received 11.28 per cent in 1960-61. However 1964-65 onwards it was dipped down to Rs. 0.04 per cent. The technical education is between 1978-79 to 1964-65 was 4.57 per cent to 2.71 per cent. The university /higher education was ranged between 1951-52 to 1993-94 was 13.70 per cent to 18.79 per cent in between there is increasing trend with the fluctuations. In Andhra Pradesh a very high emphasis was given on higher education after education on other sectors of educations the state has spent with of Rs. 8.83 per cent during 1951-52 to Rs. 13.60 per cent during 1992-93 it was increased during 1955-56 with of Rs. 21.00 per cent and dipped to 0.97 per cent during 1992-93.

Expenditure on elementary education is increased, followed by secondary and technical education with comparison, Karnataka has a very high range of gap of expenditure in all the sector of education whereas low range of gap of expenditure between various sectors of education in Andhra Pradesh.

Table 5.6

Percentage Expenditure on Each Subsector of Education to Total Expenditure on Education : Kerala

Sl No.	*Year*	*Elementary Edu.*	*Secondary Edu.*	*Adult Edu.*	*Technical Edu.*	*Univ./ Higher Edu.*	*Others*	*Total*
1	2	3	4	5	6	7	8	9
1.	1951-52	45.21	26.44	1.33	-	13.25	13.77	100.00

Contd.

1	2	3	4	5	6	7	8	9
2.	1952-53	40.91	29.17	1.11	-	15.70	13.11	100.00
3.	1953-54	41.00	31.22	1.19	-	11.54	15.04	100.00
4.	1954-55	39.12	34.90	1.12	-	9.77	15.10	100.00
5.	1955-56	32.57	36.68	0.81	-	6.67	23.26	100.00
6.	1956-57	39.25	32.73	1.06	-	5.53	21.43	100.00
7.	1957-58	48.77	29.36	3.28	-	5.39	13.20	100.00
8.	1958-59	43.28	32.10	3.61	-	5.33	15.68	100.00
9.	1959-60	62.75	21.12	2.75	-	5.50	7.88	100.00
10.	1960-61	67.31	18.10	3.01	-	5.34	6.23	100.00
11.	1961-62	62.06	16.77	3.56	-	6.57	11.04	100.00
12.	1962-63	63.37	18.86	4.17	-	6.24	7.36	100.00
13.	1963-64	59.96	18.97	5.61	-	6.26	9.20	100.00
14.	1964-65	58.87	19.51	1.52	6.05	4.42	9.62	100.00
15.	1965-66	60.47	19.59	1.33	5.08	4.18	9.35	100.00
16.	1966-67	57.58	19.14	2.30	5.13	7.53	8.31	100.00
17.	1967-68	59.46	20.93	2.32	4.34	5.66	7.29	100.00
18.	1968-69	61.43	21.04	2.23	2.86	5.09	7.34	100.00
19.	1969-70	59.75	21.16	2.15	4.05	5.00	7.89	100.00
20.	1970-71	58.25	21.25	2.13	3.77	7.08	7.51	100.00
21.	1971-72	57.77	21.50	2.11	2.80	7.40	8.42	100.00
22.	1972-73	58.36	23.84	0.97	2.78	11.82	2.22	100.00
23.	1973-74	55.92	25.39	1.24	2.78	13.12	1.56	100.00
24.	1974-75	57.70	25.82	0.61	3.21	10.92	1.75	100.00
25.	1975-76	57.15	24.80	0.95	3.50	12.16	1.44	100.00
26.	1976-77	57.40	25.36	0.74	3.57	11.55	1.37	100.00
27.	1977-78	56.87	25.60	0.01	4.01	11.36	2.15	100.00
28.	1978-79	56.87	25.60	0.01	4.01	11.36	2.15	100.00
29.	1979-80	55.27	27.60	0.10	4.25	10.50	2.29	100.00
30.	1980-81	54.48	28.37	0.04	4.22	10.63	2.28	100.00
31.	1981-82	53.82	28.68	0.03	4.01	11.28	2.18	100.00
32.	1982-83	53.25	29.22	0.04	3.51	12.07	1.92	100.00
33.	1983-84	52.38	28.74	0.04	3.80	12.99	2.05	100.00
34.	1984-85	51.70	29.07	0.04	3.98	13.20	2.00	100.00
35.	1985-86	50.97	29.65	0.23	4.67	12.93	1.54	100.00
36.	1986-87	51.20	28.87	0.26	4.78	12.79	2.11	100.00
37.	1987-88	52.34	29.11	0.29	3.98	13.53	0.75	100.00
38.	1988-89	52.77	28.46	0.23	3.79	13.41	1.34	100.00

1	2	3	4	5	6	7	8	9
39.	1989-90	51.93	29.09	0.37	3.97	13.16	1.48	100.00
40.	1990-91	52.40	29.92	0.11	4.08	12.23	1.25	100.00
41.	1991-92	49.88	29.62	0.04	4.65	14.98	0.82	100.00
42.	1992-93	47.80	30.83	0.07	4.24	16.16	0.90	100.00
43.	1993-94	47.46	31.01	0.06	4.32	16.06	1.09	100.00

Table 5.6 reveals the percentage of expenditure on each subsector of education to total expenditure on education in Kerala. Kerala stood first in education by achieving 100 per cent literacy in India. The government of Kerala spent on elementary education with the range of 32.57 per cent in 1955-56 to 67.31 per cent in 1960-61. The expenditure on elementary education shows a fluctuating trend. However, the range showed that the emphasis is more on elementary education. Because in most of the years, the percentage of expenditure on sector falls above 50 per cent. This trend is not observed in any states of South India.

It is observed that simultaneously secondary and elementary education have showed an increasing trend with fluctuations. Expenditure on secondary education of 26.44 per cent in 1951-52 has reached to 31.01 percentage in 1993-94. On this sector highest percentage was 36.68 per centage in 1955-56. The adult education is ranged between 0.01 per cent to 5.61 per cent in 1977-78 and 1963-64 respectively. After realising importance of technical education it has received 6.05 per cent in 1964-65 to 4.32 per cent in 1993-94, University/higher education has received 31.25 per cent in 1951-52 to 16.16 per cent during 1993-94. However in between, the decreasing and increasing trend were found. Other education has steadily decreasing tendency, i.e., 13.77 per cent during 1951-52 to 1.09 per cent during 1993-94 it was decreased to the lowest level 0.75 per cent in 1987-88.

The percentage of educational expenditure on elementary education is more. Followed by secondary, university/higher, technical and adult education. The percentage are higher than Karnataka in all the sectors.

Table 5.7

Percentage Expenditure on Each Subsector of Education to Total Expenditure on Education : Maharashtra

Sl No.	*Year*	*Elementary Edu.*	*Secondary Edu.*	*Adult Edu.*	*Technical Edu.*	*Univ./ Higher Edu.*	*Others*	*Total*
1	2	3	4	5	6	7	8	9
1.	1951-52	65.28	13.44	6.03	-	7.99	7.26	100.00

Contd.

1	2	3	4	5	6	7	8	9
2.	1952-53	66.10	14.34	5.18.	-	7.79	6.59	100.00
3.	1953-54	66.02	13.53	5.07	-	7.57	7.82	100.00
4.	1954-55	64.01	14.35	5.29	-	8.73	7.62	100.00
5.	1955-56	61.20	15.91	6.09	-	9.26	7.54	100.00
6.	1956-57	60.58	15.82	6.33	-	8.78	8.48	100.00
7.	1957-58	60.07	16.64	6.49	-	7.82	8.98	100.00
8.	1958-59	57.80	16.81	7.23	-	8.55	9.61	100.00
9.	1959-60	58.81	17.78	7.68	-	8.72	7.02	100.00
10.	1960-61	54.75	23.31	7.70	-	7.29	6.95	100.00
11.	1961-62	50.51	19.38	7.01	-	6.52	16.58	100.00
12.	1962-63	49.71	21.38	8.69	-	8.25	11.91	100.00
13.	1963-64	47.76	18.43	7.42	-	7.12	19.27	100.00
14.	1964-65	48.66	18.69	7.64	-	7.37	17.63	100.00
15.	1965-66	49.17	17.93	5.46	4.90	5.62	16.91	100.00
16.	1966-67	49.40	16.95	5.36	6.28	6.05	15.95	100.00
17.	1967-68	47.98	26.78	4.46	5.52	6.68	8.58	100.00
18.	1968-69	43.18	34.00	4.03	4.62	6.39	7.79	100.00
19.	1969-70	46.72	32.03	3.55	4.36	6.05	7.29	100.00
20.	1970-71	47.50	33.54	3.36	4.31	6.59	4.70	100.00
21.	1971-72	46.03	34.93	3.33	4.31	6.71	4.69	100.00
22.	1972-73	48.56	35.36	0.07	3.86	6.59	5.56	100.00
23.	1973-74	45.59	36.47	0.05	3.78	7.51	6.60	100.00
24.	1974-75	49.79	34.61	0.06	3.38	6.95	5.21	100.00
25.	1975-76	51.30	33.54	0.08	3.23	5.81	6.04	100.00
26.	1976-77	48.34	33.08	0.06	3.40	9.76	5.37	100.00
27.	1977-78	47.53	33.00	0.08	3.29	10.81	5.29	100.00
28.	1978-79	46.03	33.87	0.12	3.52	11.48	4.98	100.00
29.	1979-80	44.47	34.65	0.41	3.60	13.72	3.15	100.00
30.	1980-81	46.36	33.01	0.40	3.39	13.34	3.51	100.00
31.	1981-82	44.05	34.11	0.42	3.26	14.53	3.62	100.00
32.	1982-83	44.56	34.36	0.42	3.52	13.72	3.42	100.00
33.	1983-84	43.96	35.42	0.42	3.42	13.42	3.36	100.00
34.	1984-85	44.24	34.93	0.44	3.55	13.44	3.39	100.00

1	2	3	4	5	6	7	8	9
35.	1985-86	44.82	38.28	0.58	3.66	9.96	2.69	100.00
36.	1986-87	49.27	33.99	0.58	3.48	10.05	2.63	100.00
37.	1987-88	45.83	38.16	0.74	3.29	9.82	2.12	100.00
38.	1988-89	44.19	38.51	0.75	3.89	9.97	2.68	100.00
39.	1989-90	44.78	37.67	0.81	4.47	10.10	2.18	100.00
40.	1990-91	40.44	39.80	0.77	4.24	12.58	2.16	100.00
41.	1991-92	43.16	39.48	0.77	3.83	10.43	2.32	100.00
42.	1992-93	44.02	38.65	0.60	4.25	10.21	2.28	100.00
43.	1993-94	44.31	38.53	0.44	4.14	10.31	2.26	100.00

Table 5.7 reveals the percentage of expenditure on each sub-sector of education to total expenditure on education in the state of Maharashtra. The percentage of expenditure on elementary education is ranged between Rs. 40.44 per cent to Rs. 66.10 per cent during 1990-91 and 1952-53. Though the percentage was started with 65.28 per cent during 1951-52 it was increased up to 66.02 per cent in 1953-54. Soon after two years there is a steady decreased trend of expenditure on elementary education with fluctuations. It reached to the percentage of 44.31 per cent during 1993-94. This trend shows that the government of Maharashtra shifted its emphasis on other than the elementary education. Whereas the percentage of educational expenditure on secondary education is with fluctuations. There was 13.44 per cent during 1951-52 has reached to 38.53 per cent in 1993-94. However, with the comparison of expenditure on elementary education, secondary education received less emphasis. But its percentage share is high compared to other states like Kerala, Tamil Nadu and Karnataka.

Similarly the adult education showed a comparatively less emphasis in 1951-52 6.03 per cent. Further it was decreased to 0.44 per cent in 1993-94. Meanwhile it reached to 8.69 per cent in 1962-63 and dropped down to 0.05 per cent in 1973-74. The expenditure on technical education is steadily decreased with fluctuations 6.28 per cent to 4.90 per cent during 1966-67 and 1965-66 respectively. Further it has reached to 4.14 per cent in 1993-94.

Higher/University education has received increasing as well as decreasing expenditure. It was 7.94 per cent in 1951-52 reached to 10.31per cent in 1993-94. In other sectors of education except in few years between 1961-62 to 1966-67, in rest of the years the trend showed that expenditure on this sector was low in 1951-52 it was 7.26 and reached to 2.26 per cent in 1993-94.

The percentage of expenditure on elementary education has showed decreasing trend. Whereas secondary and higher/university education has showed increasing trend, the other sectors of education, i.e., Adult and Technical educations has showed decreasing trends.

Table 5.8
Percentage Expenditure on each Subsector of Education to Total Expenditure on Education : Tamil Nadu

Sl No.	*Year*	*Elementary Edu.*	*Secondary Edu.*	*Adult Edu.*	*Technical Edu.*	*Univ./ Higher Edu.*	*Others*	*Total*
1	2	3	4	5	6	7	8	9
1.	1951-52	63.27	11.69	6.60	-	10.89	7.54	100.00
2.	1952-53	64.16	11.79	6.69	-	9.81	7.55	100.00
3.	1953-54	62.76	12.83	6.67	-	10.08	7.66	100.00
4.	1954-55	56.49	14.64	3.63	-	8.50	16.74	100.00
5.	1955-56	51.92	17.12	2.43	-	7.93	20.59	100.00
6.	1956-57	47.79	17.64	2.07	-	7.95	24.55	100.00
7.	1957-58	47.64	20.31	5.62	-	8.64	7.79	100.00
8.	1958-59	52.83	20.47	7.25	-	8.94	10.50	100.00
9.	1959-60	53.46	21.39	6.36	-	7.96	10.83	100.00
10.	1960-61	55.15	20.84	6.16	-	7.04	10.80	100.00
11.	1961-62	49.94	22.23	4.27	-	5.48	18.08	100.00
12.	1962-63	49.79	22.70	3.98	-	5.22	18.32	100.00
13.	1963-64	47.23	24.84	3.41	-	5.73	18.79	100.00
14.	1964-65	44.67	30.97	2.17	1.57	4.56	16.06	100.00
15.	1965-66	43.41	21.10	1.98	1.49	4.72	27.30	100.00
16.	1966-67	44.02	28.93	2.18	2.52	5.01	17.34	100.00
17.	1967-68	46.86	26.08	1.93	2.63	5.08	17.42	100.00
18.	1968-69	45.31	33.42	1.94	3.18	7.18	8.98	100.00
19.	1969-70	46.60	30.89	1.66	4.61	7.48	8.76	100.00
20.	1970-71	47.19	30.11	1.44	4.27	7.31	9.68	100.00
21.	1971-72	46.32	29.62	1.28	5.67	8.03	9.09	100.00
22.	1972-73	46.16	29.51	1.33	5.74	8.00	9.26	100.00
23.	1973-74	45.20	29.74	1.46	6.12	8.50	8.98	100.00
24.	1974-75	52.23	33.54	0.57	4.01	8.63	1.03	100.00
25.	1975-76	52.75	33.61	0.60	3.85	8.05	1.14	100.00
26.	1976-77	52.93	33.14	0.57	3.75	8.56	1.05	100.00

1	2	3	4	5	6	7	8	9
27.	1977-78	51.44	32.44	0.11	3.78	10.54	1.69	100.00
28.	1978-79	51.08	31.43	0.11	3.90	12.03	1.44	100.00
29.	1979-80	48.46	27.73	0.50	4.26	17.67	1.38	100.00
30.	1980-81	49.93	26.11	0.70	3.81	17.43	2.02	100.00
31.	1981-82	47.49	28.75	0.43	3.94	17.49	1.92	100.00
32.	1982-83	50.50	26.40	0.39	4.25	17.20	1.27	100.00
33.	1983-84	48.16	27.33	0.51	3.78	17.09	3.13	100.00
34.	1984-85	49.25	27.59	0.59	3.99	17.34	1.24	100.00
35.	1985-86	51.95	26.04	0.54	3.59	16.46	1.42	100.00
36.	1986-87	51.75	26.21	-	3.73	16.66	1.64	100.00
37.	1987-88	49.58	35.56	1.00	3.89	9.46	0.51	100.00
38.	1988-89	48.62	36.04	1.04	3.48	10.03	0.79	100.00
39.	1989-90	44.78	33.82	0.82	3.80	16.26	0.52	100.00
40.	1990-91	49.45	35.48	0.71	3.41	10.39	0.57	100.00
41.	1991-92	51.39	34.32	0.66	2.97	9.20	1.46	100.00
42.	1992-93	47.75	33.22	0.50	3.50	10.73	4.31	100.00
43.	1993-94	49.96	33.77	1.45	3.15	9.77	1.90	100.00

Table 5.8 explains about the percentage of expenditure on each sub-sector of education to total expenditure on education in the state on Tamil Nadu. The percentage of expenditure on elementary education is decreasing with the fluctuations 63.27 per cent during 1951-52. The lowest percentage was Rs. 43.41 per cent during 1965-66 in between with decreasing trend it reached Rs. 49.96 per cent during 1993-94. Since elementary education plays a very significance role in the development of the nation more emphasis be laid in elementary education. Democracy has to succeed by understanding various activities of population has be state and reducedine the masses have to be taught to growth understand causes for increasing the population and as well as its consequences. This would be possible only through education. Even then the government has been showing a less emphasis on elementary education.

The percentage of expenditure on secondary education is consistently increasing from Rs. 11.69 per cent during 1951-52 to Rs. 33.77 per cent during 1993-94. The state government in Tamil Nadu have showed less emphasis towards elementary education. This gap has filled by increasing more funds on secondary education. Adult education has showed decreasing trend from 6.60 per cent during 1951-52 1.45% 1993-94.

The percentage of expenditure on technical education is incresed consistently from 1.57 per cent during 1964-65 to 3.15% in 1993-94. Even it reached to 6.12 per cent in 1973-74. For the proper a utilisation of the human capital, it has increased in industrial production. Consequently trend increase in SDP and the life the standard of living of the people in the state. The technical education was given more emphasis.

The university/higher education neither decreased nor increased. During the 1951-52 10.89 per cent and reached to 17.67 per cent during 1979-80. Mainly there are of fluctuations in expenditure on university/higher education. The percentage of expenditure on other sectors is decreasing steadily though it, reached to 24.55 per cent in 1956-57 it dropped down to 0.51 per cent during 1987-88.

The percentage of expenditure on elementary education has been given more emphasis compare to other states of Maharashtra and Kerala. Expenditure on Secondary education is also given more, emphasis, followed by technical and university higher education. However adult education and expenditure on other sector are comparatively very less.

Objective 7

3.4.1. To find out the increase, if any, in the plan allocation for education from 1951-52 to 1996-97 in Karnataka.

3.4.2. To know the extent of disparities in the plan allocation for education in different sectors.

In pursuance of these two objectives the data regarding the plan allocations was organised and tabulated using corresponding percentages. The following table shows in detail.

Table shows the percentage of expediter on each subsector of education to total expenditure on education in Pondichery. The percentage of expenditure on elementary education is ranged between 34.18% in 1963-64 to 53.93% during 1976-77. The trend showed an increasing and decreasing attitude with fluctuations. The lack of consistency of the increasing trend of expenditure on elementary education shows that the policy of government has shifted to another sector of education. i.e. secondary, adult, technical etc. The highest percentage of expenditure on elementary education is found in 1976-77 with 53.93% followed by 53.21% in 1972-73.

Elementary education is followed by secondary education is ranged between 20.41% in 1963-64 to 32.29% during 1993-94. The trend shoed an increasing and decreasing attitude with fluctuations. The highest percentage of expenditure on secondary education is found in 1980-81 with 26.40%, followed by 26.31% in 1979-80 and 25.71% in 1974-75. Moreover, the lowest

Table 5.9. Percentage Expenditure on Each Subsection of Education to Total Expenditure on Education (Revenue Account) in Pondicherry

Sl.No	Year	Elementary	Secondary	Adult	Technical	University/Higher	Other	Total
1.	1951-52	-	-	-	-	-	-	-
2.	1952-53	-	-	-	-	-	-	-
3.	1953-54	-	-	-	-	-	-	-
4.	1954-55	-	-	-	-	-	-	-
5.	1955-56	-	-	-	-	-	-	-
6.	1956-57	-	-	-	-	-	-	-
7.	1957-58	-	-	-	-			-
8.	1958-59	-	-	-	-	-	-	-
9.	1959-60	-	-	-	-	-	-	-
10.	1960-61	-	-	-	-	-	-	-
11.	1961-62	-	-	-	-	-	-	-
12.	1962-63	-	-	-	-	-	-	-
13.	1963-64	34.18	20.41	10.95	-	5.67	28.79	100.00
14.	1964-65	37.41	22.62	1.61	12.15	5.18	21.03	100.00
15.	1965-66	36.86	22.24	1.37	10.41	4.69	24.42	100.00
16.	1966-67	40.41	22.59	2.28	8.36	4.56	21.80	100.00

(Contd.)

(*Cont.*)

Sl.No	*Year*	*Elementary*	*Secondary*	*Adult*	*Technical*	*University/Higher*	*Other*	*Total*
17.	1967-68	39.16	20.15	1.96	7.34	8.58	22.81	100.00
18.	1968-69	-	-	-	-	-	-	100.00
19.	1969-70	-	-	-	-	-	-	100.00
20.	1970-71	41.17	22.11	1.54	5.74	12.09	17.35	100.00
21.	1971-72	41.08	23.18	1.42	4.96	13.19	16.20	100.00
22.	1972-73	53.21	24.44	0.12	3.20	12.98	6.05	100.00
23.	1973-74	49.40	24.76	0.17	3.49	15.75	6.43	100.00
24.	1974-75	50.45	25.71	0.12	3.96	14.24	5.52	100.00
25.	1975-76	51.81	25.51	0.12	4.02	13.23	5.31	100.00
26.	1976-77	53.93	25.45	0.10	3.61	12.21	4.71	100.00
27.	1977-78	51.40	24.82	0.23	4.23	14.22	5.10	100.00
28.	1978-79	51.08	25.45	0.54	3.99	13.70	5.25	100.00
29.	1979-80	51.57	26.31	0.67	3.98	12.53	4.94	100.00
30.	1980-81	51.28	26.40	0.98	3.48	13.02	4.85	100.00

(*Contd..*)

(*Contd.*)

Sl.No	*Year*	*Elementary*	*Secondary*	*Adult*	*Technical*	*University/Higher*	*Other*	*Total*
31.	1981-82	52.01	24.93	1.01	3.01	14.49	4.54	100.00
32.	1982-83	52.34	25.30	0.96	2.94	13.89	4.57	100.00
33.	1983-84	52.27	25.14	0.92	2.73	14.05	4.89	100.00
34.	1984-85	50.61	25.30	1.02	4.80	13.68	4.59	100.00
35.	1985-86	44.24	24.06	1.12	12.87	12.98	4.73	100.00
36.	1986-87	39.02	23.38	0.84	19.48	12.92	4.36	100.00
37.	1987-88	39.43	20.21	1..00	20.79	16.46	2.12	100.00
38.	1988-89	43.26	29.81	0.95	12.53	11.09	2.37	100.00
39.	1989-90	42.33	29.85	0.70	11.46	12.24	3.42	100.00
40.	1990-91	40.88	28.08	0.32	14.63	13.23	2.87	100.00
41.	1991-92	39.06	29.59	0.53	14.48	12.44	3.90	100.00
42.	1992-93	40.34	30.61	0.17	13.16	12.76	2.96	100.00
43.	1993-94	41.38	32.29	0.22	8.82	14.18	3.10	100.00

Source: Budgetary Resource for Education, Dept of Education, Ministry of Human Resource Development, New Delhi.

(*Contd.*)

percentage of expenditure on secondary education is found in 1967-68 with 20.15%, followed by 20.21% during 1987-88. Further, it is observed from the table that government of Pondicherry has been trying to improve elementary and secondary educations by spending more on these sectors of education comparatively to other sectors of education.

Adult education was also given more importance in the beginning years, i.e., 1963-64 with 10.95%, followed by 2.28% during 1966-67 and 1.01% during 1981-82. Nearly for 10 years, the percentage of expenditure on adult education is ranged between 0.10 % in 1976-77 to 0.96% during 1980-1981.

The percentage of expenditure on technical education is ranged between 2.73% in 1983-84 to 20.79% in 1987-88. It showed an increasing and decreasing attitude with fluctuations.

The university/higher education has given third place. After elementary and secondary educations, Pondicherry government has given importance to university /higher educations. The trend showed an increasing attitude with fluctuations. It has started with 5.67% during 1963-64 and reached to 16.46% in 1987-88. The expenditure on other sectors of education has showed decreasing trend. It has started with 28.79% during 1963-64 and reached to 2.12% in 1987-88, followed by 3.10% during 1993-94.

The over all observation of the table is that expenditure on elementary education is increased. Followed by secondary, technical and higher education. However, for two years. I.e. during 1968-69 and 1969-70, expenditure for all sectors is nil.

Table 5.10. Expenditure on Education by Education Department (Revenue Account) As percentage to Total State Domestic Product (SDP) in Pondicherry

(*Rs in Lakhs*)

Sl.No.	*Year*	*State/Union Territories*	*Centre*
1.	1951-52	-	-
2.	1952-53	-	-
3.	1953-54	-	-
4.	1954-55	-	-
5.	1955-56	-	-
6.	1956-57	-	-
7.	1957-58	-	-
8.	1958-59	-	-
9.	1959-60	-	-

Sl.No	Year	State/Union Territories	Centre
10.	1960-61	-	-
11.	1961-62	-	-
12.	1962-63	-	-
13.	1963-64	21.27	-
14.	1964-65	19.80	-
15.	1965-66	19.98	-
16.	1966-67	17.45	-
17.	1967-68	19.66	-
18.	1968-69	-	-
19.	1969-70	-	-
20.	1970-71	16.71	3.37
21.	1971-72	17.29	3.39
22.	1972-73	21.59	4.22
23.	1973-74	20.79	3.20
24.	1974-75	20.60	3.87
25.	1975-76	22.74	4.55
26.	1976-77	21.40	4.43
27.	1977-78	21.05	4.06
28.	1978-79	20.48	3.52
29.	1979-80	19.55	3.29
30.	1980-81	17.38	3.26
31.	1981-82	17.63	3.61
32.	1982-83	18.89	3.80
33.	1983-84	19.76	4.05
34.	1984-85	19.13	4.32
35.	1985-86	16.45	4.88
36.	1986-87	19.10	5.75
37.	1987-88	18.45	5.75
38.	1988-89	20.05	6.31
39.	1989-90	17.26	6.60
40.	1990-91	16.79	6.34
41.	1991-92	16.11	-
42.	1992-93	15.30	5.31
43.	1993-94	15.44	-

Source : Budgetary Resource for Education, Dept of Education, Ministry of Human Resource Development, New Delhi.

Table reveals the expenditure for education as percentage to total state budget and state domestic product (SDP) in the neighbouring union territory of Pondicherry. The percentage of expenditure for education is consistently decreasing from 22.27% in 1963-64 and reached to 15.44% in 1993-94. It is found in the table that only in one year 1975-76 the percentage of expenditure is reached to 22.74%, which is the highest amount of expenditure that has been spent for education.

The percentage of expenditure budget to SDP has been increasing from 3.37% in 1970-71 to 5.31% in 1992-93. It is found that SDP of Pondicherry has increased with fluctuation. As SDP goes on increasing and decreasing the percentage of expenditure for education is also showed increasing and decreasing trend.

Note : Rate of Growth (%) estimated on the basis of Semi-Log equation.

** Revised Estimate.

.. Data not available.

Source : www. Shikshanic.nic.in

Table reveals the expenditure on education at current and constant prices in the state of Andhra Pradesh at 1980-81 prices. In total for all sectors of education, i.e., elementary, Secondary, higher, technical, adult and other sectors of education, the plan expenditure from 1980-81 to 1991-92 has showed an increasing trend with more fluctuations. In 1980-81 it was 9.39 crores and reached to 74.34 crores in 1991-92. In between, the highest amount of 137.71 crores have been spent in 1989-90, followed by 67.03 crores in 1983-84, 75.87 crores in 1988-89 and 55.18 crores in 1984-85.On the other hand the total non-plan expenditure for all sectors of education has showed an increasing trend from 217.06 crores to 1080.38 crores in 1991-92. In total (plan + non-plan) expenditure for education has also showed an increasing trend. It has started with 226.45 crores and reached to 1154.72 crores in 1991-92. It is found that the total expenditure for all sectors of education is steadily increasing.

The plan expenditure on education at current prices has showed increasing trend with fluctuations. In 1980-81 it was 9.39 crores and reached to 39.99 crores in 1988-89. In between the highest amount of 51.71 crores are found in 1983-84. Whereas the non-plan expenditure on education has been increasing from 217.06 crores to 357.48 crores in 1988-89. In total (plan + non-plan) expenditure for education has also increased consistently from 226.45 crores in 1980-81 to 397.47 crores in 1988-89.

Note : Rate of Growth (%) estimated on the basis of Semi-Log equation.

** Revised Estimate.

Table 5.11 Total Expenditure for All Sectors of Education at Current and Constant Prices in Andhra Pradesh. At 1980-81 Prices.

(*Rs. in Crores*)

Sl.No.	Yea	At Current Prices At			Constant Prices		
		Plan	Non-Plan	Total	Plan	Non-Plan	Total
1.	1980-81	9.39	217.06	226.45	9.39	217.06	226.45
2.	1981-82	12.95	259.55	272.50	12.18	244.11	256.29
3.	1982-83	41.64	298.54	340.18	36.63	262.60	299.23
4.	1983-84	67.03	357.58	424.61	51.71	275.88	327.60
5.	1984-85	55.18	411.47	466.65	39.80	296.81	336.62
6.	1985-86	38.54	491.32	529.86	26.06	332.16	358.22
7.	1986-87	42.42	519.20	561.62	25.89	316.92	342.81
8.	1987-88	52.28	602.90	655.18	29.19	336.65	365.85
9.	1988-89	75.87	678.28	754.15	39.99	357.48	397.47
10.	1989-90	137.71	860.43	998.14	-	-	-
11.	1990-91	54.29	934.13	988.42	-	-	-
12.	1992-93**	74.34	1080.38	1154.72	-	-	-
Growth rate		22.20	15.24	15.54	12.45	6.05	6.32

Table 5.12 Total Expenditure for All Sectors of Education at Current and Constant Prices in Kerala. At 1980-81 Prices.

(*Rs. in Crores*)

Sl.No.	*Year*	At Current Prices			At Constant Prices		
		Plan	*Non-Plan*	*Total*	*Plan*	*Non-Plan*	*Total*
1.	1980-81	13.37	197.61	210.98	13.77	197.61	210.98
2.	1981-82	17.52	222.54	240.06	16.36	207.85	224.21
3.	1982-83	19.49	245.78	265.27	15.99	201.68	217.68
4.	1983-84	28.87	278.22	307.09	19.37	186.70	206.07
5.	1984-85	36.08	309.87	345.95	23.30	200.09	223.39
6.	1985-86	17.52	393.51	411.03	11.17	250.98	262.16
7.	1986-87	28.61	448.21	476.82	15.71	246.17	261.88
8.	1987-88	25.12	474.99	500.11	12.72	240.49	253.20
9.	1988-89	43.15	525.60	569.75	20.45	249.06	269.51
10.	1989-90	39.52	584.27	623.79	18.20	269.06	287.26
11.	1990-91	22.72	738.62	761.34	-	-	-
12.	1992-93**	32.78	760.88	793.66	-	-	-
Growth rate		10.57	13.39	13.20	1.11	3.69	3.52

.. Data not available.

Source :www.Shikshanic.nic.in

Table reveals the plan and non-plan expenditure on education at current and constant prices for all sectors of education in the state of Kerala at 1980-81 prices.

It is observed from the table that the plan expenditure for all sectors of education in the state of Kerala has increased with fluctuations. Kerala spends 13.37 crores in 1980-81, which is the beginning year and reached to 32.78 crores in 1991-92. In between the highest amount of 43.15 crores are spent in 1988-89. Whereas the non-plan expenditure at current prices has showed an increasing trend, i.e., from 197.61 crores to 760.88 crores in 1991-92. In total (plan+non-plan) expenditure on education at current prices is also consistently increasing from 210.98 crores to 793.66 crores in 1991-92.

The plan expenditure on education at current prices has showed increasing trend except in the year 1985-86. In which the plan expenditure on education is 11.17 crores it is less than the starting year. In 1980-81 it is 13.77 crores and reached to 18.20 crores in 1989-90. In between the highest expenditure is found in 1984-85 with 23.30 crores, followed by 20.45 crores in 1988-89. On the other hand, the non-plan expenditure on education has showed an increasing trend. It has started with 197.61 crores and reached to 269.06 crores in 1989-90. In total (plan+non-plan) is also increasing from 210.98 crores in 1980-81 and reached to 287.26 crores in 1989-90.

Over all observation of the table is that over a period the growth rate of plan expenditure is 10.57% and non-plan is 13.39 %. And at current prices the growth rate of plan expenditure is 1.11%, non-plan is 3.69%. In total, it is 3.52%.

Note : Rate of Growth (%) estimated on the basis of Semi-Log equation.

** Revised Estimate.

.. Data not available.

Source : www. Shikshanic.nic.in

Table reveals the plan and non-plan expenditure on education at current and constant prices for all sectors of education in the state of Tamil Nadu at 1980-81 prices. It is found from the table that the plan expenditure on education has showed an increasing and decreasing trend. In the year 1980-81 it was 20.55 crores and reached to 58.55 crores in 1991-92. The highest amount of 99.21 crores is found in 1989-90. It is found from the table that the growth rate of plan expenditure on education is 17.40 %. Whereas the non-plan expenditure on education has showed an increasing trend. It has started with 214.52 crores and reached to 1253.28 crores in 1991-92 with the growth rate of 16.75%. In total, the expenditure for education is also increasing consistently, from 235.07 crores to 1311.83

Table 5.13 Total Expenditure for All Sectors of Education at Current and Constant Prices In Tamil Nadu. At 1980-81 Prices.

(Rs. in Crores)

SL.No	Year	At Current Prices			At Constant Prices		
		Plan	*Non-Plan*	*Total*	*Plan*	*Non-Plan*	*Total*
1.	1980-81	20.55	214.52	235.07	20.55	214.52	235.07
2.	1981-82	24.74	239.50	264.24	22.84	221.12	243.96
3.	1982-83	40.57	297.76	338.33	34.86	255.82	290.67
4.	1983-84	31.46	339.58	371.04	24.59	265.37	289.96
5.	1984-85	46.10	388.46	434.56	34.62	291.73	326.35
6.	1985-86	51.64	473.98	525.62	35.53	326.11	361.64
7.	1986-87	55.08	475.32	530.40	34.55	298.16	332.71
8.	1987-88	70.30	607.01	677.31	40.07	346.02	386.09
9.	1988-89	74.88	693.78	768.66	42.31	392.03	434.34
10.	1989-90	99.21	943.75	1042.96	47.48	451.65	499.13
11.	1990-91	62.92	1198.99	1261.91	-	-	-
12.	1992-93**	5 8.55	1253.28	1311.83	-	-	-
Growth rate		17.40	16.75	16.80	8.59	7.99	8.03

crores in 1991-92 with growth rate of 16.80%.

The plan expenditure on education at current prices has increased with slight fluctuations. It was 20.55 crores in 1980-81 and reached to 47.48 crores in 1989-90. In addition, the overall growth is 8.59%. On the other hand the non-plan expenditure on education at current prices has consistently increased from 214.52 crores to 451.65 crores in 1989-90 with the growth rate of 7.99%. In total (plan +non-plan) expenditure on education at current prices increased from 235.07 crores to 499.13 crores in 1989-90 without fluctuations. The over all growth of total expenditure at current prices is 8.03%.

Conclusion

During the earlier period, the expenditure on education was very low. However, over a period of time the people, government and other agencies realised the importance of education. Everyone knows that without education it is difficult to achieve development. Therefore, the education expenditure has gone up at higher, which has been presented in the paper. At last one can say that concentration on primary education is the most important in underdeveloped and developed countries. Most of the population belong to very poor and poor categories.

Major Finding of the Study

Karnataka state has experienced rapid expansion in educational facilities as allocations and expenditure to education are increasing, but when the expenditureis compared with neighbouriong states, the position is not satisfactory. In all the neighbouring states the expenditure is substantially higher when compared with Karnataka.

Plan allocations to education in Karnataka are increasing. Overall trend indicates an increase in it which is also supported by the positive compound rate.The growth rate is 20.78 between 1981-82 to 1990-91 and 52.45 in post 1990 period.

Non plan allocations to education in Karnataka is increasing. It forms a significant proportion of total allocations to education sector. The overall trend indicates an increase in it which is also supported by the positive compound growth rate. It is 13.42 between 1993-94 between 1973-74 to 1982-83, 17.82 between 1983-84 to 1992-93 at 12.14 between 1993-94 to 1996-97.

Plan expenditure on education is also increasing. Trend indicates about it, compound growth rate is Rs. 0.20 to 0.25 which is higher in between 1981-82 to 1990-91 and 1991-92 to 1993-94.

Non plan expenditure on education is also increasing trend indicates about it.The compound growth rate is 13.36 between 1971-72 to 1981-82, 16.81 between 1982-83 to 1991-92 and 12.21 between 1992-93 to 1994-95.

The total allocations for education are increasing as NSDP is increasing both at current and constant prices with base year 1980-81. This is also supported by high rates of correlation coefficient between the two coefficient value is 0.9970 at current prices and constant prices 0.95.

The total allocation for education are increasing as GSDP is increasing both at current and constant prices with base year 1980-81. This is also supported by high rates correlation coefficient between the two, cofficient value is 0.99 at current and at constant prices 0.95.

The total expenditure for education are increasing as NSDP is increasing both at current and constant prices with base year 1980-81. This is also supported by high rates of correlation coefficient between the two, coefficient value is 0.99 at current prices and at the constant prices 0.96.

The total expenditure for education is increasing as GSDP is increasing both at current and constant prices with base year 1980-81. This is also supported by high rates of correlation coefficient between the two coefficient values at prices is 0.99 and at constant prices 0.96.

The allocation to education sectors optimally utilised as there is a very narrow gap between allocations and expenditure. That the percentage utilisation is 90 per cent which indicates that the educational plans are properly implemented.

The growing expenditure on education has the inflation bias in it as when the estimates are made at constant prices. The average increase in expenditure is quite low. When compared with the some figures at current prices. In the last 15 years the expenditure on education at current prices is ranged from 1047.36 to 15062.01 in 1994-95 and at constant prices 1047.36 to 2397.50 respectively. In growing at annual average rate of 2292.87 at current price but its growth at constant price is 128.91.

The total plan and non-plan allocations to education to education sector indicate that the substantial amount of resource transfer to educational sector has taken place. In 1951-52 total allocation for all sectors was 159301.41 whereas for education Rs. 308.96 lakhs which reached to Rs. 2456000.77 to all sectors and 197368.64 for education in 1996-97.

In the development process, the resource transfers to promote development in all the sectors is on increase. The plan and non-plan allocations to education also increasing. However the share of education has still remained below 10 per cent in all these years. In a developing economy like Karnataka larger resource transfers are required to develop manpower skills.

There is comparatively a higher growth in allocations and expenditure to educational sector than the actual growth in SDP both current and constant prices. This is indicated by index of education being more than that of SDP.

Index of expenditure (education) and allocation in 1960-61 is 100 and reached 11610.42 and 12437,58, in 1994-95. Whereas the index of NSDP at current and constant prices is 5116.48 and 399.41 in respective years.

The percentage variation in expenditure on education is higher than the percentage variation in NSDP. This indicates rapid fluctuations in expenditure on education. Which may be due to varying priorities assigned to education over the time period.

The elasticity of education to SDP is greater than one (1) this implies that expenditure on education is highly responsive to changes in NSDP.

Within the field of education-when sectoral observation are made it is observed that plan allocation on primary education is substantially higher than the other levels of education is substantially higher than the other levels of education with the percentage of 25.18 % during 1951-52 to 1996-97 respectively.

Within the field of education - where sectoral observations are made it is observed that though non-plan allocations on primary education is substantially higher than the other levels of education after 1990's rapid decrease is observed from 53.57 per cent to 50.02 per cent in 1996-97.

Within the field of education where sectoral observations are made it is observed that plan expenditure on primary education is substantially higher than the other level of education with the percentage of 28.86 per cent to 49.65 per cent during 1951-52 to 1994-95.

It is observed that non-plan expenditure on primary education is substantially is higher than the other levels of education with the percentage of 56.42 per cent in 1972-73 to 49.45 per cent in 1994-95.

The primary per capita educational expenditure is increasing rapidly from 188 in 1980-81 to 910 in 1994-95. This indicates, the determination of government to attain the universal primary education. It also indicates expansion in infrastructure for primary education.

Secondary education stands next in importance to primary education. However, its importance differs across the time period. After 90s the plan allocation to this level of education are average 20 per cent of total allocations.

The secondary education stands next in importance to primary education. However after 90s the non-plan allocation to this level of education is on the average 25 per cent of total allocation.

The secondary sectors stands next in importance to primary education. However, its importance differs across the time period. However after 90s the plan allocation to this level of education are average 27 per cent of total allocations.

University education was given varying importance over the time period. It was allocated (plan) a higher, total share ranging between 20 to 30 per cent of total plan allocations on education. However in post 90s the plan allocation to universityto university education have come down to single digit number percentage, i.e., less than 10 per cent (except 10.14%) in 1996-97.

The non-plan allocations for university education after the 90s has reached from 14.95 per cent is a higher in 1951-52 to 17.15 per cent in 1996-97.

University education was given varying importance over the time period. The expenditure was as higher. Total share ranging between 20 to 30 per cent of total plan expenditure on education. However, in post 90s it decreases to 11 per cent (except 14.64per cent) in 1990-91.

University education was given flexible importance over the time period. The expenditure was higher. The total share is also ranging between 20 to 30 per cent of total non-plan expenditure on education.However, in post 90s the non-plan expenditure on university education have increased from 14.95 per cent in 1951-52 to 18.24 per cent in 1994-95.

The plan allocation for the education sector is growing positively over a period of 45 years.However, the negative growth has been noticed from 1971-72 to 1980-81.

The plan expenditure is not growing on part with plan allocation. Plan allocation is higher than plan expenditure.

Non-plan allocation and non-plan expenditure are growing equally and it is a welcoming trend in the state.

One can notice the importance given to education sector.The compound growth of allocation to all sectors is lower than total allocation for education.The former is 11.01 and the latter it is 15.10 per cent per annum.

Expenditure for all sector from 1951-52 to 1960-61 is higher to expenditure on education. Even during 1991-92 to 1994-95 the same trend is noticed. However the overall growth rate is lower, i.e., 12.83 in case of all sectors and it is 16.26 per cent per annum for education.

In general the state government is giving greater importance to education but the utilisation is not upto the mark.

The following policy orientations are suggested:

It is found that educational expenditure in Andhra Pradesh, Kerala, Maharashtra and Tamil Nadu is more when compare to educational expenditure incurred in the state of Karnatka during 1993-94. But in Karnataka it was only 4.86 per cent of expenditure incurred on education during the same year, it is clearly shows that Karnataka state is lagging far behind when compared to neighbour states. Since there is lack of priority for educational expenditure. Such a trend would have a far reaching implications if no priority is given to educational expenditure return from education sector will be megre. Therefore, it should be increased keeping the incompleted tasks of education in view. Also, it has to be linked up with man power planning requirements and rates of return.

There is need for a perspective plan in education. Keeping long term requirements of education in view of total allocations and expenditure are to be worked out. It is necessary that Karnataka State Government must concentrate on the increase of financial allocations for all stages of education. It is financial source that alone strengthens the hands of academicians and economic planners to undertake progressive and constructive projects for the qualitative and quantitative education in the state. It is true that there is an increased trend, but this increase does not tune with demand and need of education sector.

There is a need to bring changes in the policy formulation itself. An economic policy should be designed in such a way that, manpower planning requirements and rate of return be channelised through productive education. There is a need for a perspective plan in education were the allocation and are to be worked out. It is necessary that Karnataka State Government are balanced in respect of view the long-term requirements of education.

It is found that the non-plan allocations as well as expenditure are more all through the year when ,compared to plan allocations and expenditure. It may be pointed out hear that, the plan expenditure includes the developmental projects which keep the sector active and to be a head. Therefore the policies are to be formulated in such a way that, the planned allocations must be spent during the same year and reach the targets fixed. There should not be ground for transmission of planned allocations and expenditure into non-plan allocation and expenditure under any circumstances. For this purpose there may be a commission similar to planning commission, to check whether allocation of funds for various schemes of education have been utilised or not before closing end of financial year.

It is interesting to note that, there is increase in the allocations and expenditure on education as there is increase in NSDPand GSDP which is supported by high rates of Coefficient of correlation. Therefore, it is a matter of common experience that, if human resource development is sought through education by providing adequate financial resources which will result in the increase of NSDP and GSDP.

The growing expenditure on education has the inflation basis in it as when the estimates are made at constant prices. The average increase in expenditure is quite low. Therefore any amount of increase in expenditure should be adequate of the price index of the current price. Otherwise quality suffers due to inflation.

It is observed too many fluctuations in the percentage of expenditure on education. The expenditure might have been arbitrary and have therefore not been related to any principle of manpower requirements of rates of return. This is not a sign of scientific and balanced planning of education in the state. Therefore, the fluctuation variations should be controlled by means of systematic approaches and time-bond strategies.

The state should have committee of economic experts including educational planners to evolve scientific strategies for the allocation of funds to different sectors in education based on their innovative project proposals for quality as well as qualitative improvements. For this purpose, directorates of different sectors in education should design developmental projects than new reporting the maintenance of the sector.

The study analyses that education sector has received less importance when compares to other sectorsin the state in terms of allocations of funds. Therefore, there is need to increase allocation of funds in equal proportion to other sectors.

The local governments should be reorganised and given more power and resources by levying educational cess and they should be compelled spend atlest 40 per cent of their revenue on education.

Suggestions for Further Study

1. As the present investigation was being conducted, a need for undertaking a few specific research studies relating to the field was felt. The suggestions for such studies are enumerated below under two categories.
   1. Studies that arise out of the limitations of the present investigation; and
   2. Studies that are related to the problem.

Studies Arising Out of the Limitations of the Present Investigation

1. The study may be conducted considering the investment and expenditure incurred by the private sector so as to know the share in the process of educating students at different levels.
2. A separate study mar be conducted to assess the retured securns out of the educational allocations and expenditure.
3. A comparative study be also taken up to know the financial allocations and expenditure during pre and post plan periods.
4. There is a need of a separate study to investigate the probable wastage if any with the allocations and expenditure of funds in the state.

Studies Related to the Problem

1. A study may be taken up to identify the reasons so to why educational expenditure did not keep pace with the increase of the total expenditure in the state.
2. The relationship of the educational expenditure and its accountability in terms of progress of education in different sectors may be found out.
3. A similar study on educational allocations and expenditure contributed by the panchayat raj system viz. Zilla Panchayats Taluk panchayats and village panchayats could be taken up.
4. The method of financial planning and financial administration for education in Karnataka may be studied.
5. The economics of disproportionate allocations for education in Karnataka may be studied.
6. A scientific study, could be taken up so as to investigate the reasons why allocations made in a particular period have not been fully utilised.

6

Expenditure on Education in India: An Over View

The development of Indias vast human resource potential is the essence of the social sector development strategy being followed in the country. Significant progress has been made over the years in human resource development which is reflected in improved demographic indicators, health care services, progress in the field of education and adult literacy levels. The Approach Paper to the Tenth Five Year Plan (2002-07) which outlines a strategy to achieve a GDP growth rate of 8 per cent, has a specific focus on human resource development. The Approach Paper stipulates that economic growth expressed in terms of increases in GDP or per capita income should be accompanied by a broader Enhancement of human well being and quality of life. This includes not only an adequate level of consumption of food and other consumer goods but also access to basic social services, especially education, health, drinking water and sanitation. It also includes the expansion of economic and social opportunities for all individuals and groups, reduction in disparities and a greater participation in the decision making process. The attainment of monitorable targets given below, set out in this regard not only necessitates a substantial allocation of resources for the social sectors but also involves an enhanced role for the government in the provision of social services and rural infrastructure, road development, etc.

Monitorable Targets for the Tenth Plan and Beyond

1. Reduction of poverty ratio by 5 percentage points by 2007 and by 15 percentage points by 2012;
2. Providing gainful high-quality employment as addition to the labour force over the Tenth Plan period;

3. All children have to be in school by 2003; all children to complete at least 5 years of schooling by 2007;
4. Reduction of gender gaps in literacy and wage rates by at least 50 per cent by 2007;
5. Reduction in the decadal rate of population growth between 2001 and 2011 to 16.2 per cent;
6. Increase in Literacy rate to 75 per cent within the Plan Period;
7. Reduction of infant mortality rate (IMR) to 45 per 1000 live births by 2007 and to 28 by 2012;
8. Reduction of Maternal mortality ratio (MMR) to 2 per 1000 live births by 2007 and to 1 by 2012;
9. Increase in forest and tree cover to 25 per cent by 2007 and 33 per cent by 2012;
10. All villages to have sustained access to potable drinking water within the Plan Period;
11. Cleaning of major polluted rivers by 2007 and other notified stretches by 2012.

Thus, in India, education occupies a very significant role in each and every of the government attempt since independence, India has achieved substantial progress in the field of education. The number of recognized educational institutions has increased more than three-fold and student enrolments at various levels of education have multiplied approximately six-fold. However, adult literacy levels in India remain very low: 44.3 per cent of India's adult population is illiterate, compared with an average of 27.6 per cent for all developing countries and 8.9 per cent in the fellow SAARC country Sri Lanka. India's overall youth literacy rate at 70.9 per cent also falls short of the average for all developing countries (84.1 per cent).

Over the years, India has expanded its effort to enhance the knowledge of its population. It has increased its public spending on education as a portion of its GNP from 3 per cent in 1980 to 3.2 per cent in 1997. Nonetheless, the expenditure seems inadequate relative to the average amount spent in developing nations (3.8 per cent) and other countries in the medium human development category (4.1 per cent).

Net enrolment rates at the primary level has increased from 65 per cent in 1980 to 77 per cent in 1997, and from 41 per cent to 60 per cent at the secondary level over the same period. However, stark disparities between genders as well as among ethnic groups exist in educational opportunity and achievement. The adult literacy rate is 67.1 per cent among men, 43.5 per cent among women, and as low as 4 per cent among some ethnic tribes in states such as Rajasthan. The combined primary, secondary and tertiary gross enrolment rate is 61 per cent for males and 46 per cent for females. However, there has been notable progress in attempting to bridge these gaps. For instance, the proportion of female teachers in primary schools has increased from 26 per cent in 1980 to 33 per cent in 1996, accompanied by a corresponding increment in the rate of girls' enrolment from 39 per cent in 1980 to 43 per cent in 1996. Limited employment opportunities and lower market returns for women are believed to discourage parents of girls from investing in education. This has given in the below table.

Table 6.1

Indicatorwise Distribution of Literacy and Expenditure on Education

Sl.No.	*Indicator*	*India*
1.	Adult literacy rate (%), 1998	
	Female	43.5
	Male	67.1
2.	Public Expenditure on Education	
	1980	3.0
	1997	3.2
3.	Expenditure per Student	
	(per centGNP Per Capita) Primary	
	1980	10.5
	1997	11.4
	Tertiary	
	1980	88.2
	1997	99.8
4.	Combined Primary,Secondary and Tertiary Gross Enrolment Ratio 1998	54
5.	Duration of Primary Education (Years)	8
6.	Teachers-Student Ratio,1997	1.64

Source : World Bank World Development Indicators, 2000; UNDO Human Development Report 2000.

Financing of Education

From 1968 onwards, goal has been to set apart 6 per cent of National Income on education. In spite of resource constraints as well as competing priorities, the Budgetary expenditure on education by Centre and States as percentage of Gross National Product has steadily increased from 0.8 per cent in 1951-52 to 3.3 per cent in 1994-95.

Para 11.4 of NPE, 1986 states "that the investment on education be gradually increased to reach a level of 6 per cent of the National Income as early as possible. Since the actual level of investment has remained far short of that target, it is important that greater determination is shown now to find the funds for the programmes laid down in this policy. While actual requirements will be computed from time to time on the basis of monitoring and review, the outlay on education will be stepped up to ensure that during the Eighth Five Year Plan and onwards it will uniformly exceed 6 per cent of the national income". The total budgetary expenditure on education by the Education Departments of the Centre and States has increased from Rs. 644.6 millions in 1951-52 to Rs. 300,000 millions in 1995-96. In terms of its share in total budgetary expenditure, it has increased from 7.9 per cent in 1951-52 to 11.1 per cent in 1995-96.

There are, at present 130 plan schemes in the department with a total Eighth Plan outlay of Rs. 74430 millions. The total plan outlay of the Department for the year 1996-97 is Rs. 33827 millions. There are 18 Centrally Sponsored Schemes which account for 65.7 per cent of the total plan outlay. Mid-Day-Meal Scheme is the major Centrally Sponsored Scheme with 1996-97 outlay of Rs. 14,000 millions. Other major Centrally Sponsored Schemes are Operation Blackboard, Non-formal Education, Teacher Education, Post Literacy and Continuing Education and Vocational Education with 1996-97 Outlay of Rs. 2790 millions, Rs. 1582.5 millions, Rs. 1170 millions, Rs. 755 millions and Rs. 820 millions respectively.

Table 6.1 shows the estimated illiteracy rate and illiterate population aged 15 years and above in India, interms of percentage and population in thousands. In 1990 in total there are 279006 illiterate people in this country. Among the total male population consists of 105054 and female is 173952. Whereas percentage of illiterate population is 51.5 per cent in total. Out of the total male illiterates is 37.6 per cent and female is 66.5 per cent with the age of 15 years and above. Which clearly shows that there is a need on the part of government, planners and policy makers to cut down the percentage of illiterate population of the country. Even after the 50 years of Indias independence, i.e. in the year 2000 the estimated illiteracy rate is 44.2 per cent in total. Out of the total male is 31.4 per cent and female is 57.9 per cent.

It is revealed from the above table that over a period of 10 years, i.e., from 1990-2000, only 7.3 per cent of illiteracy rate has come down. The male illiteracy is just 6.2 per cent and female illiteracy is 8.6 per cent is increased.

Thus from the above table it is necessary to concentrate on the educational expenditure in order to reduce rate of illiteracy in India. Due to the high rate of illiteracy, Central government and the state governments have been allocating more budgets for education for the improvement in all sectors of education.

Table 6.2

Estimated Illiteracy Rate and Illiterate Population Aged 15 Years and Above

Sl.No	*Year of Survey*	*Age*	*Illiteracy Rate (%)*			*Illiterate Population (000)*		
			Total	*Male*	*Female*	*Total*	*Male*	*Female*
1.	1990	15+	51.5	37.6	66.5	279006	105054	173952
2.	2000	15+	44.2	31.4	57.9	299327	109681	189645

Source: www.education.org

Table 6.3

Expenditure on Education by Education Department (Revenue Account) As Percentage to Total State Budget

(Rs in Lakhs)

Sl.No.	Year	% Of Edu.Exp.To State/Union Territories	Total Bud. Centre	Grand Total 7.92
1.	1951-52	14.75	1.01	8.42
2.	1952-53	15.42	0.81	8.81
3.	1953-54	15.54	1.02	9.84
4.	1954-55	16.20	2.14	10.65
5.	1955-56	16.53	2.96	11.48
6.	1956-57	17.78	3.74	10.61
7.	1957-58	18.17	2.97	10.90
8.	1958-59	18.04	3.55	11.73
9.	1959-60	18.65	4.30	11.99
10.	1960-61	18.81	4.58	11.70
11.	1961-62	19.96	2.47	9.47
12.	1962-63	18.51	1.78	9.00
13.	1963-64	18.45	1.56	9.60
14.	1964-65	18.82	1.98	9.82
15.	1965-66	18.55	2.11	9.56
16.	1966-67	18.08	2.02	10.55
17.	1967-68	19.84	2.11	9.38
18.	1968-69	22.01	1.06	9.61
19.	1969-70	20.74	1.23	10.16
20.	1970-71	21.39	1.34	9.38
21.	1971-72	20.31	1.19	9.51
22.	1972-73	20.14	1.31	9.89
23.	1973-74	20.57	1.11	10.53
24.	1974-75	23.22	1.20	10.07
25.	1975-76	22.37	1.21	9.70
26.	1976-77	22.49	1.17	9.95
27.	1977-78	22.74	1.14	9.80
28.	1978-79	21.65	1.36	9.28
29.	1979-80	20.52	1.16	9.27
30.	1980-81	20.59	1.06	9.09

Contd.

Sl.No.	*Year*	*% Of Edu.Exp.To State/Union Territories*	*Total Bud. Centre*	*Grand Total 7.92*
31.	1981-82	20.03	1.00	9.57
32.	1982-83	21.28	1.05	8.81
33.	1983-84	20.75	0.95	9.32
34.	1984-85	20.46	1.12	11.11
35.	1985-86	20.55	1.58	10.50
36.	1986-87	19.82	1.58	11.27
37.	1987-88	19.99	2.59	11.54
38.	1988-89	20.24	2.95	11.94
39.	1989-90	21.88	2.35	7.93
40.	1990-91	10.86	2.24	11.01
41.	1991-92	19.35	2.08	11.11
42.	1992-93	20.06	1.92	11.46
43.	1993-94	20.36	2.12	-

Source : Budgetary resource for Education, Dept. of Education, Ministry of Human Resource Development, New Delhi.

Table 6.4 intends to analyse the expenditure on education by education department (Revenue Account) as percentage to total state budget.

It is evident from the table that over period the educational expenditure for all sectors by the states and union territories has increased with fluctuations. It has started with 14.75 lakhs in 1951-52 and reached to Rs. 20.36 lakhs in 1993-94. In between lakhs has been spent for education in the year 1974-75, followed by Rs. 22.74 lakhs in 1997-98, Rs. 22.49 lakhs in 1976-77 and Rs. 22.37 lakhs in 1975-76. And the lowest amount of Rs. 10.86 lakhs was spent for education in the year 1990-91.

The expenditure for education for all sectors by the central government with Rs. 1.01 lakhs in the year 1951-52 and reached to the Rs. 2.12 lakhs in 1993-94. In between there exists fluctuations. The highest amount of 4.58 lakhs were spent on education in the year 1960-61, followed by Rs. 4.30 lakhs in 1959-60. And the lowest amount of Rs. 0.81 lakhs in 1952-53 and Rs. 0.95 lakhs in 1983-84 are found. The expenditure by the central government is relatively lesser than state and union territories. It is because, education is being managed by the states and respective union territories with assistance of central government.

The total expenditure of states, union territories and centre on education has started with Rs. 7.92 lakhs in the year 1951-52 and reached to Rs. 11.46 lakhs in 1993-94. The trend showed that an increasing attitude on educational expenditure. It is found from the table that the highest amount of Rs. 11.99 lakhs in 1961-61 followed by Rs. 11.94 lakhs in 1989-90, Rs. 11.73 lakhs during 1959-60 and RS 11.70 lakhs during 61-62. And the lowest amount of Rs. 7.92 is found in the beginning year, i.e., 1951-52. The over all finding of the table shows that the total expenditure on education is between 7 to 12 lakhs.

Table 6.4

Expenditure on Education by Education Department (Revenue Account) As Percentage to Total State Domestic Product (SDP)

Sl.No	*Year*	*% of Edu. Exp.To State/Union Territories*	*SDP Centre*	*Grand Total*
1.	1951-52	-	-	0.68
2.	1952-53	-	-	0.77
3.	1953-54	-	-	0.79
4.	1954-55	-	-	1.01
5.	1955-56	-	-	1.22
6.	1956-57	-	-	1.15
7.	1957-58	-	-	1.27
8.	1958-59	-	-	1.31
9.	1959-60	-	-	1.50
10.	1960-61	-	-	1.58
11.	1961-62	-	-	1.63
12.	1962-63	-	-	1.63
13.	1963-64	-	-	1.61
14.	1964-65	-	-	1.62
15.	1965-66	-	-	1.81
16.	1966-67	-	-	1.80
17.	1967-68	-	-	1.86

Contd.

Contd.

Sl.No.	*Year*	*per cent of Edu.Exp.To State/Union Territories*	*Center*	*SDP Grand Total*
18.	1968-69	-	-	1.93
19.	1969-70	-	-	2.05
20.	1970-71	-	-	2.26
21.	1971-72	-	-	2.37
22.	1972-73	-	-	2.44
23.	1973-74	-	-	2.25
24.	1974-75	-	-	2.31
25.	1975-76	-	-	2.55
26.	1976-77	-	-	2.60
27.	1977-78	-	-	2.59
28.	1978-79	-	-	2.73
29.	1979-80	-	-	2.80
30.	1980-81	-	-	2.75
31.	1981-82	-	-	2.65
32.	1982-83	-	-	3.00
33.	1983-84	-	-	2.94
34.	1984-85	-	-	3.11
35.	1985-86	-	-	3.21
36.	1986-87	-	-	3.27
37.	1987-88	-	-	3.57
38.	1988-89	-	-	3.56
39.	1989-90	-	-	3.76
40.	1990-91	-	-	3.69
41.	1991-92	-	-	3.47
42.	1992-93	-	-	3.47
43.	1993-94	-	-	-

Source : Budgetary Resource for Education, Dept. of Education, Ministry of Human Resource Development, New Delhi.

Table 6.5
Percentage Expenditure on each Subsection of Education to Total Expenditure on Education (Revenue Account) by Central Government

Sl.No	*Year*	*Elementary*	*Secondary*	*Adult*	*Technical*	*University/Higher*	*Other*	*Total*
1.	1951-52	18.66	26.22	4.18	-	22.31	28.63	100.00
2.	1952-53	4.81	9.05	4.15	-	31.38	50.61	100.00
3.	1953-54	5.65	5.79	3.03	-	21.62	64.91	100.00
4.	1954-55	2.29	2.38	1.84	-	10.91	82.58	100.00
5.	1955-56	1.79	1.46	1.40	-	19.61	75.77	100.00
6.	1956-57	3.95	4.95	1.24	-	18.58	71.27	100.00
7.	1957-58	4.17	7.17	3.92	-	17.41	67.33	100.00
8.	1958-59	1.51	4.55	4.06	-	23.17	66.71	100.00
9.	1959-60	1.43	3.28	0.63	-	23.15	71.50	100.00
10.	1960-61	1.12	2.50	0.57	-	19.34	76.47	100.00
11.	1961-62	4.53	10.18	0.91	-	44.06	40.32	100.00
12.	1962-63	4.98	10.53	0.85	-	39.10	44.54	100.00
13.	1963-64	5.04	9.59	0.19	-	39.11	46.07	100.00
14.	1964-65	2.67	7.77	0.03	32.23	33.94	23.36	100.00
15.	1965-66	2.36	7.19	0.03	30.76	36.02	23.64	100.00
16.	1966-67	4.00	11.65	0.08	30.80	33.91	19.55	100.00
17.	1967-68	3.72	11.00	0.13	31.74	33.06	20.36	100.00

Contd.

Contd.

Sl.No	Year	Elementary	Secondary	Adult	Technical	University/Higher	Other	Total
18.	1968-69	-	1.09	-	22.71	48.40	27.80	100.00
19.	1969-70	-	0.87	-	29.16	45.92	24.05	100.00
20.	1970-71	-	0.85	-	25.31	49.20	24.64	100.00
21.	1971-72	-	0.68	-	28.77	47.10	23.45	100.00
22.	1972-73	-	0.71	-	25.47	44.62	29.19	100.00
23.	1973-74	-	8.95	2.92	26.07	46.62	15.44	100.00
24.	1974-75	-	9.26	2.85	24.25	50.31	13.33	100.00
25.	1975-76	-	9.00	2.86	25.24	50.74	12.16	100.00
26.	1976-77	-	10.55	2.76	22.35	52.18	12.16	100.00
27.	1977-78	-	11.02	2.99	23.62	54.03	8.34	100.00
28.	1978-79	-	9.07	2.89	21.51	43.94	22.58	100.00
29.	1979-80	-	9.51	11.52	19.87	45.45	13.65	100.00
30.	1980-81	3.99	9.22	3.40	22.16	44.11	17.11	100.00
31.	1981-82	4.42	9.82	4.24	24.23	45.56	11.72	100.00
32.	1982-83	7.59	11.07	5.33	24.70	41.69	9.61	100.00
33.	1983-84	6.66	12.18	7.58	22.71	40.03	10.83	100.00

Contd.

Contd.

Sl.No	*Year*	*Elementary*	*Secondary*	*Adult*	*Technical*	*University/Higher*	*Other*	*Total*
34.	1984-85	6.47	11.86	2.05	22.72	40.67	16.22	100.00
35.	1985-86	4.49	15.41	7.90	28.27	38.96	4.98	100.00
36.	1986-87	5.11	20.13	7.01	23.55	39.05	5.14	100.00
37.	1987-88	17.75	20.35	4.90	21.92	27.45	7.62	100.00
38.	1988-89	15.02	19.58	5.44	17.68	35.26	7.01	100.00
39.	1989-90	14.35	20.99	6.02	18.43	32.16	8.06	100.00
40.	1990-91	13.74	23.52	8.26	18.74	28.94	6.81	100.00
41.	1991-92	16.50	23.77	6.07	18.43	28.92	6.31	100.00
42.	1992-93	18.79	25.01	6.29	18.76	27.68	3.46	100.00
43.	1993-94	20.76	26.19	8.36	18.57	22.98	3.14	100.00

Source: Budgetary resource for Education ,Dept of Education. Ministry of Human resource Development. New Delhi.

(Contd.)

Table 6.4 indicate the expenditure by education department (Revenue Account) as percentage to total state domestic product (SDP) by states, union territories and central government. It indicates that with fluctuations an increasing and decreasing trends ranging between Rs. 0.68 lakhs during 1951-52 to Rs. 3.76 lakhs during 1989-90. It is evident from the table that the increasing trend is found from 1951-52 to 1972-73 with Rs. 0.68 lakhs to Rs. 2.44 lakhs. From the 1974-75 there exists fluctuations with increasing and decreasing trends.

Table 6.5 shows the percentage expenditure on education on each subsector of education to total expenditure on education (Revenue Account) by the central government. It is found from the table that central Government has given more emphasis on University/Higher education. The central government started to spend on higher/university education along with the other sectors of education, i.e., primary, secondary, adult, technical and other. For university education the central government has spent 22.31 per cent in 1951-52 and reached to 22.98 per cent in 1993-94. In between, the highest percentage of 50.74 per cent in 19745-76, followed by 50.31 per cent in 1974-75 is found. Moreover, the lowest percentage of expenditure on university/higher education is found in 1954-55 with 10.91 per cent.

After university education, second emphasis has given to technical education. It has started to spent on technical education from 1964-65 onwards. Further, it showed that the percentage of expenditure on technical education only the decreasing trend. It has started with 32.23 per cent in 1964-65 and reached to 18.57 per cent in 1993-94.

On the other hand, central government paid less attention on elementary and secondary education. From 1968-69 to 1979-80 the percentage of expenditure on education is nil. Whereas the percentage of expenditure on secondary education showed stagnation. It has started with 26.22 per cent in 1951-52 and reached to 26.19 per cent in 1993-94. In between the lowest percentage of 0.71 per cent is found in 1972-73. Which shows that, elementary and secondary education have become the responsibility of respective states and union territories. On the other hand, higher/university and technical education have become the responsibiliy of the central government.

Table 6.6

Educational Expenditure as Percentage of GDP

Sl.No	*Year*	*GDP (Rs. Crores)*	*Educational Expenditure (Crores)*	*Educational Expenditure as Percentage of GDP*
1.	1950-51	8979	114	1.27
2.	1960-61	15254	344	2.26
3.	1970-71	39708	1118	2.82
4.	1975-76	71201	2105	2.96
5.	1980-81	122427	3641	2.97
6.	1985-86	233799	7457	3.19
7.	1986-87	260030	8450	3.25
8.	1987-88	294851	10430	3.54
9.	1988-89	352706	12409	3.52
10.	1989-90	408662	15292	3.74
11.	1990-91	477814	20761	4.3
12.	1991-92	552768	22639	4.10
13.	1992-93	630772	25303	4.01
14.	1993-94	732874	28599	3.90
15.	1994-95	868019	32875	3.79
16.	1995-96	1006286	39299(R.E)	3.91
17.	1996-97	1149215	43723(B.E)	3.80

Note : R.E. Revised Estimates B.E. Budget Estimate GDP: Gross Domestic Product.

Source : 1. Central Statistical Organisation, National Accounts Statistics – 1998.

2. Ministry of Human Resource Development.

Table 5 reveals the expenditure for education as percentage of Gross Domestic Product (GDP) by states, union territories and central governments. The expenditure for education is consistently increasing from Rs. 114 crores in 1950-51 to Rs. 43.723 crores of budget estimates in 1996-97. The GDP of the country is also consistently increasing from

Rs. 8979 crores to Rs. 1,149,215 crores in 1996-97. It is revealed from the table that as GDP goes on increasing the expenditure for education is also increasing.

The educational expenditure as percentage of GDP is increasing with fluctuations. The highest percentage of 4.34 is found in 1990-91, followed by 4.10 per cent in 1991-92 and 4.01 per cent in 1992-93. The lowest percentage of 1.27 per cent is found in 1950-51.

Table 6 reveals the average annual cost per student by type of institutions at all India level. It is found in the table that the average annual cost per student has been calculated at decades. The average annual cost per student on primary schools is ranged from rupees 19.5 in 1950-51 to rupees 407.0 in 1989-90. It is evident from the table that there is an increasing trend on the primary school institutions.

Table 6.7

Average Annual Cost Per Student by Type of Institution

Sl. No	*Year*	*Primary*	*Middle*	*Higher/Hr Secondary*	*Colleges for General Education*
1.	1950-51	19.5	31.8	73.4	225.1
2.	1960-61	27.6	40.5	91.8	302.4
3.	1970-71	57.0	84.9	168.6	421.6
4.	1980-81	164.2	200.0	427.6	1031.7
5.	1985-86	262.7	344.3	654.0	1257.7
6.	1986-87	327.7	400.0	730.3	1324.0
7.	1987-88	332.6	418.9	780.1	NA
8.	1988-89	352.8	466.5	785.2	NA
9.	1989-90	407.0	550.0	939.3*	NA

* Includes Intermediate

Source: Ministry of Human Resource Development, Education in India, vol. II (S), 1989-90.

The average annual cost per student on middle schools is also showed increasing trend. It has started with Rs. 31.8 in 1950-51 and reached to Rs. 550.0 in 1989-90.

On the higher and secondary institutions The average annual cost per student has also showed increasing trend from Rs. 73.4 in

1950-51 and reached to Rs. 939.3 in 1989-90. Whereas on the college and general educations, the average annual cost per student is showed an increasing trend. It has started with Rs. 225.1 in 1950-51 and reached to Rs. 1324.0 in 1986-87.

Table 6.8
International Comparison of Public Expenditure on Education

Sl.No	*Countries*	*Year*	*% of GNP*	*% of Total Governmental Expenditure*
1.	Canada	1994	6.9	12.9
2.	Mexico	1995	4.9	23.0
3.	U.S.	1994	5.4	14.4
4.	Brazil	1995	5.1	-
5.	Brunei Darussalam	1990	2.5	
6.	China	1996	2.3	-
7.	Hong Kong	1995	2.9	-
8.	India	1996	3.2	-
9.	Indonesia	1996	1.4	7.9
10.	Japan	1994	3.6	9.9
11.	Korea	1995	3.7	17.5
12.	Malaysia	1997	4.9	-
13.	Philippines	1997	3.4	15.7
14.	Singapore	1995	3.0	23.4
15.	Thailand	1996	4.8	-
16.	Austria	1996	5.4	10.4
17.	Belgium	1996	3.1	6.0
18.	Denmark	1996	8.1	-
19.	Finland	1996	7.5	12.2
20.	France	1996	6.0	10.9
21.	Germany	1996	4.8	9.6
22.	Ireland	1996	6.0	-
23.	Italy	1996	4.9	9.1
24.	Netherlands	1996	5.1	9.8
25.	Norway	1996	7.4	15.8
26.	Sweden	1996	8.3	12.2
27.	Switzerland	1996	5.4	15.4
28.	United Kingdom	1995	5.3	11.6
29.	Australia	1995	5.5	13.5

30.	New Zealand	1996	7.3	-
31.	Russia	1995	3.5	-

Source: UNESCO Statistical Year Book 1999 Edition. UNESCO (April 25,2000).

Table 7 reveals the international comparison of public expenditure on education as percentage of GNP and percentage of total governmental expenditure for education.

It is evident from the table that the public expenditure on education as percentage of GNP is ranged between 1.4 per cent to 8.3 per cent from 1990-1996, which nearly compare about 35 countries. The highest percentage of educational expenditure as percentage of GNP is 8.3 per cent in Sweden in the year 1996, followed by 8.1 per cent in Denmark in the year 1996, 7.5 per cent in Finland in the year 1996, 7.4 per cent in Norway in 1996 and 7.3 per cent in New Zealand in 1996. The highest amount of expenditure on education as percentage to GNP is 1.4 per cent in Indonesia in 1996, followed by 2.3 per cent in China in 1996.

Over all the comparison of the table reveals that India stands just above the countries, which falls on the lowest expenditure on education as percentage to GNP. i.e., at third place with 3.2 per cent in 1996.

The above table also intends to identify the percentage of educational expenditure to the total expenditure at the international countries. The highest percentage of educational expenditure to the total expenditure is found in Norway in 1996 with 15.8 per cent, followed by Korea in the year 1995 with 17.5 per cent, Philippines with 15.7 per cent in the year 1997, Switzerland with 15.4 per cent in 1996 and Brazil with 14.4 per cent in 1996. And the lowest amount as percentage to total expenditure is found in Belgium with 6.0 per cent in 1996, followed by Indonesia with 7.9 per cent in 1996.

Bibliography

Abu Baker, M., *The Union and the States in Education: A Study in Educational Finance and Planning,* Shabad Sanchar, New Delhi, 1976.

Aggrawal, J.C. *The Progress of Education in Free India,* Agra Book Depot, New Delhi, 1996.

Aggrawal, J.C. *Educational Research in Introducation,* Agra Book Depot, New Delhi, 1996.

Aher, H., *"Critical Analysis of University Finances in Maharashtra",* Buch,M.B., (Ed.)Fourth Survey of Research in Education 1983-88, Vol.1, New Delhi; NCERT, 1991.

Aijay, R.,Mattoo, *Management of Price Fluctuations,* Anmon Publications, New Delhi, 1990.

Anderson, J.et al., *Thesis and Assignment Writting :* Wiley Earborn Limited, New Delhi, 1881.

Ashok Kumar, *Current Trends in Indian Education,* Ashish Publishing House, New Delhi, 1981.

Azad, J.L., *" Financing of Higher Education in India",* Sterling Publisher Pvt. Ltd., New Delhi, 1975.

Backe, S. Garry, *Human Capital,* New York: Columbia University Press, 1964.

Barr, A.S. and Others, *Educational Research and Appraisal,* J.B. Lippincott Company, New York, 1953.

Bert J. Ward Khan J.V. *Research in Education* (Sixth Edition): New Delhi:Prentice Hall of India Private Limited, 1989.

Bhaskar, V.V., *"Management of Higher Education: Financing of Universities and Resources Allocation",* Paper presented at the Second International Conference of Registrars/University Administrators held in Hong Kong, Aug. 3-Sept. 4, 1982.

Blaug, M.(Ed.), *Economics of Education,* London : Penguin Books Ltd.,1978.

Buch M.B., (Ed.) *Fourth Survey of Research in Education* 1983-88, Vol. 1, NCERT, New Delhi, 1991.

Cambell W.G. al. Forms Style : *Thesis, Reports, Term Papers.* (Seventh Edition) Boston; Haugton Miflin company, 1986.

Chalam, K.S. *"Expenditure on University Education* : A Unit Cost Analysis", *Journal of Higher Education,* Vol. 4 (2), Autumn 1978.

Chaube, S.P.*History and Problems of Indian Education,* Vinod Pustak Mandir, Agra, 1980.

Chaudhri, D.P., *"A Crucial Input in Indian Agricultural Development",* Social Change, Vol.1, August, 1971.

Chaudhri, D.P. *Education and Agricultural Productivity in India,* Unpublished Ph.D.Thesis, Delhi University, 1968, in Jandhyala B.G.Tilak,"Approaches to Educational Planning and the applications in India", *The India Economic Journal,* Vol. 24(3), January-March , 1977.

Chauhan, C.P.S., *Higher Education in India,* Ashish Publishing House, New Delhi, 1990.

Choch, B.N. *Scientific Method and Social Research,* Sterling Publishers, New Delhi, 1982.

Department of Education, *Budgetary Resources for Education* 1951-52 to 1993-94, Ministry of Human Resource Development, New Delhi, 1995.

Desai, D.M. *Universal, Compulsory and Free Primary Education in India, Indian* Institute of Education, Bombay, 1853.

Dissertation abstract international : *The Humanities and Social Sciences,* University microfilms international, Michigan, volume 5 number 5, November 1996.

Ibid., Volume -51, Number 5, November 1990.

Ibid., Volume -50, Number 5, November 1989.

Ibid., Volume - 50, Number 9, March 1990.

Ibid., Volume -50, Number 6, December 1989.

Ibid., Volume -50, Number 8, February 1990.

Ibid., Volume -49, Number 9, March 1989.

Ibid., Volume -55, Number 11, May 1995.

Ibid., Volume -50, Number 2, August 1995.

Ibid., Volume -52, Number 3, September 1991.

Ibid., Volume -52, Number 6, December 1991.

Ibid., Volume -55, Number 12, January 1995.

Ibid., Volume -52, Number 4, October 1991.

Ibid., Volume -51, Number 4, October 1990.

Ibid., Volume -56, Number 5, November 1995.

Ibid., Volume -56, Number 4, October 1995.

Ibid., Volume -55, Number 8, February 1995.

Ibid., Volume -56, Number 6, December 1995.

Ibid., Volume -52, Number 9, March 1992.

Ibid., Volume -55, Number 10, April 1995.

Ibid., Volume -55, Number 9, March 1995.

Ibid., Volume -55, Number 7, January 1995.

Ibid., Volume -56, Number 3, September 1995.

Ibid., Volume -56, Number 1, July 1995.

The Cause of India in Education and Economic Development, Aldini Pub Co. Chicago, 1963.

Harbison, F. and C.A. Myers, *Education, Manpower and Economic Growth,* Oxford & IBH Pub Co. New Delhi, 1964.

Hayavadana Rao C. (ed.) *Mysore Gazetter (Compiled for Government), Vol. IV (Administrative),* New Education, 1929, Printed at the Government Press, Bangalore.

Hemalata Rao, *Centre State Financial Relations, Criteria of Federal Fiscal transfers and their application in India.* Allied Publishers Private Limited, New Delhi, 1981.

Heyneman, Stephen, P., *Investment in Indian Education: Uneconomic ?* World Bank Staff Working Paper, No. 327, World Bank, Washington DC, May 1979.

Houthakker, H.S., "*Education and Income", Review of Economics and Statistics,* Vol. 41(1)Table 3, p. 26, February 1959.

Jena, S.L., "*University Finance : A Case Study of the Maharaja Sayajirao University of Baroda*", Buch, M.B.(Ed) *Fourth Survey of Research in Education 1983-88,* Vol.1, New Delhi : NCERT 1991.

Khajapeer, M., "*Financing of Education in India*", Unpublished, Bangalore, 1982.

Kothari, C.A., *Research Methology-Methods and Techniques (Second Edition),* Wiley Earpron Limited, New Delhi, 1990.

Koul, Lokesh, *Methodology of Educational Research (Second Edition),* Vilkas Publishing House Private Limited, New Delhi, 1988.

Lakshmidevamma, V., " *A Critical Analysis of Outlays and Expenditure on Education during the Plan period*" , Unpublished M.Ed., Dissertation, Bangalore University, Bangalore, May 1982.

Lathamma, T., "*Progress of Women's Education in the state of Karnataka from 1946-47 to 1979-80*, Bangalore, Unpublished M.Ed.,

Dissertation, Bangalore University, Bangalore, December 1984.

Lerner, Daniel, *The Passing of Traditional Society : The Role of Mass Media in Modernizing the Middle East,* Glencol : The Free Press, 1962.

————, "*Towards a communication Theory on Modernization,*" , cited in Lucian W.Pye (Ed.)Communications and Political Development, Princeton, New Jersey, Princeton University Press, 1963.

Lockheed, ME., Januson, D.T. and L. J. Lau, Farmer, *Education and Farm Efficiency : A Survey,* Washington D.C. The World Bank, October, 1980.

Malyarov. O.V., *The Role of the State in the Socio-economic Structure of India*, Vikas Publishing House, Pvt. Ltd., 1983.

Mathur, M.V., *A Study in Costs of Education in India During the period 1951-61, Unpublished Ph.D.Thesis in Education*, Rajasthan University, 1968.

Mehrotra L.P. and Mehrotra K., *First Course in Educational and statisties.* Allahabad, 1954.

Milton Friedman, Price Theory : *A Provisional Text, Kalyani Publishers,* New Delhi, 1988.

Ministry of Education and Culture, *Government of India, Expenditure on Education as Shown in Central and State Annual Budgets* 1977-78 to 1979-80, New Delhi,1980

————, *Selected Educational Statistics,* 1980-81, New Delhi, 1982.

————, *Trends of Expenditure on Education* 1968-69 -1978-79, New Delhi, 1980.

Ministry of Education and Social Welfare, *Government of India, Report of the Secondary Education Commission* (1952-53), Seventh Reprint, New Delhi, May 1972.

————, *Enrolment Trends in the States*, 1968-69 - 1978-79, Government of Misra, Atmanada, The financing if Indian Education, Asia Publishing House, Bombay, 1967.

Misra, Atmananda, *The Financial of Indian Education*, Asia Publishing House, Bombay, 1986.

Moonis Raza, *Educational Planning, Concept Publishing Company*, New Delhi, 1986.

Mukerji, K., and Krishnarao, N.,"*An Empirical Investigation of the Relationship between Education and Economic Development in India between 1951-61*", cited in Baljit Singh (ed.), Education as Investment, Delhi, Meenakshi Prakashan, 1967.

Murthy Sreenivasa, H.V., and Ramakrishnan R., *A History of Karnataka (from the Earliest Times to the Present Day)*, S. Chand and Co. Ltd., New Delhi,1978.

Mushkin, J.Selma, *"Health as an Investment"*, *Journal of Political Economy,* Vol. 70, (5, Part 2), 1962.

Nagaraja, G.P. *"Inter-state Disparities in Educational expenditure in India"*, Bangalore, Unpublished M.Ed., Project, Bangalore University, April 1983.

Naik, J.P., *"Broad-based planning process consisting of Integrated plans at the Institutional, District, State and National level"*, *Education Quarterly,* 20(1), 1968.

Nair, P.R., Pillai, N.P., *" A Study of the History and Problems of Educational Finance in Kerala"* Department of Education, Kerala University, 1962

Nanda S.K. *Indian Education and its Problems Today*, Kalyani Publisher, New Delhi, 1982.

Nanjundappa, D.M., *"A Study of University Finance"*, Department of Economics, Karnataka University, 1975 (ICSSR financed).

Natarajan, S., *Introduction to Economics and Education,* Sterling Publishers Private Limited, New Delhi, 1990.

Narayanaswamy, A. *"A Study of the Relationship between Education and Equity"*, Bangalore : Unpublished, M. Phil. Thesis, Bangalore University, April 1983.

Navaneetha Rao, T. *"Report of the Karnataka Universities Review Commission, Karnataka Universities Review Commission,* Bangalore, March 1994.

——————, *"Contros of Karnataka's New Sixth Plan"*, *Southern Economics*, Vol. 19(13), No. 1, 1980.

NCERT, *Education and National Development: Report of the Education Commission 1964-66, Reprint Edition*, New Delhi, May 1970.

Nigan, M.S., *"A Study of the Finances of University of Rajashthan,"* Unpublished, Rajasthan University, 1974.

Nural Hasan, *"Challanges in Education"*, *Culture and Social Welfare,* Allied Publisher Pvt. Ltd. , Bombay, 1971.

Padmanabhan, C.B., *Economics of Educational Planning in India,* Arya Book Depot., New Delhi, 1971.

Panchmukhi, P.R., *"Economics of University Finances"*, Unpublished, Bombay University, 1974.

—————— , *"Educational Finance in Federal Framework"*, Unpublished Paper, Bombay University.

Pandit, H.N., *"Effectiveness and Financing of Investment in Education*

1950-51 to 1965-66" : Unpublished Thesis, Delhi University, 1972.

Parlokar, J.S. (Pardesi), *"Education of Young Farmers and its Impact on Agriculture Production", Literacy Work* Vol. 1 (6), May 1972.

Planning Department, *Annual Financial Statement, Govt. of Mysore,* Bangalore for the year 1950-51.

Ibdi., for the year, 1951-74.

Planning Department, *Annual Finnacial Statement,* Govt. of Karnataka, Bangalore for the year 1974-75.

Ibdi., for the year, 1975-97.

——————, *First Five Year Plan of Mysore* (1951-56), Government of Mysore, Bangalore.

—————— *The Progress of the First Five Year Plan of Mysore,* Government of Mysore, Bangalore, 1951-56.

——————, *Second Five Year Plan of Mysore* (1956-61), Government of Mysore, Bangalore.

——————, *Mysore State Draft Fifth Five Year Plan* (1974-79), Government of Karnataka, Bangalore.

——————, *Karnataka Draft Fifth Five Year Plan* 1978-83, Government of Karnataka, Bangalore.

——————, *Annual Plan 1980-81*, Government of Karnataka

Sharama G.D., " *Research allocations of Education*", in Buch, M.B. (ed), Fourth Survey and Research in Education, 1983-88, Vol. 1, New Delhi, NCERT 1991.

——————, *Annual Plan 1982-83*, Government of Karnataka.

—————— , *Karnataka Draft Annual Year Plan 1983-84 Part II Statements,* Government of Karnataka, Bangalore.

—————— , *Eight Five Year Plan Draft 1990-95*,Vol. I Planning Department, Government of Karnataka

——————, *Eight Plan Document - Government of India, 1992-93*

——————, *Budget Estimate, Government of Mysore,* Bangalore for the year, 1950-51

Ibdi., for the year, 1951-74.

——————, *Budget Estimate, Government of Karnataka,* Bangalore for the year 1974-75.

Ibdi., for the year, 1975-84

—————— , *Detailed estimate of the expenditure,* Government of Karnataka, Bnagalor Vol. II, for the year 1974-75

Ibdi., for the year, 1975-92.

______________ , *Detailed estimated of the expenditure,* Government of Karnataka, Bnagalor Vol. II, for the year 1974-75.

Ibdi., for the year, 1993-97.

———————, *Statistical Abstract of Mysore*, 1962-63, Bureau of Economics and Statistics, Bangalore.

———————, *Statistical Abstract of Mysore,* 1970-71, Government of Mysore, Bangalore.

———————, *Bureau of Economics and Statistical,* Statistical Abstract of Mysore, 1973-74, Government of Mysore, Bangalore.

———————, *Statistical Abstract of Karnataka,* 1976-77, Government of Karnataka, Bangalore.

———————, *Statistical Abstract of Karnataka*, 1978-79, Government of Karnataka, Bangalore.

———————, *Statistical Abstract of Karnataka*, 1979-80, Government of Karnrtaka, Bangalore.

———————, *Directorate Economics and Statistics Statistical* Abstract of Karnataka, 1983-84, Government of Karnataka, Bangalore.

———————, *Directorate Economics and Statistics Statistical* Abstract of Karnataka, 1988-89, Government of Karnataka, Bangalore.

———————, *Directorate Economics and Statistics Statistical*, Outline of Karnataka, 1989-90, Government of Karnataka, Bangalore.

———————, *Directorate Economics and Statistics Statistical,* Karnataka Economics Review, 1992-93, Government of Karnataka.

———————, *Directorate Economics and Statistics Statistical*, Karnataka At a Glance, 1993-94, Bangalore.

———————, *Directorate Economics and Statistics Statistical,* Karnataka -India, Basic Statstics, Government of Karnataka, Bangalore, April 1994.

———————, *Directorate Economics and Statistics* State Domestic Product Karnataka - 1980-81 to 1992-93,Bangalore.

Planning, Housing and Social Welfare Department, *Third Five Year Plan, Programme for 1965-66*. Government of Karnataka, Bangalore.

Planning, Montoring and Statistics Division, *Ministry of Education and Culture,* Selected Educational Statistics : 1979-80, New Delhi, 1981.

Provisional Population Totals, *Census of India,* 1981, Series 9, Karnataka Paper 2 of 1981(B.K.Das, Diectorate of Census Operations), Government of Karnataka, Bangalore.

Shah, K.R., *Outlays on Education and its Financing in India,* 1950-51 to 1960-61, Unpublished Ph. D. Thesis, Baroda, MS University, 1969.

Shivanna, K. "*Trends of Expenditure for Education in Karnataka during 1980-81 to 1991-92*", Unpublished M. Ed., Project Bangalore University, April 1993.

Statistical Brochure, *Karnataka State Education Progress* (1975-76)

Government of Karnataka, Bangalore.

Statistical Brochure, *Karnataka State Education Progress* (1978-79) Government of Karnataka Bangalore.

Subramanya, K.N.(ed.) "*Is Karanataka Model State or a Soft State*", Southen Economist Vol. 21 (13), No.1, 1982.

Sunitya, B.P., "*Expenditure on Education in Karnataka*", Unpublished M.Ed., Dissertation, Bangalore University, December 1983.

Thimmaiah, G., "*Growth of Public Expenditure in Karnataka*", Southern Economist, Karnataka Number 1, 1977.

Tilak, Jandhyala, "*Education and Economic Growth in India between 1950-51 and 1969-70 : An Empirical Investigation*", *Indian Educational Review*, Vol. X, No. 1, 1975.

——————, "*Investment in Education in India*", *Eastern Economics* Annual Number, 1980.

——————, "*On Allocating Plan Resources to Education in India*", paper prepared (unpublished) for the seminar the seminar mobilisation of additional resources for education in India, NIEPA, July 21-31, 1982.

Vaizey, John., *The Economics of Education,* London, Feber and Faber, 1962.

Udaya Kumar, D.M. "*A Study of the Relative Priority Accorded to Allocations for Education in India during the Planning Era*", Unpublished M.Ed., Project, Bangalore University, April 1989.

Waienser, Jerome, B., "*Planning Policies for Investing in Scientific and Technological Education*". Human Resources Training of Scientific and Technical, Personnel, United States Papers preared for the United Nations Conference on the Application of Science and Technology for the Benefit of Less Developed, Areas (Geneva, Switzerland, February, 1963), Vol. XI, Superintendent of Documents, Washington, 1962, p. 132.

Watson and Holman, *Price Theory and its uses-IV Edition,* Haughton Mifflin Company Boston, Atlanta Dallas Geneva, Illinois Hopewell, New Jersey Palo Alto London, 1977.

Index

K

L

M

N